Arthurian Poets

E. A. Robinson

Arthurian Poets

EDWIN ARLINGTON ROBINSON

THE ARTHURIAN POEMS of E.A. Robinson were first published in America between 1917 and 1929, to considerable popular acclaim: *Tristram* won a Pulitzer prize. Yet they are almost unknown today, and the present volume restores a powerful and individual writer to his rightful place among Arthurian authors.

Robinson's introspective New England style and quiet tone are often classical rather than romantic, and he has little time for heroics. But he has also inherited much from Swinburne and Tennyson, and the tension between reason and passion that drives the characters of the Arthurian stories is brilliantly caught. These poems are above all studies in personality, and unforgettable for their vivid portraits, which are often unexpected – Merlin, cheerful and fierce; Vivian, enchanting rather than an enchantress; Lancelot in search of 'the Light'.

The sense of vision, and the feeling that the world of Arthur mirrors the fate of all mankind, binds these diverse characters together, and makes Robinson's poems essential reading for everyone interested in the Arthurian legend in the twentieth century.

'E.A. Robinson is too good a poet to be widely popular; his vision is too personal, too relentless to appeal to a crowd. Traditional yet original, realistic but not in the reductive sense, he is too good to be forgotten.'

ROBERTSON DAVIES

JAMES CARLEY is Professor of Medieval Studies, York University, Toronto.

Arthurian Poets

MATTHEW ARNOLD AND WILLIAM MORRIS
Introduced by James P. Carley
ALGERNON CHARLES SWINBURNE
Introduced by James P. Carley

Arthurian Poets

EDWIN ARLINGTON ROBINSON

Introduced by
JAMES P. CARLEY

THE BOYDELL PRESS

First published 1990 by The Boydell Press, Woodbridge

The Boydell Press is an imprint of Boydell & Brewer Ltd
PO Box 9, Woodbridge, Suffolk IP12 3DF
and of Boydell & Brewer Inc.
PO Box 41026, Rochester, NY 14604, USA

ISBN 0 85115 545 6

British Library Cataloguing in Publication Data
Robinson, Edwin Arlington
   Edwin Arlington Robinson. – (Arthurian poets).
   I. Title II. Series
   811.4
   ISBN 0–85115–545–6

Library of Congress Cataloging-in-Publication Data
Robinson, Edwin Arlington, 1869–1925.
   [Poems. Selections]
   Edwin Arlington Robinson / introduced by James P. Carley.
      p. cm. – (Arthurian poets)
   Includes bibliographical references.
   Contents: Tristram – Merlin – Lancelot.
   ISBN 0–85115–545–6 (alk. paper)
   1. Tristan (Legendary character) – Poetry. 2. Merlin (Legendary
character) – Poetry. 3. Lancelot (Legendary character) – Poetry.
4. Arthurian romances – Adaptations. I. Carley, James P.
II. Title. III. Series: Carley, James P. Arthurian poets.
PS3535.025A6   1990
811'.52–dc20   89–71263
                                                                      CIP

This publication is printed on acid-free paper

Printed in Great Britain by
St Edmundsbury Press, Bury St Edmunds, Suffolk

CONTENTS

Robertson Davies writes:

'I am glad you are bringing Edwin Arlington Robinson's notions about Arthur back into circulation. They are a fine corrective to the nineteenth century romanticism of Tennyson and the arch whimsy of T. H. White. Robinson cuts out the supernatural element in the great tale, which robs it of much of its splendour; indeed, one feels that he was an existentialist before that mushy term came into fashion. But he gives us a fresh look at what had become familiar in pre-Raphaelite fancy dress, and thus not really human. Of course, when people say 'human' they so often mean commonplace, or 'flawed' to use another cant term, and they cannot see that when a great story has dropped backward in time it is not the quotidian silliness that remains, but the skeleton structure, which may be of overwhelming nobility. Robinson was too good a poet to miss the nobility, even if he rejected some of what lay at the root of it. Indeed, he is too good a poet to be widely popular; his vision is too personal, too relentless to appeal to a crowd. Great poets have been popular, but there are also some who have not, and whose claims are just as cogent, and Edwin Arlington Robinson is one. Traditional yet original, realistic but not in the reductive sense, he is too good to be forgotten.'

INTRODUCTION

A New Englander by birth and in poetic inspiration, Edwin Arlington Robinson (1869–1935) is probably best remembered for his shorter verse depicting 'Tilbury town'. Perhaps simply because of their length, his powerfully evocative Arthurian poems – *Merlin*, published in 1917, *Lancelot*, appearing in 1920, and *Tristram*, which won the Pulitzer prize in 1927 – have fallen into relative oblivion. In the wake of what has been called the 'Arthurian renascence of the late twentieth century', however, there has been a revival of enthusiasm for these poems and the time seems ripe for their reissue. As Robinson himself predicted as early as 1920: 'I shall begin to live, if all goes well, about twenty-fiuve years after I'm dead. And that isn't a bad time to begin.'

By the time Robinson came to write his Arthurian trilogy the numerous editions and adaptations of Malory had made the legend a major part of the culture of the English-speaking world and his reader is expected to know how the moment described fits into the whole cycle of the rise and fall of Camelot; also who is who and what is going on in general. Individuals come on stage, as it were, with their pedigrees provided. Robinson had, of course, also read Tennyson, Morris, Arnold and Swinburne and had seen how they had transformed the story. His verisons – what he does with Merlin's enchantment, Lancelot's vision of the Grail and so forth – show not only a desire to put new wine in old bottles as they had done, but also to provide an altogether different brew. And in this he has succeeded. His Arthurian poems read very differently from any of their predecessors: the characters are modern in every sense, their psychological makeup closely defined (we are well into the Freudian world here), the aura of a romantic and exotic Middle Ages cast aside. In spite of their setting, therefore, the poems are securely located in the American tradition; more similar in many ways to Twain (even if lacking the latter's cutting irony) than to Arnold or Swinburne.

Robinson saw *Merlin* and *Lancelot* as a matched pair – 'the two should be read together', he wrote – with *Tristram* standing quite apart: 'There is no symbolic significance in it, although there is a certain amount in *Merlin* and *Lancelot*, which were suggested by the world war – Camelot representing in a way the going of a world that is now pretty much gone.' In both the earlier poems the dominant mood is dark and apocalyptic; they focus on the grimness of war and the wanton destruction it unleashes to maintain ideals which do not always seem worth salvaging. As Guinevere remarks during her singularly miserable sojourn at Joyous Gard:

> Tomorrow it will be
> The King's move, I suppose, and we shall have
> One more magnificent waste of nameless pawns,
> And of a few more knights.

The emphasis on the pawns, too, contributes to the feeling of disillusionment: the great deeds and stubborn pride of the knights are paid for in the blood of their nameless followers:

> How many thousand men
> Are going to their death before Gawaine
> And Arthur go to theirs – and I to mine?

Ultimately – the kingdom shrouded in rain and fog, a moonlight burial with no tangible promise of resurrection in Avalon, only unfounded 'tales told of a ship' – the reader must agree with Gawain's bitter observation that 'The world has paid enough / For Camelot.'

There is, nevertheless, no sense that war can be avoided; Robinson does not suggest that an alternative can be found. As

Gawaine adds after his judgement on Camelot: 'It is the world's turn now – / Or so it would be if the world were not / The world.' The cycle of rising fortune, temporary peace, followed by collapse into dissention and chaos is inevitable. *Merlin* and *Lancelot* are topical, then, in that they arise out of Robinson's reaction to the First World War, but they also have a wider philosophical base in their concern with the cyclical nature of war itself:

> When the world sees,
> The world will have in turn another madness:
> And so, as I've a glimpse, *ad infinitum.*

Given this thesis, it is not surprising that no post-war euphoria entered into the spirit of *Lancelot* – even though it was published two years after Armistice – and that Robinson could foresee a new war quite clearly on the horizon as early as 1934: 'Today I have been thinking of Hitler, and of what one neurotic fanatic may yet do to us and drag us into. It's all right to say it can't happen, but unfortunately it can.' From Robinson's perspective, nevertheless, Merlin's vision and the Light – that is, seeing the world and the human psyche as they really are – lead to a spirit of acceptance. Even as everything around him is collapsing, Lancelot can foretell that 'There are worlds enough to follow.' Or, as Robinson would formulate it in his own voice: 'The world is a hell of a place; and if life and universe mean anything, there is no reason to suppose it will be anything else. This, as I understand it, is the true optimism.'

In both *Merlin* and *Lancelot* the basic narrative framework comes from Malory, who provided – as Robinson's biographer Hermann Hagedorn put it – 'a parable into which he could pour his sense of cosmic disaster, his grief and his hope.' There are, however, additions and deletions as well as significant changes in characterisation. Many of these take their inception in Robinson's reading of later versions of the legend. In his transformation of Vivian into a loving companion to Merlin, for example, Robinson appears to have used S.Humphreys

Gurteen's summary of the Vulgate *Merlin*, found in *The Arthurian Epic* (New York, 1895). After Merlin has met Vivian, according to this retelling, he twice returns to Britain on affairs of state. It is Vivian's love, and fear of having him leave again, that makes her entrap him. The spell becomes a symbol of fully reciprocated love and the two are bound together eternally, love prisoners 'in an enchanted castle, reposing on a couch of flowers'.

From Gurteen's synopsis of the Vulgate text Robinson borrows the love motif as well as many specific details. He makes, however, one radical change – one for which there is no precedent in the romances – when he as Merlin escape from his 'esplumoir'. Why? To understand this change, one must first examine the nature of the original enchantment in *Merlin*. The most obvious thing is that Merlin and Vivian are a matched pair – as their balancing dialogue of courtship makes clear. Vivian announces that:

> I'm cruel and I'm cold, and I like snakes;
> And some have said my mother was a fairy,
> Though I believe it not.

To which Merlin responds

> I'm cheerful and I'm fierce, and I've made kings;
> And some have said my father was the Devil,
> Though I believe it not.

Merlin accepts his imprisonment in Broceliande not because it is an external fate; he has come willingly and enthusiastically because he wants to be with the one individual with whom he shares 'sight'. Both he and Vivian see beyond the petty world of the self – self which inevitably wishes to transform itself to a kind of cosmic will, making war of love, of madness, of hate, of ambition:

> Now Arthur, Modred, Lancelot, and Gawaine
> Are swollen thoughts of this eternal will
> Which have no other way to find the way

> That leads them in to their inheritance
> Than by the time-infuriating flame
> Of a wrecked empire, lighted by the torch
> Of woman ...

Vivian and Guinevere form an instructive contrast here. Earthbound, Guinevere fears the Light of the Grail:

> The Light you saw
> Was not the light of Rome; the word you had
> Of Rome was not the word of God – though Rome
> Has refuge for the weary and heavy-laden.
> Were I to live too long I might seek Rome
> Myself, and be the happier when I found it.

In the last scene, a nun at Amesbury, she assures Lancelot that she does not stand any longer in the way of his quest, that 'There is nothing now / That I can see between you and the Light / That I have dimmed so long.' As she realizes, the torch of woman stands in direct contrast to the spiritual Grail – 'the light / That Galahad found.' Lancelot must choose between Woman and the Light: 'Time, tide, and twilight – and the dark' he muses (in what is almost certainly an echo of Tennyson's 'Crossing the Bar'), 'And then, for me, the Light. But what for her?'

In Vivian's character, on the other hand, there seems to be a hint of how this dichotomy could be resolved – the choice between 'two fires that are to light the world' – and it is this that draws Merlin's admiration. Vivian is a hope for the future.

> In time to be,
> The like of her shall have another name
> Than Vivian, and her laugh shall be a fire,
> Not shining only to consume itself
> With what it burns.

It is this Vivian too who does not block the gate when Merlin at last leaves Broceliande, the timeless Eden which she tried to create for them: at the end 'She closed the gate again so quietly / That Merlin could have heard no sound of it.'

In *Merlin* especially, the mirror image turns up again and again. Merlin elevated Arthur, so he tells Vivian, 'to be a mirror for the world'. Arthur's subsequent adultery is, therefore, much worse than a simple personal failing because it 'set the pace' for the others. The whole rise and fall itself becomes a pattern in the last sad story Merlin tells Vivian:

> Of one wise counsellor who loved the king,
> And loved the world and therefore made him king
> To be a mirror for it, – the king reigned well
> For certain years, awaiting a sure doom . . .

Merlin, as he comes to realize, is himself a mirror of the inevitable cycle:

> He wondered, when she was away from him,
> If his avenging injured intellect
> Might shine with Arthur's kingdom a twin mirror,
> Fate's plaything, for new ages without eyes
> To see therein themselves and their declension.

On a more general level the poem itself is a mirror: 'I wrote *Merlin* because I saw a world symbol in the situation and used the Arthurian period merely as a peg to hang the picture on.' As in the world of the Great War, Fate seems malign:

> The seeds of history
> Are small, but given a few gouts of warm blood
> For quickening, they sprout out wondrously
> And have a leaping growth whereof no man
> May shun such harvesting of change or death,
> Or life, as may fall on him to be borne.

In the final analysis Merlin is – as he must teach Arthur – neither 'Fate nor God', but mankind (both within the poem and outside it) must gain hope from the very fact of his existence and of his vision, his eyes in which

> There was a mystic and intrinsic peace
> Of one who sees where men of nearer sight
> See nothing.

For Robinson, the vision is overpowering, beyond the power of words, but it is not transcendent as in the medieval *Queste del Saint Graal*, for example, since it is entirely human in its manifestations: 'Galahad's light is simply the light of the Grail, interpreted universally as a spiritual realization of Things and their significance. I don't see how this can be made any more concrete, for it is not the same thing to any two individuals.' By the end Lancelot attains this understanding – even if it reveals itself as 'not the same thing' as it was for Merlin: 'always in the darkness he rode on, / Alone; and in the darkness came the Light.' The great heroes of Arthurian romance, then, exemplify Robinson's belief that 'the man who fixes on something definite in life that he must do, at the expense of everything else, if necessary, has presumably got something that, for him, should be recognized as the Inner Fire. For him, that is the Gleam, the Vision and the Word! He'd better follow it. The greatest adventure he'll ever have on this side is following where it leads.'

By Robinson's own account his publishers, Seltzer, found *Lancelot* too long and he decided to remove one small self-contained section – i.e. the episode which signals the period of 'Slander and Strife' where

> King Arthur rode on hunting and sent word to the queen that he would be out all that night. Then Sir Agravaine and Sir Mordred gat to them twelve knights, and hid themselves in a chambir in the Castle of Carlisle.

Robinson had elaborated on this scene, dramatizing it and filling it with dialogue, as a means of probing Modred's essential and all-consuming corruption. The decision to excise probably had a beneficial effect on *Lancelot* itself since, as Beverly Taylor and Elisabeth Brewer argue in *The Return of King Arthur*: 'Deleting this scene proved fortunate, for Modred, who never appears in the poem, remains horrifying as a disembodied force of evil.' Nevertheless, the fragment stands on its own and Robinson decided in 1929 to publish it separately as

Modred: A Fragment in a limited edition of two hundred and fifty copies.

In Robinson's poem Modred is Iago-like, an arch manipulator who invites 'admirable Colgrevance' and 'gentle Agravaine' into the garden, and arranges them as on a stage in the two chairs recently vacated by Lancelot and Guinevere and then drives them into action with his 'tongue / That sang an evil music while it spoke'. Modred plays with images of harvest and blindness, using irony and understatement in his attempt to win the others over to his plot. In Robinson, as in Malory, Agravaine is already part of Modred's conspiracy, although he lacks the latter's duplicity. Colgrevance, on the other hand, is disgusted and resists strongly and bitterly, in terms which emphasize Modred's own dark nature: 'I'll be / This night no poisonous inhabitant / Of alcoves in your play'. Hiding his anger, Modred responds 'musically' and uses powerful erotic imagery to drive them forward to his plans. His success finally assured he leads them out to the banquet and potent drink, 'humming lowly to himself / A chant of satisfaction'. In spite of all his manipulating, however, Modred is himself – as Gawaine will come to realize – not as free as he thought; he is in fact the agent of Fate, of the universal pattern where war and peace are themselves in eternal conflict:

> and all the time
> His evil it was that grew, the King not seeing
> In Modred the Almighty's instrument
> Of a world's overthrow.

In a recent paper Rebecca Cochran has contrasted Robinson's Arthurian world with the self-conscious medievalism of his nineteenth-century English predecessors, and has concluded that '*Merlin* and *Lancelot* possess a modern spirit and tone, one that renders them ineligible as examples of either Pater's "profounder medievalism" or [Alice] Chandler's "medieval ideal" . . . . With its emphasis upon the importance of a stoic resolve to accept an unalterable fate, *Tristram* achieves greater fidelity to the spirit of its medieval antecedents than *Merlin* or *Lancelot*.' Certainly, *Tristram* is much less a *roman à thèse* than the two earlier poems and differs significantly, as Robinson himself put it, in 'key and color'. It is a sustained meditation upon the relation of love and fate – i.e. precisely the same themes Swinburne had earlier explored in his *Tristram of Lyonesse* – and Robinson himself notes that: 'The outlines of Tristram are taken mostly from Malory, with certain elements of the French version as followed by Swinburne'. Unlike Swinburne's sustained *cri de coeur*, however, the mode of exploration here is through dialogue and analysis. The characters explain their feelings, contemplate and discuss their predicament.

Apart from plot changes – and, in particular, the invention of Andred's role as Tristram's murderer – the most fascinating transformation of the legend comes in Robinson's depiction of Isolt of the White Hands, whose meditations frame the whole poem. Isolt's unwavering devotion to Tristram can evoke nothing but pity and kindness in him, but she accepts this as her lot. She moves from a childlike fixation (and an agate Tristram once gave her is her perpetual talisman) to a stoic acceptance of her fate:

> It was like that
> For women, sometimes, and might be so too often
> For women like her. She hoped there were not many
> Of them, or many of them to be . . .

She is the white rose – white in virginity but also in the intensity of her gray/white burning eyes – which cannot touch Tristram who is in turn under the spell – but a psychological spell, not one induced by an external potion – of her dark, wild adversary 'Dark and love-red for ever, and not there, / Where the white rose was queen.'

As there are two contrasting women, so too does Robinson use Gawaine's traditional reputation for worldliness and lightness in love to provide a foil to Tristram's unalterable devotion.

Gawaine, unlike Tristram, can be deeply moved by the beauty of Isolt of the White Hands, but his feelings fade the moment his ship departs from Brittany. And later he can be equally drawn to Brangwaine even in the midst of Tristram's collapse: ' "Gawaine, Brangwaine," Brangwaine was fair to see'. Nor does he have a nature which can understand the agony suffered by the distraught Tristram: 'Why must a man, where there are loaves and fishes, / See only as far as one crumb on his table? . . . Here is no place for me.' The Light, as he well realizes, is not for him and he does not desire it.

For all three lovers the sea acts as an agent of fate, the bringer of change; it separates and it unites. It also stands as a symbol of their own inner feelings. Exiled in Brittany, Tristram hears Isolt's name on every wave. For Isolt of the White Hands, in contrast, the waves call out 'unceasingly', ' "Tristram – / Tristram." ' After she has been brought back to Tintagel, Isolt of Ireland feels that the still, nightmarish sea, reflects her own state: ' "It is like something after life, / And it is not like death." ' Mark, in return, realizes that 'Perhaps the sea is like ourselves . . . And has as much to say of calms / That shake or make it still, as we have power / To shake or to be still.' Resolution for Isolt and for Tristram comes in death as fulfillment of their love: '... silence within, / Silence without, dark silence everywhere – / And peace.' For the other Isolt the sea also brings peace. The poem ends (as it began) with her contemplation of the gulls. At this point, however, there is no longer expectation, no anticipation of ships on the horizon:

> She watched them [the gulls] there till even her
>   thoughts were white,
> And there was nothing alive but white birds flying.
> Flying, and always flying, and still flying,
> And the white sunlight flashing on the sea.

'Öd' und leer das Meer.'

In his use of Arthurian themes, then, Robinson does not

escape into a nostalgic past, as even his first reviewers were quick to observe. *The Yale Review* of 6 July, 1917, for example, noted that: 'The characters are not figures in armor; they are men and women no further removed from us than the characters in Meredith's "Modern Love".' In the poems there are times when modernity and social relevance almost take over: symbol can merge into allegory, demystification can overlap with reductionism, distress with Arthur's reign, say, appear an appeal for republicanism. At their best, however, the poems are compelling evocations of the philosophical and psychological concerns of the early twentieth century. After reading them one does not feel – as in the case of the romances – 'how I've dreamt of that world and how I wish I could enter it', but rather 'I've been there before'.

SELECT BIBLIOGRAPHY

Adler, Jacon. 'Robinson's Gawaine'. *English Studies* 39 (1958), 1–20.

Barnard, Ellsworth, ed. *Edwin Arlington Robinson Centenary Essays* (Athens. Ga, 1969).

Chandler, Alice. *A Dream of Order: The Medieval Ideal in Nineteenth-Century English Literature* (Lincoln, 1970).

Cochran, Rebecca. 'Edwin Arlington Robinson's Arthurian Poems: Studies in Medievalisms?'. *Arthurian Interpretations* 3 (1988), 49–60.

Cox, Don. 'The Vision of Robinson's Merlin'. *Colby Library Quarterly* 10 (1974), 495–504.

Fisher, John Hurt. 'Edwin Arlington Robinson and Arthurian Tradition'. In Mieczyslaw Brahmer, Stanislow Helsztynski, and Julian Kryzanowski, eds. *Studies in Language and Literature in Honor of Margaret Schlauch* (Warsaw, 1966), pp. 117–131.

Hagedorn, Hermann. *Edwin Arlington Robinson: A Biography* (New York, 1938).

Lagorio, Valerie M. 'Edwin Arlington Robinson: Arthurian Pacifist'. In Valerie M. Lagorio and Mildred Leake Day, eds. *King Arthur Through the Ages*. 2 vols. New York, 1990.

Perrine, Laurence. 'Contemporary Reference of Robinson's Arthurian Poems'. *Twentieth Century Literature* 8 (1962), 74–82.

Perrine, Laurence. 'The Sources of Robinson's *Merlin*'. *American Literature* 44 (1972–3), 313–321.

Starr, Nathan C. 'Edwin Arlington Robinson's Arthurian Heroines: Vivian, Guinevere and the Two Isolts'. *Philological Quarterly* 56 (1977), 253–258.

Thompson, W. R. 'Broceliande: E. A. Robinson's Palace of Art.' *The New England Quarterly* 43 (1970), 231–49.

Torrence, Ridgely, ed. *Selected Letters of Edwin Arlington Robinson* (New York, 1940).

MERLIN

I

"GAWAINE, GAWAINE, what look ye for to see,
So far beyond the faint edge of the world?
D'ye look to see the lady Vivian,
Pursued by divers ominous vile demons
That have another king more fierce than ours?
Or think ye that if ye look far enough
And hard enough into the feathery west
Ye'll have a glimmer of the Grail itself?
And if ye look for neither Grail nor lady,
What look ye for to see, Gawaine, Gawaine?"

So Dagonet, whom Arthur made a knight
Because he loved him as he laughed at him,
Intoned his idle presence on a day
To Gawaine, who had thought himself alone,
Had there been in him thought of anything
Save what was murmured now in Camelot
Of Merlin's hushed and all but unconfirmed
Appearance out of Brittany. It was heard
At first there was a ghost in Arthur's palace,
But soon among the scullions and anon
Among the knights a firmer credit held
All tongues from uttering what all glances told—
Though not for long. Gawaine, this afternoon,
Fearing he might say more to Lancelot

Of Merlin's rumor-laden resurrection
Than Lancelot would have an ear to cherish,
Had sauntered off with his imagination
To Merlin's Rock, where now there was no Merlin
To meditate upon a whispering town
Below him in the silence.—Once he said
To Gawaine: "You are young; and that being so,
Behold the shining city of our dreams
And of our King."—"Long live the King," said Gawaine.—
"Long live the King," said Merlin after him;
"Better for me that I shall not be King;
Wherefore I say again, Long live the King,
And add, God save him, also, and all kings—
All kings and queens. I speak in general.
Kings have I known that were but weary men
With no stout appetite for more than peace
That was not made for them."—"Nor were they made
For kings," Gawaine said, laughing.—"You are young,
Gawaine, and you may one day hold the world
Between your fingers, knowing not what it is
That you are holding. Better for you and me,
I think, that we shall not be kings."

                                        Gawaine,
Remembering Merlin's words of long ago,
Frowned as he thought, and having frowned again,
He smiled and threw an acorn at a lizard:
"There's more afoot and in the air to-day
Than what is good for Camelot. Merlin
May or may not know all, but he said well
To say to me that he would not be King.
Nor more would I be King." Far down he gazed
On Camelot, until he made of it
A phantom town of many stillnesses,

Not reared for men to dwell in, or for kings
To reign in, without omens and obscure
Familiars to bring terror to their days;
For though a knight, and one as hard at arms
As any, save the fate-begotten few
That all acknowledged or in envy loathed,
He felt a foreign sort of creeping up
And down him, as of moist things in the dark,—
When Dagonet, coming on him unawares,
Presuming on his title of Sir Fool,
Addressed him and crooned on till he was done:
"What look ye for to see, Gawaine, Gawaine?"

"Sir Dagonet, you best and wariest
Of all dishonest men, I look through Time,
For sight of what it is that is to be.
I look to see it, though I see it not.
I see a town down there that holds a king,
And over it I see a few small clouds—
Like feathers in the west, as you observe;
And I shall see no more this afternoon
Than what there is around us every day,
Unless you have a skill that I have not
To ferret the invisible for rats."

"If you see what's around us every day,
You need no other showing to go mad.
Remember that and take it home with you;
And say tonight, 'I had it of a fool—
With no immediate obliquity
For this one or for that one, or for me.' "
Gawaine, having risen, eyed the fool curiously:
"I'll not forget I had it of a knight,
Whose only folly is to fool himself;
And as for making other men to laugh,

And so forget their sins and selves a little,
There's no great folly there. So keep it up,
As long as you've a legend or a song,
And have whatever sport of us you like
Till havoc is the word and we fall howling.
For I've a guess there may not be so loud
A sound of laughing here in Camelot
When Merlin goes again to his gay grave
In Brittany. To mention lesser terrors,
Men say his beard is gone."

                    "Do men say that?"
A twitch of an impatient weariness
Played for a moment over the lean face
Of Dagonet, who reasoned inwardly:
"The friendly zeal of this inquiring knight
Will overtake his tact and leave it squealing,
One of these days."—Gawaine looked hard at him:
"If I be too familiar with a fool,
I'm on the way to be another fool,"
He mused, and owned a rueful qualm within him:
"Yes, Dagonet," he ventured, with a laugh,
"Men tell me that his beard has vanished wholly,
And that he shines now as the Lord's anointed,
And wears the valiance of an ageless youth
Crowned with a glory of eternal peace."

Dagonet, smiling strangely, shook his head:
"I grant your valiance of a kind of youth
To Merlin, but your crown of peace I question;
For, though I know no more than any churl
Who pinches any chambermaid soever
In the King's palace, I look not to Merlin
For peace, when out of his peculiar tomb
He comes again to Camelot. Time swings

A mighty scythe, and some day all your peace
Goes down before its edge like so much clover.
No, it is not for peace that Merlin comes,
Without a trumpet—and without a beard,
If what you say men say of him be true—
Nor yet for sudden war."

                              Gawaine, for a moment,
Met then the ambiguous gaze of Dagonet,
And, making nothing of it, looked abroad
As if at something cheerful on all sides,
And back again to the fool's unasking eyes:
"Well, Dagonet, if Merlin would have peace,
Let Merlin stay away from Brittany,"
Said he, with admiration for the man
Whom Folly called a fool: "And we have known him;
We knew him once when he knew everything."

"He knew as much as God would let him know
Until he met the lady Vivian.
I tell you that, for the world knows all that;
Also it knows he told the King one day
That he was to be buried, and alive,
In Brittany; and that the King should see
The face of him no more. Then Merlin sailed
Away to Vivian in Broceliande,
Where now she crowns him and herself with flowers
And feeds him fruits and wines and many foods
Of many savors, and sweet ortolans.
Wise books of every lore of every land
Are there to fill his days, if he require them,
And there are players of all instruments—
Flutes, hautboys, drums, and viols; and she sings
To Merlin, till he trembles in her arms

And there forgets that any town alive
Had ever such a name as Camelot.
So Vivian holds him with her love, they say,
And he, who has no age, has not grown old.
I swear to nothing, but that's what they say.
That's being buried in Broceliande
For too much wisdom and clairvoyancy.
But you and all who live, Gawaine, have heard
This tale, or many like it, more than once;
And you must know that Love, when Love invites
Philosophy to play, plays high and wins,
Or low and loses. And you say to me,
'If Merlin would have peace, let Merlin stay
Away from Brittany.' Gawaine, you are young,
And Merlin's in his grave."

       "Merlin said once
That I was young, and it's a joy for me
That I am here to listen while you say it.
Young or not young, if that be burial,
May I be buried long before I die.
I might be worse than young; I might be old."—
Dagonet answered, and without a smile:
"Somehow I fancy Merlin saying that;
A fancy—a mere fancy." Then he smiled:
"And such a doom as his may be for you,
Gawaine, should your untiring divination
Delve in the veiled eternal mysteries
Too far to be a pleasure for the Lord.
And when you stake your wisdom for a woman,
Compute the woman to be worth a grave,
As Merlin did, and say no more about it.
But Vivian, she played high. Oh, very high!
Flutes, hautboys, drums, and viols,—and her love.
Gawaine, farewell."

"Farewell, Sir Dagonet,
And may the devil take you presently."
He followed with a vexed and envious eye,
And with an arid laugh, Sir Dagonet's
Departure, till his gaunt obscurity
Was cloaked and lost amid the glimmering trees.
"Poor fool!" he murmured. "Or am I the fool?
With all my fast ascendency in arms,
That ominous clown is nearer to the King
Than I am—yet; and God knows what he knows,
And what his wits infer from what he sees
And feels and hears. I wonder what he knows
Of Lancelot, or what I might know now,
Could I have sunk myself to sound a fool
To springe a friend. . . . No, I like not this day.
There's a cloud coming over Camelot
Larger than any that is in the sky,—
Or Merlin would be still in Brittany,
With Vivian and the viols. It's all too strange."

And later, when descending to the city,
Through unavailing casements he could hear
The roaring of a mighty voice within,
Confirming fervidly his own conviction:
"It's all too strange, and half the world's half crazy!"—
He scowled: "Well, I agree with Lamorak."
He frowned, and passed: "And I like not this day."

II

SIR LAMORAK, the man of oak and iron,
Had with him now, as a care-laden guest,
Sir Bedivere, a man whom Arthur loved
As he had loved no man save Lancelot.

Like one whose late-flown shaft of argument
Had glanced and fallen afield innocuously,
He turned upon his host a sudden eye
That met from Lamorak's an even shaft
Of native and unused authority;
And each man held the other till at length
Each turned away, shutting his heavy jaws
Again together, prisoning thus two tongues
That might forget and might not be forgiven.
Then Bedivere, to find a plain way out,
Said, "Lamorak, let us drink to some one here,
And end this dryness. Who shall it be—the King,
The Queen, or Lancelot?"—"Merlin," Lamorak growled;
And then there were more wrinkles round his eyes
Than Bedivere had said were possible.
"There's no refusal in me now for that,"
The guest replied; "so, 'Merlin' let it be.
We've not yet seen him, but if he be here,
And even if he should not be here, say 'Merlin.'"
They drank to the unseen from two new tankards,
And fell straightway to sighing for the past,
And what was yet before them. Silence laid
A cogent finger on the lips of each
Impatient veteran, whose hard hands lay clenched
And restless on his midriff, until words
Were stronger than strong Lamorak:

                                        "Bedivere,"

Began the solid host, "you may as well
Say now as at another time hereafter
That all your certainties have bruises on 'em,
And all your pestilent asseverations
Will never make a man a salamander—
Who's born, as we are told, so fire won't bite him,—
Or a slippery queen a nun who counts and burns

Herself to nothing with her beads and candles.
There's nature, and what's in us, to be sifted
Before we know ourselves, or any man
Or woman that God suffers to be born.
That's how I speak; and while you strain your mazard,
Like Father Jove, big with a new Minerva,
We'll say, to pass the time, that I speak well.
God's fish! The King had eyes; and Lancelot
Won't ride home to his mother, for she's dead.
The story is that Merlin warned the King
Of what's come now to pass; and I believe it
And Arthur, he being Arthur and a king,
Has made a more pernicious mess than one,
We're told, for being so great and amorous:
It's that unwholesome and inclement cub
Young Modred I'd see first in hell before
I'd hang too high the Queen or Lancelot;
The King, if one may say it, set the pace,
And we've two strapping bastards here to prove it.
Young Borre, he's well enough; but as for Modred,
I squirm as often as I look at him.
And there again did Merlin warn the King,
The story goes abroad; and I believe it."

Sir Bedivere, as one who caught no more
Than what he would of Lamorak's outpouring,
Inclined his grizzled head and closed his eyes
Before he sighed and rubbed his beard and spoke:
"For all I know to make it otherwise,
The Queen may be a nun some day or other;
I'd pray to God for such a thing to be,
If prayer for that were not a mockery.
We're late now for much praying, Lamorak,
When you and I can feel upon our faces
A wind that has been blowing over ruins

That we had said were castles and high towers—
Till Merlin, or the spirit of him, came
As the dead come in dreams. I saw the King
This morning, and I saw his face. Therefore,
I tell you, if a state shall have a king,
The king must have the state, and be the state;
Or then shall we have neither king nor state,
But bones and ashes, and high towers all fallen:
And we shall have, where late there was a kingdom,
A dusty wreck of what was once a glory—
A wilderness whereon to crouch and mourn
And moralize, or else to build once more
For something better or for something worse.
Therefore again, I say that Lancelot
Has wrought a potent wrong upon the King,
And all who serve and recognize the King,
And all who follow him and all who love him.
Whatever the stormy faults he may have had,
To look on him today is to forget them;
And if it be too late for sorrow now
To save him—for it was a broken man
I saw this morning, and a broken king—
The God who sets a day for desolation
Will not forsake him in Avilion,
Or whatsoever shadowy land there be
Where peace awaits him on its healing shores."

Sir Lamorak, shifting in his oaken chair,
Growled like a dog and shook himself like one:
"For the stone-chested, helmet-cracking knight
That you are known to be from Lyonnesse
To northward, Bedivere, you fol-de-rol
When days are rancid, and you fiddle-faddle
More like a woman than a man with hands
Fit for the smiting of a crazy giant

With armor an inch thick, as we all know
You are, when you're not sermonizing at us.
As for the King, I say the King, no doubt,
Is angry, sorry, and all sorts of things,
For Lancelot, and for his easy Queen,
Whom he took knowing she'd thrown sparks already
On that same piece of tinder, Lancelot,
Who fetched her with him from Leodogran
Because the King—God save poor human reason!—
Would prove to Merlin, who knew everything
Worth knowing in those days, that he was wrong.
I'll drink now and be quiet,—but, by God,
I'll have to tell you, Brother Bedivere,
Once more, to make you listen properly,
That crowns and orders, and high palaces,
And all the manifold ingredients
Of this good solid kingdom, where we sit
And spit now at each other with our eyes,
Will not go rolling down to hell just yet
Because a pretty woman is a fool.
And here's Kay coming with his fiddle face
As long now as two fiddles. Sit ye down,
Sir Man, and tell us everything you know
Of Merlin—or his ghost without a beard.
What mostly is it?"

                      Sir Kay, the seneschal,
Sat wearily while he gazed upon the two:
"To you it mostly is, if I err not,
That what you hear of Merlin's coming back
Is nothing more or less than heavy truth.
But ask me nothing of the Queen, I say,
For I know nothing. All I know of her
Is what her eyes have told the silences
That now attend her; and that her estate

Is one for less complacent execration
Than quips and innuendoes of the city
Would augur for her sin—if there be sin—
Or for her name—if now she have a name.
And where, I say, is this to lead the King,
And after him, the kingdom and ourselves?
Here be we, three men of a certain strength
And some confessed intelligence, who know
That Merlin has come out of Brittany—
Out of his grave, as he would say it for us—
Because the King has now a desperation
More strong upon him than a woman's net
Was over Merlin—for now Merlin's here,
And two of us who knew him know how well
His wisdom, if he have it any longer,
Will by this hour have sounded and appraised
The grief and wrath and anguish of the King,
Requiring mercy and inspiring fear
Lest he forego the vigil now most urgent,
And leave unwatched a cranny where some worm
Or serpent may come in to speculate."

"I know your worm, and his worm's name is Modred—
Albeit the streets are not yet saying so,"
Said Lamorak, as he lowered his wrath and laughed
A sort of poisonous apology
To Kay: "And in the meantime, I'll be gyved!
Here's Bedivere a-wailing for the King,
And you, Kay, with a moist eye for the Queen.
I think I'll blow a horn for Lancelot;
For by my soul a man's in sorry case
When Guineveres are out with eyes to scorch him:
I'm not so ancient or so frozen certain
That I'd ride horses down to skeletons

If she were after me. Has Merlin seen him—
This Lancelot, this Queen-fed friend of ours?"

Kay answered sighing, with a lonely scowl:
"The picture that I conjure leaves him out;
The King and Merlin are this hour together,
And I can say no more; for I know nothing.
But how the King persuaded or beguiled
The stricken wizard from across the water
Outriddles my poor wits. It's all too strange."

"It's all too strange, and half the world's half crazy!"
Roared Lamorak, forgetting once again
The devastating carriage of his voice.
"Is the King sick?" he said, more quietly;
"Is he to let one damned scratch be enough
To paralyze the force that heretofore
Would operate a way through hell and iron,
And iron already slimy with his blood?
Is the King blind—with Modred watching him?
Does he forget the crown for Lancelot?
Does he forget that every woman mewing
Shall some day be a handful of small ashes?"

"You speak as one for whom the god of Love
Has yet a mighty trap in preparation.
We know you, Lamorak," said Bedivere:
"We know you for a short man, Lamorak,—
In deeds, if not in inches or in words;
But there are fens and heights and distances
That your capricious ranging has not yet
Essayed in this weird region of man's love.
Forgive me, Lamorak, but your words are words.
Your deeds are what they are; and ages hence
Will men remember your illustriousness,

If there be gratitude in history.
For me, I see the shadow of the end,
Wherein to serve King Arthur to the end,
And, if God have it so, to see the Grail
Before I die."

                    But Lamorak shook his head:
"See what you will, or what you may. For me,
I see no other than a stinking mess—
With Modred stirring it, and Agravaine
Spattering Camelot with as much of it
As he can throw. The Devil got somehow
Into God's workshop once upon a time,
And out of the red clay that he found there
He made a shape like Modred, and another
As like as eyes are to this Agravaine.
'I never made 'em,' said the good Lord God,
'But let 'em go, and see what comes of 'em.'
And that's what we're to do. As for the Grail,
I've never worried it, and so the Grail
Has never worried me."

                         Kay sighed. "I see
With Bedivere the coming of the end,"
He murmured; "for the King I saw today
Was not, nor shall he ever be again,
The King we knew. I say the King is dead;
The man is living, but the King is dead.
The wheel is broken."

                    "Faugh!" said Lamorak;
"There are no dead kings yet in Camelot;
But there is Modred who is hatching ruin,—
And when it hatches I may not be here.
There's Gawaine too, and he does not forget

My father, who killed his. King Arthur's house
Has more divisions in it than I like
In houses; and if Modred's aim be good
For backs like mine, I'm not long for the scene."

III

KING ARTHUR, as he paced a lonely floor
That rolled a muffled echo, as he fancied,
All through the palace and out through the world,
Might now have wondered hard, could he have heard
Sir Lamorak's apathetic disregard
Of what Fate's knocking made so manifest
And ominous to others near the King—
If any, indeed, were near him at this hour
Save Merlin, once the wisest of all men,
And weary Dagonet, whom he had made
A knight for love of him and his abused
Integrity. He might have wondered hard
And wondered much; and after wondering,
He might have summoned, with as little heart
As he had now for crowns, the fond, lost Merlin,
Whose Nemesis had made of him a slave,
A man of dalliance, and a sybarite.

"Men change in Brittany, Merlin," said the King;
And even his grief had strife to freeze again
A dreary smile for the transmuted seer
Now robed in heavy wealth of purple silk,
With frogs and foreign tassels. On his face,
Too smooth now for a wizard or a sage,
Lay written, for the King's remembering eyes,
A pathos of a lost authority
Long faded, and unconscionably gone;
And on the King's heart lay a sudden cold:

"I might as well have left him in his grave,
As he would say it, saying what was true,—
As death is true. This Merlin is not mine,
But Vivian's. My crown is less than hers,
And I am less than woman to this man."

Then Merlin, as one reading Arthur's words
On viewless tablets in the air before him:
"Now, Arthur, since you are a child of mine—
A foster-child, and that's a kind of child—
Be not from hearsay or despair too eager
To dash your meat with bitter seasoning,
So none that are more famished than yourself
Shall have what you refuse. For you are King,
And if you starve yourself, you starve the state;
And then by sundry looks and silences
Of those you loved, and by the lax regard
Of those you knew for fawning enemies,
You may learn soon that you are King no more,
But a slack, blasted, and sad-fronted man,
Made sadder with a crown. No other friend
Than I could say this to you, and say more;
And if you bid me say no more, so be it."

The King, who sat with folded arms, now bowed
His head and felt, unfought and all aflame
Like immanent hell-fire, the wretchedness
That only those who are to lead may feel—
And only they when they are maimed and worn
Too sore to covet without shuddering
The fixed impending eminence where death
Itself were victory, could they but lead
Unbitten by the serpents they had fed.
Turning, he spoke: "Merlin, you say the truth:
There is no man who could say more to me

Today, or say so much to me, and live.
But you are Merlin still, or part of him;
I did you wrong when I thought otherwise,
And I am sorry now. Say what you will.
We are alone, and I shall be alone
As long as Time shall hide a reason here
For me to stay in this infested world
Where I have sinned and erred and heeded not
Your counsel; and where you yourself—God save us!—
Have gone down smiling to the smaller life
That you and your incongruous laughter called
Your living grave. God save us all, Merlin,
When you, the seer, the founder, and the prophet,
May throw the gold of your immortal treasure
Back to the God that gave it, and then laugh
Because a woman has you in her arms . . .
Why do you sting me now with a small hive
Of words that are all poison? I do not ask
Much honey; but why poison me for nothing,
And with a venom that I know already
As I know crowns and wars? Why tell a king—
A poor, foiled, flouted, miserable king—
That if he lets rats eat his fingers off
He'll have no fingers to fight battles with?
I know as much as that, for I am still
A king—who thought himself a little less
Than God; a king who built him palaces
On sand and mud, and hears them crumbling now,
And sees them tottering, as he knew they must.
You are the man who made me to be King—
Therefore, say anything."

                              Merlin, stricken deep
With pity that was old, being born of old
Foreshadowings, made answer to the King:

"This coil of Lancelot and Guinevere
Is not for any mortal to undo,
Or to deny, or to make otherwise;
But your most violent years are on their way
To days, and to a sounding of loud hours
That are to strike for war. Let not the time
Between this hour and then be lost in fears,
Or told in obscurations and vain faith
In what has been your long security;
For should your force be slower then than hate,
And your regret be sharper than your sight,
And your remorse fall heavier than your sword,—
Then say farewell to Camelot, and the crown.
But say not you have lost, or failed in aught
Your golden horoscope of imperfection
Has held in starry words that I have read.
I see no farther now than I saw then,
For no man shall be given of everything
Together in one life; yet I may say
The time is imminent when he shall come
For whom I founded the Siege Perilous;
And he shall be too much a living part
Of what he brings, and what he burns away in,
To be for long a vexed inhabitant
Of this mad realm of stains and lower trials.
And here the ways of God again are mixed:
For this new knight who is to find the Grail
For you, and for the least who pray for you
In such lost coombs and hollows of the world
As you have never entered, is to be
The son of him you trusted—Lancelot,
Of all who ever jeopardized a throne
Sure the most evil-fated, saving one,
Your son, begotten, though you knew not then
Your leman was your sister, of Morgause;

For it is Modred now, not Lancelot,
Whose native hate plans your annihilation—
Though he may smile till he be sick, and swear
Allegiance to an unforgiven father
Until at last he shake an empty tongue
Talked out with too much lying—though his lies
Will have a truth to steer them. Trust him not,
For unto you the father, he the son
Is like enough to be the last of terrors—
If in a field of time that looms to you
Far larger than it is you fail to plant
And harvest the old seeds of what I say,
And so be nourished and adept again
For what may come to be. But Lancelot
Will have you first; and you need starve no more
For the Queen's love, the love that never was.
Your Queen is now your Kingdom, and hereafter
Let no man take it from you, or you die.
Let no man take it from you for a day;
For days are long when we are far from what
We love, and mischief's other name is distance.
Let :hat be all, for I can say no more;
Not even to Blaise the Hermit, were he living,
Could I say more than I have given you now
To hear; and he alone was my confessor."

The King arose and paced the floor again.
"I get gray comfort of dark words," he said;
"But tell me not that you can say no more:
You can, for I can hear you saying it.
Yet I'll not ask for more. I have enough—
Until my new knight comes to prove and find
The promise and the glory of the Grail,
Though I shall see no Grail. For I have built
On sand and mud, and I shall see no Grail."—

"Nor I," said Merlin. "Once I dreamed of it,
But I was buried. I shall see no Grail,
Nor would I have it otherwise. I saw
Too much, and that was never good for man.
The man who goes alone too far goes mad—
In one way or another. God knew best,
And he knows what is coming yet for me.
I do not ask. Like you, I have enough."

That night King Arthur's apprehension found
In Merlin an obscure and restive guest,
Whose only thought was on the hour of dawn,
When he should see the last of Camelot
And ride again for Brittany; and what words
Were said before the King was left alone
Were only darker for reiteration.
They parted, all provision made secure
For Merlin's early convoy to the coast,
And Arthur tramped the past. The loneliness
Of kings, around him like the unseen dead,
Lay everywhere; and he was loath to move,
As if in fear to meet with his cold hand
The touch of something colder. Then a whim,
Begotten of intolerable doubt,
Seized him and stung him until he was asking
If any longer lived among his knights
A man to trust as once he trusted all,
And Lancelot more than all. "And it is he
Who is to have me first," so Merlin says,—
"As if he had me not in hell already.
Lancelot! Lancelot!" He cursed the tears
That cooled his misery, and then he asked
Himself again if he had one to trust
Among his knights, till even Bedivere,
Tor, Bors, and Percival, rough Lamorak,

Griflet, and Gareth, and gay Gawaine, all
Were dubious knaves,—or they were like to be,
For cause to make them so; and he had made
Himself to be the cause. "God set me right,
Before this folly carry me on farther,"
He murmured; and he smiled unhappily,
Though fondly, as he thought: "Yes, there is one
Whom I may trust with even my soul's last shred;
And Dagonet will sing for me tonight
An old song, not too merry or too sad."

When Dagonet, having entered, stood before
The King as one affrighted, the King smiled:
"You think because I call for you so late
That I am angry, Dagonet? Why so?
Have you been saying what I say to you,
And telling men that you brought Merlin here?
No? So I fancied; and if you report
No syllable of anything I speak,
You will have no regrets, and I no anger.
What word of Merlin was abroad today?"

"Today have I heard no man save Gawaine,
And to him I said only what all men
Are saying to their neighbors. They believe
That you have Merlin here, and that his coming
Denotes no good. Gawaine was curious,
But ever mindful of your majesty.
He pressed me not, and we made light of it."

"Gawaine, I fear, makes light of everything,"
The King said, looking down. "Sometimes I wish
I had a full Round Table of Gawaines.
But that's a freak of midnight,—never mind it.
Sing me a song—one of those endless things

That Merlin liked of old, when men were younger
And there were more stars twinkling in the sky.
I see no stars that are alive tonight,
And I am not the king of sleep. So then,
Sing me an old song."

                              Dagonet's quick eye
Caught sorrow in the King's; and he knew more,
In a fool's way, than even the King himself
Of what was hovering over Camelot.
"O King," he said, "I cannot sing tonight.
If you command me I shall try to sing,
But I shall fail; for there are no songs now
In my old throat, or even in these poor strings
That I can hardly follow with my fingers.
Forgive me—kill me—but I cannot sing."
Dagonet fell down then on both his knees
And shook there while he clutched the King's cold hand
And wept for what he knew.

                              "There, Dagonet;
I shall not kill my knight, or make him sing.
No more; get up, and get you off to bed.
There'll be another time for you to sing,
So get you to your covers and sleep well."
Alone again, the King said, bitterly:
"Yes, I have one friend left, and they who know
As much of him as of themselves believe
That he's a fool. Poor Dagonet's a fool.
And if he be a fool, what else am I
Than one fool more to make the world complete?
'The love that never was!' . . . Fool, fool, fool, fool!"

The King was long awake. No covenant
With peace was his tonight; and he knew sleep

As he knew the cold eyes of Guinevere
That yesterday had stabbed him, having first
On Lancelot's name struck fire, and left him then
As now they left him—with a wounded heart,
A wounded pride, and a sickening pang worse yet
Of lost possession. He thought wearily
Of watchers by the dead, late wayfarers,
Rough-handed mariners on ships at sea,
Lone-yawning sentries, wastrels, and all others
Who might be saying somewhere to themselves,
"The King is now asleep in Camelot;
God save the King."—"God save the King, indeed,
If there be now a king to save," he said.
Then he saw giants rising in the dark,
Born horribly of memories and new fears
That in the gray-lit irony of dawn
Were partly to fade out and be forgotten;
And then there might be sleep, and for a time
There might again be peace. His head was hot
And throbbing; but the rest of him was cold,
As he lay staring hard where nothing stood,
And hearing what was not, even while he saw
And heard, like dust and thunder far away,
The coming confirmation of the words
Of him who saw so much and feared so little
Of all that was to be. No spoken doom
That ever chilled the last night of a felon
Prepared a dragging anguish more profound
And absolute than Arthur, in these hours,
Made out of darkness and of Merlin's words;
No tide that ever crashed on Lyonnesse
Drove echoes inland that were lonelier
For widowed ears among the fisher-folk,
Than for the King were memories tonight
Of old illusions that were dead for ever.

IV

THE tortured King—seeing Merlin wholly meshed
In his defection, even to indifference,
And all the while attended and exalted
By some unfathomable obscurity
Of divination, where the Grail, unseen,
Broke yet the darkness where a king saw nothing—
Feared now the lady Vivian more than Fate;
For now he knew that Modred, Lancelot,
The Queen, the King, the Kingdom, and the World,
Were less to Merlin, who had made him King,
Than one small woman in Broceliande.
Whereas the lady Vivian, seeing Merlin
Acclaimed and tempted and allured again
To service in his old magnificence,
Feared now King Arthur more than storms and robbers;
For Merlin, though he knew himself immune
To no least whispered little wish of hers
That might afflict his ear with ecstasy,
Had yet sufficient of his old command
Of all around him to invest an eye
With quiet lightning, and a spoken word
With easy thunder, so accomplishing
A profit and a pastime for himself—
And for the lady Vivian, when her guile
Outlived at intervals her graciousness;
And this equipment of uncertainty,
Which now had gone away with him to Britain
With Dagonet, so plagued her memory
That soon a phantom brood of goblin doubts
Inhabited his absence, which had else
Been empty waiting and a few brave fears,
And a few more, she knew, that were not brave,
Or long to be disowned, or manageable.

She thought of him as he had looked at her
When first he had acquainted her alarm
At sight of the King's letter with its import;
And she remembered now his very words:
"The King believes today as in his boyhood
That I am Fate," he said; and when they parted
She had not even asked him not to go;
She might as well, she thought, have bid the wind
Throw no more clouds across a lonely sky
Between her and the moon,—so great he seemed
In his oppressed solemnity, and she,
In her excess of wrong imagining,
So trivial in an hour, and, after all
A creature of a smaller consequence
Than kings to Merlin, who made kings and kingdoms
And had them as a father; and so she feared
King Arthur more than robbers while she waited
For Merlin's promise to fulfil itself,
And for the rest that was to follow after:
"He said he would come back, and so he will.
He will because he must, and he is Merlin,
The master of the world—or so he was;
And he is coming back again to me
Because he must and I am Vivian.
It's all as easy as two added numbers:
Some day I'll hear him ringing at the gate,
As he rang on that morning in the spring,
Ten years ago; and I shall have him then
For ever. He shall never go away
Though kings come walking on their hands and knees
To take him on their backs." When Merlin came,
She told him that, and laughed; and he said strangely:
"Be glad or sorry, but no kings are coming.
Not Arthur, surely; for now Arthur knows
That I am less than Fate."

Ten years ago
The King had heard, with unbelieving ears
At first, what Merlin said would be the last
Reiteration of his going down
To find a living grave in Brittany:
"Buried alive I told you I should be,
By love made little and by woman shorn,
Like Samson, of my glory; and the time
Is now at hand. I follow in the morning
Where I am led. I see behind me now
The last of crossways, and I see before me
A straight and final highway to the end
Of all my divination. You are King,
And in your kingdom I am what I was.
Wherever I have warned you, see as far
As I have seen; for I have shown the worst
There is to see. Require no more of me,
For I can be no more than what I was."
So, on the morrow, the King said farewell;
And he was never more to Merlin's eye
The King than at that hour; for Merlin knew
How much was going out of Arthur's life
With him, as he went southward to the sea.

Over the waves and into Brittany
Went Merlin, to Broceliande. Gay birds
Were singing high to greet him all along
A broad and sanded woodland avenue
That led him on forever, so he thought,
Until at last there was an end of it;
And at the end there was a gate of iron,
Wrought heavily and invidiously barred.
He pulled a cord that rang somewhere a bell
Of many echoes, and sat down to rest,
Outside. the keeper's house, upon a bench

Of carven stone that might for centuries
Have waited there in silence to receive him.
The birds were singing still; leaves flashed and swung
Before him in the sunlight; a soft breeze
Made intermittent whisperings around him
Of love and fate and danger, and faint waves
Of many sweetly-stinging fragile odors
Broke lightly as they touched him; cherry-boughs
Above him snowed white petals down upon him,
And under their slow falling Merlin smiled
Contentedly, as one who contemplates
No longer fear, confusion, or regret,
May smile at ruin or at revelation.

A stately fellow with a forest air
Now hailed him from within, with searching words
And curious looks, till Merlin's glowing eye
 Transfixed him and he flinched: "My compliments
And homage to the lady Vivian.
Say Merlin from King Arthur's Court is here,
A pilgrim and a stranger in appearance,
Though in effect her friend and humble servant.
Convey to her my speech as I have said it,
Without abbreviation or delay,
And so deserve my gratitude forever."
"But Merlin?" the man stammered; "Merlin?   Merlin?"—
"One Merlin is enough. I know no other.
Now go you to the lady Vivian
And bring to me her word, for I am weary."
Still smiling at the cherry-blossoms falling
Down on him and around him in the sunlight,
He waited, never moving, never glancing
This way or that, until his messenger
Came jingling into vision, weighed with keys,
And inly shaken with much wondering

At this great wizard's coming unannounced
And unattended. When the way was open
The stately messenger, now bowing low
In reverence and awe, bade Merlin enter;
And Merlin, having entered, heard the gate
Clang back behind him; and he swore no gate
Like that had ever clanged in Camelot,
Or any other place if not in hell.
"I may be dead; and this good fellow here,
With all his keys," he thought, "may be the Devil,—
Though I were loath to say so, for the keys
Would make him rather more akin to Peter;
And that's fair reasoning for this fair weather."

"The lady Vivian says you are most welcome,"
Said now the stately-favored servitor,
"And are to follow me. She said, 'Say Merlin—
A pilgrim and a stranger in appearance,
Though in effect my friend and humble servant—
Is welcome for himself, and for the sound
Of his great name that echoes everywhere.' "—
"I like you and I like your memory,"
Said Merlin, curiously, "but not your gate.
Why forge for this elysian wilderness
A thing so vicious with unholy noise?"—
"There's a way out of every wilderness
For those who dare or care enough to find it,"
The guide said: and they moved along together,
Down shaded ways, through open ways with hedgerows.
And into shade again more deep than ever,
But edged anon with rays of broken sunshine
In which a fountain, raining crystal music,
Made faery magic of it through green leafage,
Till Merlin's eyes were dim with preparation
For sight now of the lady Vivian.

He saw at first a bit of living green
That might have been a part of all the green
Around the tinkling fountain where she gazed
Upon the circling pool as if her thoughts
Were not so much on Merlin—whose advance
Betrayed through his enormity of hair
The cheeks and eyes of youth—as on the fishes.
But soon she turned and found him, now alone,
And held him while her beauty and her grace
Made passing trash of empires, and his eyes
Told hers of what a splendid emptiness
Her tedious world had been without him in it
Whose love and service were to be her school,
Her triumph, and her history: "This is Merlin,"
She thought; "and I shall dream of him no more.
And he has come, he thinks, to frighten me
With beards and robes and his immortal fame;
Or is it I who think so? I know not.
I'm frightened, sure enough, but if I show it,
I'll be no more the Vivian for whose love
He tossed away his glory, or the Vivian
Who saw no man alive to make her love him
Till she saw Merlin once in Camelot,
And seeing him, saw no other. In an age
That has no plan for me that I can read
Without him, shall he tell me what I am,
And why I am, I wonder?" While she thought,
And feared the man whom her perverse negation
Must overcome somehow to soothe her fancy,
She smiled and welcomed him; and so they stood,
Each finding in the other's eyes a gleam
Of what eternity had hidden there.

"Are you always all in green, as you are now?"
Said Merlin, more employed with her complexion,

Where blood and olive made wild harmony
With eyes and wayward hair that were too dark
For peace if they were not subordinated;
"If so you are, then so you make yourself
A danger in a world of many dangers.
If I were young, God knows if I were safe
Concerning you in green, like a slim cedar,
As you are now, to say my life was mine:
Were you to say to me that I should end it,
Longevity for me were jeopardized.
Have you your green on always and all over?"

"Come here, and I will tell you about that,"
Said Vivian, leading Merlin with a laugh
To an arbored seat where they made opposites:
"If you are Merlin—and I know you are,
For I remember you in Camelot,—
You know that I am Vivian, as I am;
And if I go in green, why, let me go so,
And say at once why you have come to me
Cloaked over like a monk, and with a beard
As long as Jeremiah's. I don't like it.
I'll never like a man with hair like that
While I can feed a carp with little frogs.
I'm rather sure to hate you if you keep it,
And when I hate a man I poison him."

"You've never fed a carp with little frogs,"
Said Merlin; "I can see it in your eyes."—
"I might then, if I haven't," said the lady;
"For I'm a savage, and I love no man
As I have seen him yet. I'm here alone,
With some three hundred others, all of whom
Are ready, I dare say, to die for me;
I'm cruel and I'm cold, and I like snakes;

And some have said my mother was a fairy,
Though I believe it not."

                              "Why not believe it?"
Said Merlin; "I believe it. I believe
Also that you divine, as I had wished,
In my surviving ornament of office
A needless imposition on your wits,
If not yet on the scope of your regard.
Even so, you cannot say how old I am,
Or yet how young. I'm willing cheerfully
To fight, left-handed, Hell's three headed hound
If you but whistle him up from where he lives;
I'm cheerful and I'm fierce, and I've made kings;
And some have said my father was the Devil,
Though I believe it not. Whatever I am,
I have not lived in Time until to-day."
A moment's worth of wisdom there escaped him,
But Vivian seized it, and it was not lost.

Embroidering doom with many levities,
Till now the fountain's crystal silver, fading,
Became a splash and a mere chilliness,
They mocked their fate with easy pleasantries
That were too false and small to be forgotten,
And with ingenious insincerities
That had no repetition or revival.
At last the lady Vivian arose,
And with a crying of how late it was
Took Merlin's hand and led him like a child
Along a dusky way between tall cones
Of tight green cedars: "Am I like one of these?
You said I was, though I deny it wholly."—
"Very," said Merlin, to his bearded lips
Uplifting her small fingers.—"O, that hair!"

She moaned, as if in sorrow: "Must it be?
Must every prophet and important wizard
Be clouded so that nothing but his nose
And eyes, and intimations of his ears,
Are there to make us know him when we see him?
Praise heaven I'm not a prophet!   Are you glad?"—

He did not say that he was glad or sorry;
For suddenly came flashing into vision
A thing that was a manor and a castle,
With walls and roofs that had a flaming sky
Behind them, like a sky that he remembered,
And one that had from his rock-sheltered haunt
Above the roofs of his forsaken city
Made flame as if all Camelot were on fire.
The glow brought with it a brief memory
Of Arthur as he left him, and the pain
That fought in Arthur's eyes for losing him,
And must have overflowed when he had vanished.
But now the eyes that looked hard into his
Were Vivian's, not the King's; and he could see,
Or so he thought, a shade of sorrow in them.
She took his two hands: "You are sad," she said.—
He smiled: "Your western lights bring memories
Of Camelot. We all have memories—
Prophets, and women who are like slim cedars;
But you are wrong to say that I am sad."—
"Would you go back to Camelot?" she asked,
Her fingers tightening. Merlin shook his head.
"Then listen while I tell you that I'm glad,"
She purred, as if assured that he would listen:
"At your first warning, much too long ago,
Of this quaint pilgrimage of yours to see
'The fairest and most orgulous of ladies'—
No language for a prophet, I am sure—

Said I, 'When this great Merlin comes to me,
My task and avocation for some time
Will be to make him willing, if I can,
To teach and feed me with an ounce of wisdom.'
For I have eaten to an empty shell,
After a weary feast of observation
Among the glories of a tinsel world
That had for me no glory till you came,
A life that is no life. Would you go back
To Camelot?"—Merlin shook his head again,
And the two smiled together in the sunset.

They moved along in silence to the door,
Where Merlin said: "Of your three hundred here
There is but one I know, and him I favor;
I mean the stately one who shakes the keys
Of that most evil sounding gate of yours,
Which has a clang as if it shut forever."—
"If there be need, I'll shut the gate myself,"
She said. "And you like Blaise? Then you shall have him.
He was not born to serve, but serve he must,
It seems, and be enamoured of my shadow.
He cherishes the taint of some high folly
That haunts him with a name he cannot know,
And I could fear his wits are paying for it.
Forgive his tongue, and humor it a little."—
"I knew another one whose name was Blaise,"
He said; and she said lightly, "Well, what of it?"—
"And he was nigh the learnedest of hermits;
His home was far away from everywhere,
And he was all alone there when he died."—
"Now be a pleasant Merlin," Vivian said,
Patting his arm, "and have no more of that;
For I'll not hear of dead men far away,
Or dead men anywhere this afternoon.

There'll be a trifle in the way of supper
This evening, but the dead shall not have any.
Blaise and this man will tell you all there is
For you to know. Then you'll know everything."
She laughed, and vanished like a humming-bird.

V

THE sun went down, and the dark after it
Starred Merlin's new abode with many a sconced
And many a moving candle, in whose light
The prisoned wizard, mirrored in amazement,
Saw fronting him a stranger, falcon-eyed,
Firm-featured, of a negligible age,
And fair enough to look upon, he fancied,
Though not a warrior born, nor more a courtier.
A native humor resting in his long
And solemn jaws now stirred, and Merlin smiled
To see himself in purple, touched with gold,
And fledged with snowy lace.—The careful Blaise,
Having drawn some time before from Merlin's wallet
The sable raiment of a royal scholar,
Had eyed it with a long mistrust and said:
"The lady Vivian would be vexed, I fear,
To meet you vested in these learned weeds
Of gravity and death; for she abhors
Mortality in all its hues and emblems—
Black wear, long argument, and all the cold
And solemn things that appertain to graves."—
And Merlin, listening, to himself had said,
"This fellow has a freedom, yet I like him;"
And then aloud: "I trust you. Deck me out,
However, with a temperate regard
For what your candid eye may find in me
Of inward coloring. Let them reap my beard,

Moreover, with a sort of reverence,
For I shall never look on it again.
And though your lady frown her face away
To think of me in black, for God's indulgence,
Array me not in scarlet or in yellow."—
And so it came to pass that Merlin sat
At ease in purple, even though his chin
Reproached him as he pinched it, and seemed yet
A little fearful of its nakedness.
He might have sat and scanned himself for ever
Had not the careful Blaise, regarding him,
Remarked again that in his proper judgment,
And on the valid word of his attendants,
No more was to be done. "Then do no more,"
Said Merlin, with a last look at his chin;
"Never do more when there's no more to do,
And you may shun thereby the bitter taste
Of many disillusions and regrets.
God's pity on us that our words have wings
And leave our deeds to crawl so far below them;
For we have all two heights, we men who dream,
Whether we lead or follow, rule or serve."—
"God's pity on us anyhow," Blaise answered,
"Or most of us. Meanwhile, I have to say,
As long as you are here, and I'm alive,
Your summons will assure the loyalty
Of all my diligence and expedition.
The gong that you hear singing in the distance
Was rung for your attention and your presence."—
"I wonder at this fellow, yet I like him,"
Said Merlin; and he rose to follow him.

The lady Vivian in a fragile sheath
Of crimson, dimmed and veiled ineffably
By the flame-shaken gloom wherein she sat,

And twinkled if she moved, heard Merlin coming,
And smiled as if to make herself believe
Her joy was all a triumph; yet her blood
Confessed a tingling of more wonderment
Than all her five and twenty worldly years
Of waiting for this triumph could remember;
And when she knew and felt the slower tread
Of his unseen advance among the shadows
To the small haven of uncertain light
That held her in it as a torch-lit shoal
Might hold a smooth red fish, her listening skin
Responded with a creeping underneath it,
And a crinkling that was incident alike
To darkness, love, and mice. When he was there,
She looked up at him in a whirl of mirth
And wonder, as in childhood she had gazed
Wide-eyed on royal mountebanks who made
So brief a shift of the impossible
That kings and queens would laugh and shake themselves;
Then rising slowly on her little feet,
Like a slim creature lifted, she thrust out
Her two small hands as if to push him back—
Whereon he seized them. "Go away," she said;
"I never saw you in my life before."—
"You say the truth," he answered; "when I met
Myself an hour ago, my words were yours.
God made the man you see for you to like,
If possible. If otherwise, turn down
These two prodigious and remorseless thumbs
And leave your lions to annihilate him."—

"I have no other lion than yourself,"
She said; "and since you cannot eat yourself,
Pray do a lonely woman, who is, you say,
More like a tree than any other thing

In your discrimination, the large honor
Of sharing with her a small kind of supper."—
"Yes, you are like a tree,—or like a flower;
More like a flower to-night." He bowed his head
And kissed the ten small fingers he was holding,
As calmly as if each had been a son;
Although his heart was leaping and his eyes
Had sight for nothing save a swimming crimson
Between two glimmering arms. "More like a flower
To-night," he said, as now he scanned again
The immemorial meaning of her face
And drew it nearer to his eyes. It seemed
A flower of wonder with a crimson stem
Came leaning slowly and regretfully
To meet his will—a flower of change and peril
That had a clinging blossom of warm olive
Half stifled with a tyranny of black,
And held the wayward fragrance of a rose
Made woman by delirious alchemy.
She raised her face and yoked his willing neck
With half her weight; and with hot lips that left
The world with only one philosophy
For Merlin or for Anaxagoras,
Called his to meet them and in one long hush
Of capture to surrender and make hers
The last of anything that might remain
Of what was now their beardless wizardry.
Then slowly she began to push herself
Away, and slowly Merlin let her go
As far from him as his outreaching hands
Could hold her fingers while his eyes had all
The beauty of the woodland and the world
Before him in the firelight, like a nymph
Of cities, or a queen a little weary
Of inland stillness and immortal trees.

"Are you to let me go again sometime,"
She said,—"before I starve to death, I wonder?
If not, I'll have to bite the lion's paws,
And make him roar. He cannot shake his mane,
For now the lion has no mane to shake;
The lion hardly knows himself without it,
And thinks he has no face, but there's a lady
Who says he had no face until he lost it.
So there we are. And there's a flute somewhere,
Playing a strange old tune. You know the words:
'The Lion and the Lady are both hungry.'"

Fatigue and hunger—tempered leisurely
With food that some devout magician's oven
Might after many failures have delivered,
And wine that had for decades in the dark
Of Merlin's grave been slowly quickening,
And with half-heard, dream-weaving interludes
Of distant flutes and viols, made more distant
By far, nostalgic hautboys blown from nowhere,—
Were tempered not so leisurely, may be,
With Vivian's inextinguishable eyes
Between two shining silver candlesticks
That lifted each a trembling flame to make
The rest of her a dusky loveliness
Against a bank of shadow. Merlin made,
As well as he was able while he ate,
A fair division of the fealty due
To food and beauty, albeit more times than one
Was he at odds with his urbanity
In honoring too long the grosser viand.
"The best invention in Broceliande
Has not been over-taxed in vain, I see,"
She told him, with her chin propped on her fingers
And her eyes flashing blindness into his:

"I put myself out cruelly to please you,
And you, for that, forget almost at once
The name and image of me altogether.
You needn't, for when all is analyzed,
It's only a bird-pie that you are eating."

"I know not what you call it," Merlin said;
"Nor more do I forget your name and image,
Though I do eat; and if I did not eat,
Your sending out of ships and caravans
To get whatever 'tis that's in this thing
Would be a sorrow for you all your days;
And my great love, which you have seen by now,
Might look to you a lie; and like as not
You'd actuate some sinewed mercenary
To carry me away to God knows where
And seal me in a fearsome hole to starve,
Because I made of this insidious picking
An idle circumstance. My dear fair lady—
And there is not another under heaven
So fair as you are as I see you now—
I cannot look at you too much and eat;
And I must eat, or be untimely ashes,
Whereon the light of your celestial gaze
Would fall, I fear me, for no longer time
Than on the solemn dust of Jeremiah—
Whose beard you likened once, in heathen jest,
To mine that now is no man's."

                              "Are you sorry?"
Said Vivian, filling Merlin's empty goblet;
"If you are sorry for the loss of it,
Drink more of this and you may tell me lies
Enough to make me sure that you are glad;
But if your love is what you say it is,

Be never sorry that my love took off
That horrid hair to make your face at last
A human fact. Since I have had your name
To dream of and say over to myself,
The visitations of that awful beard
Have been a terror for my nights and days—
For twenty years. I've seen it like an ocean,
Blown seven ways at once and wrecking ships,
With men and women screaming for their lives;
I've seen it woven into shining ladders
That ran up out of sight and so to heaven,
All covered with white ghosts with hanging robes
Like folded wings,—and there were millions of them,
Climbing, climbing, climbing, all the time;
And all the time that I was watching them
I thought how far above me Merlin was,
And wondered always what his face was like.
But even then, as a child, I knew the day
Would come some time when I should see his face
And hear his voice, and have him in my house
Till he should care no more to stay in it,
And go away to found another kingdom."—
"Not that," he said; and, sighing, drank more wine;
"One kingdom for one Merlin is enough."—
"One Merlin for one Vivian is enough,"
She said. "If you care much, remember that;
But the Lord knows how many Vivians
One Merlin's entertaining eye might favor,
Indifferently well and all at once,
If they were all at hand. Praise heaven they're not."

"If they were in the world—praise heaven they're not—
And if one Merlin's entertaining eye
Saw two of them, there might be left him then
The sight of no eye to see anything—

Not even the Vivian who is everything,
She being Beauty, Beauty being She,
She being Vivian, and so on for ever."—
"I'm glad you don't see two of me," she said;
"For there's a whole world yet for you to eat
And drink and say to me before I know
The sort of creature that you see in me.
I'm withering for a little more attention,
But, being woman, I can wait. These cups
That you see coming are for the last there is
Of what my father gave to kings alone,
And far from always. You are more than kings
To me; therefore I give it all to you,
Imploring you to spare no more of it
Than a small cockle-shell would hold for me
To pledge your love and mine in. Take the rest,
That I may see tonight the end of it.
I'll have no living remnant of the dead
Annoying me until it fades and sours
Of too long cherishing; for Time enjoys
The look that's on our faces when we scowl
On unexpected ruins, and thrift itself
May be a sort of slow unwholesome fire
That eats away to dust the life that feeds it.
You smile, I see, but I said what I said.
One hardly has to live a thousand years
To contemplate a lost economy;
So let us drink it while it's yet alive
And you and I are not untimely ashes.
My last words are your own, and I don't like 'em."—
A sudden laughter scattered from her eyes
A threatening wisdom. He smiled and let her laugh,
Then looked into the dark where there was nothing:
"There's more in this than I have seen," he thought,
"Though I shall see it."—"Drink," she said again;

"There's only this much in the world of it,
And I am near to giving all to you
Because you are so great and I so little."

With a long-kindling gaze that caught from hers
A laughing flame, and with a hand that shook
Like Arthur's kingdom, Merlin slowly raised
A golden cup that for a golden moment
Was twinned in air with hers; and Vivian,
Who smiled at him across their gleaming rims,
From eyes that made a fuel of the night
Surrounding her, shot glory over gold
At Merlin, while their cups touched and his trembled.
He drank, not knowing what, nor caring much
For kings who might have cared less for themselves,
He thought, had all the darkness and wild light
That fell together to make Vivian
Been there before them then to flower anew
Through sheathing crimson into candle-light
With each new leer of their loose, liquorish eyes.
Again he drank, and he cursed every king
Who might have touched her even in her cradle;
For what were kings to such as he, who made them
And saw them totter—for the world to see,
And heed, if the world would? He drank again,
And yet again—to make himself assured
No manner of king should have the last of it—
The cup that Vivian filled unfailingly
Until she poured for nothing. "At the end
Of this incomparable flowing gold,"
She prattled on to Merlin, who observed
Her solemnly, "I fear there may be specks."—
He sighed aloud, whereat she laughed at him
And pushed the golden cup a little nearer.
He scanned it with a sad anxiety,

And then her face likewise, and shook his head
As if at her concern for such a matter:
"Specks? What are specks? Are you afraid of them?"
He murmured slowly, with a drowsy tongue;
"There are specks everywhere. I fear them not.
If I were king in Camelot, I might
Fear more than specks. But now I fear them not.
You are too strange a lady to fear specks."

He stared a long time at the cup of gold
Before him but he drank no more. There came
Between him and the world a crumbling sky
Of black and crimson, with a crimson cloud
That held a far off town of many towers.
All swayed and shaken, till at last they fell,
And there was nothing but a crimson cloud
That crumbled into nothing, like the sky
That vanished with it, carrying away
The world, the woman, and all memory of them,
Until a slow light of another sky
Made gray an open casement, showing him
Faint shapes of an exotic furniture
That glimmered with a dim magnificence,
And letting in the sound of many birds
That were, as he lay there remembering,
The only occupation of his ears
Until it seemed they shared a fainter sound,
As if a sleeping child with a black head
Beside him drew the breath of innocence.

One shining afternoon around the fountain,
As on the shining day of his arrival,
The sunlight was alive with flying silver
That had for Merlin a more dazzling flash
Than jewels rained in dreams, and a richer sound

Than harps, and all the morning stars together,—
When jewels and harps and stars and everything
That flashed and sang and was not Vivian,
Seemed less than echoes of her least of words—
For she was coming. Suddenly, somewhere
Behind him, she was coming; that was all
He knew until she came and took his hand
And held it while she talked about the fishes.
When she looked up he thought a softer light
Was in her eyes than once he had found there;
And had there been left yet for dusky women
A beauty that was heretofore not hers,
He told himself he must have seen it then
Before him in the face at which he smiled
And trembled. "Many men have called me wise,"
He said, "but you are wiser than all wisdom
If you know what you are."—"I don't," she said;
"I know that you and I are here together;
I know that I have known for twenty years
That life would be almost a constant yawning
Until you came; and now that you are here,
I know that you are not to go away
Until you tell me that I'm hideous;
I know that I like fishes, ferns, and snakes,—
Maybe because I liked them when the world
Was young and you and I were salamanders;
I know, too, a cool place not far from here,
Where there are ferns that are like marching men
Who never march away. Come now and see them,
And do as they do—never march away.
When they are gone, some others, crisp and green,
Will have their place, but never march away."—
He smoothed her silky fingers, one by one:
"Some other Merlin, also, do you think,
Will have his place—and never march away?"—

Then Vivian laid a finger on his lips
And shook her head at him before she laughed:
"There is no other Merlin than yourself,
And you are never going to be old."

Oblivious of a world that made of him
A jest, a legend, and a long regret,
And with a more commanding wizardry
Than his to rule a kingdom where the king
Was Love and the queen Vivian, Merlin found
His queen without the blemish of a word
That was more rough than honey from her lips,
Or the first adumbration of a frown
To cloud the night-wild fire that in her eyes
Had yet a smoky friendliness of home,
And a foreknowing care for mighty trifles.
"There are miles and miles for you to wander in,"
She told him once: "Your prison yard is large,
And I would rather take my two ears off
And feed them to the fishes in the fountain
Than buzz like an incorrigible bee
For always around yours, and have you hate
The sound of me; for some day then, for certain,
Your philosophic rage would see in me
A bee in earnest, and your hand would smite
My life away. And what would you do then?
I know: for years and years you'd sit alone
Upon my grave, and be the grieving image
Of lean remorse, and suffer miserably;
And often, all day long, you'd only shake
Your celebrated head and all it holds,
Or beat it with your fist the while you groaned
Aloud and went on saying to yourself:
'Never should I have killed her, or believed
She was a bee that buzzed herself to death,

First having made me crazy, had there been
Judicious distance and wise absences
To keep the two of us inquisitive.' "—
"I fear you bow your unoffending head
Before a load that should be mine," said he;
"If so, you led me on by listening.
You should have shrieked and jumped, and then fled yelling
That's the best way when a man talks too long.
God's pity on me if I love your feet
More now than I could ever love the face
Of any one of all those Vivians
You summoned out of nothing on the night
When I saw towers. I'll wander and amend."—
At that she flung the noose of her soft arms
Around his neck and kissed him instantly:
"You are the wisest man that ever was,
And I've a prayer to make: May all you say
To Vivian be a part of what you knew
Before the curse of her unquiet head
Was on your shoulder, as you have it now,
To punish you for knowing beyond knowledge.
You are the only one who sees enough
To make me see how far away I am
From all that I have seen and have not been;
You are the only thing there is alive
Between me as I am and as I was
When Merlin was a dream. You are to listen
When I say now to you that I'm alone.
Like you, I saw too much; and unlike you
I made no kingdom out of what I saw—
Or none save this one here that you must rule,
Believing you are ruled. I see too far
To rule myself. Time's way with you and me
Is our way, in that we are out of Time
And out of tune with Time. We have this place,

And you must hold us in it or we die.
Look at me now and say if what I say
Be folly or not; for my unquiet head
Is no conceit of mine. I had it first
When I was born; and I shall have it with me
Till my unquiet soul is on its way
To be, I hope, where souls are quieter.
So let the first and last activity
Of what you say so often is your love
Be always to remember that our lyres
Are not strung for Today. On you it falls
To keep them in accord here with each other,
For you have wisdom, I have only sight
For distant things—and you. And you are Merlin.
Poor wizard! Vivian is your punishment
For making kings of men who are not kings;
And you are mine, by the same reasoning,
For living out of Time and out of tune
With anything but you. No other man
Could make me say so much of what I know
As I say now to you. And you are Merlin!"

She looked up at him till his way was lost
Again in the familiar wilderness
Of night that love made for him in her eyes,
And there he wandered as he said he would;
He wandered also in his prison-yard,
And, when he found her coming after him,
Beguiled her with her own admonishing
And frowned upon her with a fierce reproof
That many a time in the old world outside
Had set the mark of silence on strong men—
Whereat she laughed, not always wholly sure,
Nor always wholly glad, that he who played
So lightly was the wizard of her dreams:

"No matter—if only Merlin keep the world
Away," she thought. "Our lyres have many strings,
But he must know them all, for he is Merlin."

And so for years, till ten of them were gone,—
Ten years, ten seasons, or ten flying ages—
Fate made Broceliande a paradise,
By none invaded, until Dagonet,
Like a discordant, awkward bird of doom,
Flew in with Arthur's message. For the King,
In sorrow cleaving to simplicity,
And having in his love a quick remembrance
Of Merlin's old affection for the fellow,
Had for this vain, reluctant enterprise
Appointed him—the knight who made men laugh,
And was a fool because he played the fool.

"The King believes today, as in his boyhood,
That I am Fate; and I can do no more
Than show again what in his heart he knows,"
Said Merlin to himself and Vivian:
"This time I go because I made him King,
Thereby to be a mirror for the world;
This time I go, but never after this,
For I can be no more than what I was,
And I can do no more than I have done."
He took her slowly in his arms and felt
Her body throbbing like a bird against him:
"This time I go; I go because I must."

And in the morning, when he rode away
With Dagonet and Blaise through the same gate
That once had clanged as if to shut for ever,
She had not even asked him not to go;
For it was then that in his lonely gaze

Of helpless love and sad authority
She found the gleam of his imprisoned power
That Fate withheld; and, pitying herself,
She pitied the fond Merlin she had changed,
And saw the Merlin who had changed the world.

VI

"No kings are coming on their hands and knees,
Nor yet on horses or in chariots,
To carry me away from you again,"
Said Merlin, winding around Vivian's ear
A shred of her black hair. "King Arthur knows
That I have done with kings, and that I speak
No more their crafty language. Once I knew it,
But now the only language I have left
Is one that I must never let you hear
Too long, or know too well. When towering deeds
Once done shall only out of dust and words
Be done again, the doer may then be wary
Lest in the complement of his new fabric
There be more words than dust."

       "Why tell me so?"
Said Vivian; and a singular thin laugh
Came after her thin question. "Do you think
That I'm so far away from history
That I require, even of the wisest man
Who ever said the wrong thing to a woman,
So large a light on what I know already—
When all I seek is here before me now
In your new eyes that you have brought for me
From Camelot? The eyes you took away
Were sad and old; and I could see in them
A Merlin who remembered all the kings

He ever saw, and wished himself, almost,
Away from Vivian, to make other kings,
And shake the world again in the old manner.
I saw myself no bigger than a beetle
For several days, and wondered if your love
Were large enough to make me any larger
When you came back. Am I a beetle still?"
She stood up on her toes and held her cheek
For some time against his, and let him go.

"I fear the time has come for me to wander
A little in my prison-yard," he said.—
"No, tell me everything that you have seen
And heard and done, and seen done, and heard done,
Since you deserted me. And tell me first
What the King thinks of me."—"The King believes
That you are almost what you are," he told her:
"The beauty of all ages that are vanished,
Reborn to be the wonder of one woman."—
"I knew he hated me. What else of him?"—
"And all that I have seen and heard and done,
Which is not much, would make a weary telling;
And all your part of it would be to sleep,
And dream that Merlin had his beard again."—
"Then tell me more about your good fool knight,
Sir Dagonet. If Blaise were not half-mad
Already with his pondering on the name
And shield of his unshielding nameless father,
I'd make a fool of him. I'd call him Ajax;
I'd have him shake his fist at thunder-storms,
And dance a jig as long as there was lightning,
And so till I forgot myself entirely.
Not even your love may do so much as that."—
"Thunder and lightning are no friends of mine,"
Said Merlin slowly, "more than they are yours;

They bring me nearer to the elements
From which I came than I care now to be."—
"You owe a service to those elements;
For by their service you outwitted age
And made the world a kingdom of your will."—
He touched her hand, smiling: "Whatever service
Of mine awaits them will not be forgotten,"
He said; and the smile faded on his face.—
"Now of all graceless and ungrateful wizards—"
But there she ceased, for she found in his eyes
The first of a new fear. "The wrong word rules
Today," she said; "and we'll have no more journeys."

Although he wandered rather more than ever
Since he had come again to Brittany
From Camelot, Merlin found eternally
Before him a new loneliness that made
Of garden, park, and woodland, all alike,
A desolation and a changelessness
Defying reason, without Vivian
Beside him, like a child with a black head,
Or moving on before him, or somewhere
So near him that, although he saw it not
With eyes, he felt the picture of her beauty
And shivered at the nearness of her being.
Without her now there was no past or future,
And a vague, soul-consuming premonition
He found the only tenant of the present;
He wondered, when she was away from him,
If his avenging injured intellect
Might shine with Arthur's kingdom a twin mirror,
Fate's plaything, for new ages without eyes
To see therein themselves and their declension.
Love made his hours a martyrdom without her;
The world was like an empty house without her,

Where Merlin was a prisoner of love
Confined within himself by too much freedom,
Repeating an unending exploration
Of many solitary silent rooms,
And only in a way remembering now
That once their very solitude and silence
Had by the magic of expectancy
Made sure what now he doubted—though his doubts,
Day after day, were founded on a shadow.

For now to Merlin, in his paradise,
Had come an unseen angel with a sword
Unseen, the touch of which was a long fear
For longer sorrow that had never come,
Yet might if he compelled it. He discovered,
One golden day in autumn as he wandered,
That he had made the radiance of two years
A misty twilight when he might as well
Have had no mist between him and the sun,
The sun being Vivian. On his coming then
To find her all in green against a wall
Of green and yellow leaves, and crumbling bread
For birds around the fountain while she sang
And the birds ate the bread, he told himself
That everything today was as it was
At first, and for a minute he believed it.
"I'd have you always all in green out here,"
He said, "if I had much to say about it."—
She clapped her crumbs away and laughed at him:
"I've covered up my bones with every color
That I can carry on them without screaming,
And you have liked them all—or made me think so."—
"I must have liked them if you thought I did,"
He answered, sighing; "but the sight of you

Today as on the day I saw you first,
All green, all wonderful" . . . He tore a leaf
To pieces with a melancholy care
That made her smile.—"Why pause at 'wonderful'?
You've hardly been yourself since you came back
From Camelot, where that unpleasant King
Said things that you have never said to me."—
He looked upon her with a worn reproach:
"The King said nothing that I keep from you."—
"What is it then?" she asked, imploringly;
"You man of moods and miracles, what is it?"—
He shook his head and tore another leaf:
"There is no need of asking what it is;
Whatever you or I may choose to name it,
The name of it is Fate, who played with me
And gave me eyes to read of the unwritten
More lines than I have read. I see no more
Today than yesterday, but I remember.
My ways are not the ways of other men;
My memories go forward. It was you
Who said that we were not in tune with Time;
It was not I who said it."—"But you knew it;
What matter then who said it?"—"It was you
Who said that Merlin was your punishment
For being in tune with him and not with Time—
With Time or with the world; and it was you
Who said you were alone, even here with Merlin;
It was not I who said it. It is I
Who tell you now my inmost thoughts." He laughed
As if at hidden pain around his heart,
But there was not much laughing in his eyes.
They walked, and for a season they were silent:
"I shall know what you mean by that," she said,
"When you have told me. Here's an oak you like,
And here's a place that fits me wondrous well

To sit in. You sit there. I've seen you there
Before; and I have spoiled your noble thoughts
By walking all my fingers up and down
Your countenance, as if they were the feet
Of a small animal with no great claws.
Tell me a story now about the world,
And the men in it, what they do in it,
And why it is they do it all so badly."—
"I've told you every story that I know,
Almost," he said.—"O, don't begin like that."—
"Well, once upon a time there was a King."—
"That has a more commendable address;
Go on, and tell me all about the King;
I'll bet the King had warts or carbuncles,
Or something wrong in his divine insides,
To make him wish that Adam had died young."

Merlin observed her slowly with a frown
Of saddened wonder. She laughed rather lightly,
And at his heart he felt again the sword
Whose touch was a long fear for longer sorrow.
"Well, once upon a time there was a king,"
He said again, but now in a dry voice
That wavered and betrayed a venturing.
He paused, and would have hesitated longer,
But something in him that was not himself
Compelled an utterance that his tongue obeyed,
As an unwilling child obeys a father
Who might be richer for obedience
If he obeyed the child: "There was a king
Who would have made his reign a monument
For kings and peoples of the waiting ages
To reverence and remember, and to this end
He coveted and won, with no ado
To make a story of, a neighbor queen

Who limed him with her smile and had of him,
In token of their sin, what he found soon
To be a sort of mongrel son and nephew—
And a most precious reptile in addition—
To ornament his court and carry arms,
And latterly to be the darker half
Of ruin. Also the king, who made of love
More than he made of life and death together,
Forgot the world and his example in it
For yet another woman—one of many—
And this one he made Queen, albeit he knew
That her unsworn allegiance to the knight
That he had loved the best of all his order
Must one day bring along the coming end
Of love and honor and of everything;
And with a kingdom builded on two pits
Of living sin,—so founded by the will
Of one wise counsellor who loved the king,
And loved the world and therefore made him king
To be a mirror for it,—the king reigned well
For certain years, awaiting a sure doom;
For certain years he waved across the world
A royal banner with a Dragon on it;
And men of every land fell worshipping
The Dragon as it were the living God,
And not the living sin."

                                        She rose at that,
And after a calm yawn, she looked at Merlin:
"Why all this new insistence upon sin?"
She said; "I wonder if I understand
This king of yours, with all his pits and dragons;
I know I do not like him." A thinner light
Was in her eyes than he had found in them
Since he became the willing prisoner

That she had made of him; and on her mouth
Lay now a colder line of irony
Than all his fears or nightmares could have drawn
Before today: "What reason do you know
For me to listen to this king of yours?
What reading has a man of woman's days,
Even though the man be Merlin and a prophet?"

"I know no call for you to love the king,"
Said Merlin, driven ruinously along
By the vindictive urging of his fate;
"I know no call for you to love the king,
Although you serve him, knowing not yet the king
You serve. There is no man, or any woman,
For whom the story of the living king
Is not the story of the living sin.
I thought my story was the common one,
For common recognition and regard."

"Then let us have no more of it," she said;
"For we are not so common, I believe,
That we need kings and pits and flags and dragons
To make us know that we have let the world
Go by us. Have you missed the world so much
That you must have it in with all its clots
And wounds and bristles on to make us happy—
Like Blaise, with shouts and horns and seven men
Triumphant with a most unlovely boar?
Is there no other story in the world
Than this one of a man that you made king
To be a moral for the speckled ages?
You said once long ago, if you remember,
'You are too strange a lady to fear specks';
And it was you, you said, who feared them not.
Why do you look at me as at a snake

All coiled to spring at you and strike you dead?
I am not going to spring at you, or bite you;
I'm going home. And you, if you are kind,
Will have no fear to wander for an hour.
I'm sure the time has come for you to wander;
And there may come a time for you to say
What most you think it is that we need here
To make of this Broceliande a refuge
Where two disheartened sinners may forget
A world that has today no place for them."

A melancholy wave of revelation
Broke over Merlin like a rising sea,
Long viewed unwillingly and long denied.
He saw what he had seen, but would not feel,
Till now the bitterness of what he felt
Was in his throat, and all the coldness of it
Was on him and around him like a flood
Of lonelier memories than he had said
Were memories, although he knew them now
For what they were—for what his eyes had seen,
For what his ears had heard and what his heart
Had felt, with him not knowing what it felt.
But now he knew that his cold angel's name
Was Change, and that a mightier will than his
Or Vivian's had ordained that he be there.
To Vivian he could not say anything
But words that had no more of hope in them
Than anguish had of peace: "I meant the world . . .
I meant the world," he groaned; "not you—not me."

Again the frozen line of irony
Was on her mouth. He looked up once at it.
And then away—too fearful of her eyes
To see what he could hear now in her laugh

That melted slowly into what she said,
Like snow in icy water: "This world of yours
Will surely be the end of us. And why not?
I'm overmuch afraid we're part of it,—
Or why do we build walls up all around us,
With gates of iron that make us think the day
Of judgment's coming when they clang behind us?
And yet you tell me that you fear no specks!
With you I never cared for them enough
To think of them. I was too strange a lady.
And your return is now a speckled king
And something that you call a living sin—
That's like an uninvited poor relation
Who comes without a welcome, rather late,
And on a foundered horse."

                              "Specks? What are specks?"
He gazed at her in a forlorn wonderment
That made her say: "You said, 'I fear them not.'
'If I were king in Camelot,' you said,
'I might fear more than specks.' Have you forgotten?
Don't tell me, Merlin, you are growing old.
Why don't you make somehow a queen of me,
And give me half the world? I'd wager thrushes
That I should reign, with you to turn the wheel,
As well as any king that ever was.
The curse on me is that I cannot serve
A ruler who forgets that he is king."

In his bewildered misery Merlin then
Stared hard at Vivian's face, more like a slave
Who sought for common mercy than like Merlin:
"You speak a language that was never mine,
Or I have lost my wits. Why do you seize
The flimsiest of opportunities

To make of what I said another thing
Than love or reason could have let me say,
Or let me fancy? Why do you keep the truth
So far away from me, when all your gates
Will open at your word and let me go
To some place where no fear or weariness
Of yours need ever dwell? Why does a woman,
Made otherwise a miracle of love
And loveliness, and of immortal beauty,
Tear one word by the roots out of a thousand,
And worry it, and torture it, and shake it,
Like a small dog that has a rag to play with?
What coil of an ingenious destiny
Is this that makes of what I never meant
A meaning as remote as hell from heaven?"

"I don't know," Vivian said reluctantly,
And half as if in pain; "I'm going home.
I'm going home and leave you here to wander,
Pray take your kings and sins away somewhere
And bury them, and bury the Queen in also.
I know this king; he lives in Camelot,
And I shall never like him. There are specks
Almost all over him. Long live the king,
But not the king who lives in Camelot,
With Modred, Lancelot, and Guinevere—
And all four speckled like a merry nest
Of addled eggs together. You made him King
Because you loved the world and saw in him
From infancy a mirror for the millions.
The world will see itself in him, and then
The world will say its prayers and wash its face,
And build for some new king a new foundation.
Long live the King! . . . But now I apprehend
A time for me to shudder and grow old

And garrulous—and so become a fright
For Blaise to take out walking in warm weather—
Should I give way to long considering
Of worlds you may have lost while prisoned here
With me and my light mind. I contemplate
Another name for this forbidden place,
And one more fitting. Tell me, if you find it,
Some fitter name than Eden. We have had
A man and woman in it for some time,
And now, it seems, we have a Tree of Knowledge."
She looked up at the branches overhead
And shrugged her shoulders. Then she went away;
And what was left of Merlin's happiness,
Like a disloyal phantom, followed her.

He felt the sword of his cold angel thrust
And twisted in his heart, as if the end
Were coming next, but the cold angel passed
Invisibly and left him desolate,
With misty brow and eyes. "The man who sees
May see too far, and he may see too late
The path he takes unseen," he told himself
When he found thought again. "The man who sees
May go on seeing till the immortal flame
That lights and lures him folds him in its heart,
And leaves of what there was of him to die
An item of inhospitable dust
That love and hate alike must hide away;
Or there may still be charted for his feet
A dimmer faring, where the touch of time
Were like the passing of a twilight moth
From flower to flower into oblivion,
If there were not somewhere a barren end
Of moths and flowers, and glimmering far away
Beyond a desert where the flowerless days

Are told in slow defeats and agonies,
The guiding of a nameless light that once
Had made him see too much—and has by now
Revealed in death, to the undying child
Of Lancelot, the Grail. For this pure light
Has many rays to throw, for many men
To follow; and the wise are not all pure,
Nor are the pure all wise who follow it.
There are more rays than men. But let the man
Who saw too much, and was to drive himself
From paradise, play too lightly or too long
Among the moths and flowers, he finds at last
There is a dim way out; and he shall grope
Where pleasant shadows lead him to the plain
That has no shadow save his own behind him.
And there, with no complaint, nor much regret,
Shall he plod on, with death between him now
And the far light that guides him, till he falls
And has an empty thought of empty rest;
Then Fate will put a mattock in his hands
And lash him while he digs himself the grave
That is to be the pallet and the shroud
Of his poor blundering bones. The man who saw
Too much must have an eye to see at last
Where Fate has marked the clay; and he shall delve,
Although his hand may slacken, and his knees
May rock without a method as he toils;
For there's a delving that is to be done—
If not for God, for man. I see the light,
But I shall fall before I come to it;
For I am old. I was young yesterday.
Time's hand that I have held away so long
Grips hard now on my shoulder. Time has won.
Tomorrow I shall say to Vivian

That I am old and gaunt and garrulous,
And tell her one more story: I am old."

There were long hours for Merlin after that,
And much long wandering in his prison-yard,
Where now the progress of each heavy step
Confirmed a stillness of impending change
And imminent farewell. To Vivian's ear
There came for many days no other story
Than Merlin's iteration of his love
And his departure from Broceliande,
Where Merlin still remained. In Vivian's eye,
There was a quiet kindness, and at times
A smoky flash of incredulity
That faded into pain. Was this the Merlin—
This incarnation of idolatry
And all but supplicating deference—
This bowed and reverential contradiction
Of all her dreams and her realities—
Was this the Merlin who for years and years
Before she found him had so made her love him
That kings and princes, thrones and diadems,
And honorable men who drowned themselves
For love, were less to her than melon-shells?
Was this the Merlin whom her fate had sent
One spring day to come ringing at her gate,
Bewildering her love with happy terror
That later was to be all happiness?
Was this the Merlin who had made the world
Half over, and then left it with a laugh
To be the youngest, oldest, weirdest, gayest,
And wisest, and sometimes the foolishest
Of all the men of her consideration?
Was this the man who had made other men
As ordinary as arithmetic?

Was this man Merlin who came now so slowly
Towards the fountain where she stood again
In shimmering green? Trembling, he took her hands
And pressed them fondly, one upon the other,
Between his:

                    "I was wrong that other day,
For I have one more story. I am old."
He waited like one hungry for the word
Not said; and she found in his eyes a light
As patient as a candle in a window
That looks upon the sea and is a mark
For ships that have gone down. "Tomorrow," he said;
"Tomorrow I shall go away again
To Camelot; and I shall see the King
Once more; and I may come to you again
Once more; and I shall go away again
For ever. There is now no more than that
For me to do; and I shall do no more.
I saw too much when I saw Camelot;
And I saw farther backward into Time,
And forward, than a man may see and live,
When I made Arthur king. I saw too far,
But not so far as this. Fate played with me
As I have played with Time; and Time, like me,
Being less than Fate, will have on me his vengeance.
On Fate there is no vengeance, even for God."
He drew her slowly into his embrace
And held her there, but when he kissed her lips
They were as cold as leaves and had no answer;
For Time had given him then, to prove his words,
A frozen moment of a woman's life.

When Merlin the next morning came again
In the same pilgrim robe that he had worn

While he sat waiting where the cherry-blossoms
Outside the gate fell on him and around him
Grief came to Vivian at the sight of him;
And like a flash of a swift ugly knife,
A blinding fear came with it. "Are you going?"
She said, more with her lips than with her voice;
And he said, "I am going. Blaise and I
Are going down together to the shore,
And Blaise is coming back. For this one day
Be good enough to spare him, for I like him.
I tell you now, as once I told the King,
That I can be no more than what I was,
And I can say no more than I have said.
Sometimes you told me that I spoke too long
And sent me off to wander. That was good.
I go now for another wandering,
And I pray God that all be well with you."

For long there was a whining in her ears
Of distant wheels departing. When it ceased,
She closed the gate again so quietly
That Merlin could have heard no sound of it.

VII

By Merlin's Rock, where Dagonet the fool
Was given through many a dying afternoon
To sit and meditate on human ways
And ways divine, Gawaine and Bedivere
Stood silent, gazing down on Camelot.
The two had risen and were going home:
"It hits me sore, Gawaine," said Bedivere,
"To think on all the tumult and affliction
Down there, and all the noise and preparation

That hums of coming death, and, if my fears
Be born of reason, of what's more than death.
Wherefore, I say to you again, Gawaine,—
To you—that this late hour is not too late
For you to change yourself and change the King:
For though the King may love me with a love
More tried, and older, and more sure, may be,
Than for another, for such a time as this
The friend who turns him to the world again
Shall have a tongue more gracious and an eye
More shrewd than mine. For such a time as this
The King must have a glamour to persuade him."

"The King shall have a glamour, and anon,"
Gawaine said, and he shot death from his eyes;
"If you were King, as Arthur is—or was—
And Lancelot had carried off your Queen,
And killed a score or so of your best knights—
Not mentioning my two brothers, whom he slew
Unarmored and unarmed—God save your wits!
Two stewards with skewers could have done as much,
And you and I might now be rotting for it."

"But Lancelot's men were crowded,—they were crushed;
And there was nothing for them but to strike
Or die, not seeing where they struck. Think you
They would have slain Gareth and Gaheris,
And Tor, and all those other friends of theirs?
God's mercy for the world he made, I say,
And for the blood that writes the story of it.
Gareth and Gaheris, Tor and Lamorak,—
All dead, with all the others that are dead!
These years have made me turn to Lamorak
For counsel—and now Lamorak is dead."

"Why do you fling those two names in my face?
'Twas Modred made an end of Lamorak,
Not I; and Lancelot now has done for Tor.
I'll urge no king on after Lancelot
For such a two as Tor and Lamorak:
Their father killed my father, and their friend
Was Lancelot, not I. I'll own my fault—
I'm living; and while I've a tongue can talk,
I'll say this to the King: 'Burn Lancelot
By inches till he give you back the Queen;
Then hang him—drown him—or do anything
To rid the world of him.' He killed my brothers,
And he was once my friend. Now damn the soul
Of him who killed my brothers! There you have me."

"You are a strong man, Gawaine, and your strength
Goes ill where foes are. You may cleave their limbs
And heads off, but you cannot damn their souls;
What you may do now is to save their souls,
And bodies too, and like enough your own.
Remember that King Arthur is a king,
And where there is a king there is a kingdom.
Is not the kingdom any more to you
Than one brief enemy? Would you see it fall
And the King with it, for one mortal hate
That burns out reason? Gawaine, you are king
Today. Another day may see no king
But Havoc, if you have no other word
For Arthur now than hate for Lancelot.
Is not the world as large as Lancelot?
Is Lancelot, because one woman's eyes
Are brighter when they look on him, to sluice
The world with angry blood? Poor flesh! Poor flesh!
And you, Gawaine,—are you so gaffed with hate
You cannot leave it and so plunge away

To stiller places and there see, for once,
What hangs on this pernicious expedition
The King in his insane forgetfulness.
Would undertake—with you to drum him on?
Are you as mad as he and Lancelot
Made ravening into one man twice as mad
As either? Is the kingdom of the world,
Now rocking, to go down in sound and blood
And ashes and sick ruin, and for the sake
Of three men and a woman? If it be so,
God's mercy for the world he made, I say,—
And say again to Dagonet. Sir Fool,
Your throne is empty, and you may as well
Sit on it and be ruler of the world
From now till supper-time."

       Sir Dagonet,
Appearing, made reply to Bedivere's
Dry welcome with a famished look of pain,
On which he built a smile: "If I were King,
You, Bedivere, should be my counsellor;
And we should have no more wars over women.
I'll sit me down and meditate on that."
Gawaine, for all his anger, laughed a little,
And clapped the fool's lean shoulder; for he loved him
And was with Arthur when he made him knight.
Then Dagonet said on to Bedivere,
As if his tongue would make a jest of sorrow:
"Sometime I'll tell you what I might have done
Had I been Lancelot and you King Arthur—
Each having in himself the vicious essence
That now lives in the other and makes war.
When all men are like you and me, my lord,
When all are rational or rickety,
There may be no more war. But what's here now?

Lancelot loves the Queen, and he makes war
Of love; the King, being bitten to the soul
By love and hate that work in him together,
Makes war of madness; Gawaine hates Lancelot,
And he, to be in tune, makes war of hate;
Modred hates everything, yet he can see
With one damned illegitimate small eye
His father's crown, and with another like it
He sees the beauty of the Queen herself;
He needs the two for his ambitious pleasure,
And therefore he makes war of his ambition;
And somewhere in the middle of all this
There's a squeezed world that elbows for attention.
Poor Merlin, buried in Broceliande!
He must have had an academic eye
For woman when he founded Arthur's kingdom,
And in Broceliande he may be sorry.
Flutes, hautboys, drums, and viols. God be with him!
I'm glad they tell me there's another world,
For this one's a disease without a doctor."

"No, not so bad as that," said Bedivere;
The doctor, like ourselves, may now be learning;
And Merlin may have gauged his enterprise
Whatever the cost he may have paid for knowing.
We pass, but many are to follow us,
And what they build may stay; though I believe
Another age will have another Merlin,
Another Camelot, and another King.
Sir Dagonet, farewell."

                              "Farewell, Sir Knight,
And you, Sir Knight: Gawaine, you have the world
Now in your fingers—an uncommon toy,
Albeit a small persuasion in the balance

With one man's hate. I'm glad you're not a fool,
For then you might be rickety, as I am,
And rational as Bedivere. Farewell.
I'll sit here and be king. God save the King!"

But Gawaine scowled and frowned and answered nothing
As he went slowly down with Bedivere
To Camelot, where Arthur's army waited
The King's word for the melancholy march
To Joyous Gard, where Lancelot hid the Queen
And armed his host, and there was now no joy,
As there was now no joy for Dagonet
While he sat brooding, with his wan cheek-bones
Hooked with his bony fingers: "Go, Gawaine,"
He mumbled: "Go your way, and drag the world
Along down with you. What's a world or so
To you if you can hide an ell of iron
Somewhere in Lancelot, and hear him wheeze
And sputter once or twice before he goes
Wherever the Queen sends him? There's a man
Who should have been a king, and would have been,
Had he been born so. So should I have been
A king, had I been born so, fool or no:
King Dagonet, or Dagonet the King;
King-Fool, Fool-King; 'twere not impossible.
I'll meditate on that and pray for Arthur,
Who made me all I am, except a fool.
Now he goes mad for love, as I might go
Had I been born a king and not a fool.
Today I think I'd rather be a fool;
Today the world is less than one scared woman—
Wherefore a field of waving men may soon
Be shorn by Time's indifferent scythe, because
The King is mad. The seeds of history
Are small, but given a few gouts of warm blood

For quickening, they sprout out wondrously
And have a leaping growth whereof no man
May shun such harvesting of change or death,
Or life, as may fall on him to be borne
When I am still alive and rickety,
And Bedivere's alive and rational—
If he come out of this, and there's a doubt,—
The King, Gawaine, Modred, and Lancelot
May all be lying underneath a weight
Of bloody sheaves too heavy for their shoulders
All spent, and all dishonored, and all dead;
And if it come to be that this be so,
And it be true that Merlin saw the truth,
Such harvest were the best. Your fool sees not
So far as Merlin sees: yet if he saw
The truth—why then, such harvest were the best.
I'll pray for Arthur; I can do no more."

"Why not for Merlin? Or do you count him,
In this extreme, so foreign to salvation
That prayer would be a stranger to his name?"

Poor Dagonet, with terror shaking him,
Stood up and saw before him an old face
Made older with an inch of silver beard,
And faded eyes more eloquent of pain
And ruin than all the faded eyes of age
Till now had ever been, although in them
There was a mystic and intrinsic peace
Of one who sees where men of nearer sight
See nothing. On their way to Camelot,
Gawaine and Bedivere had passed him by,
With lax attention for the pilgrim cloak
They passed, and what it hid: yet Merlin saw

Their faces, and he saw the tale was true
That he had lately drawn from solemn strangers.

"Well, Dagonet, and by your leave," he said,
"I'll rest my lonely relics for a while
On this rock that was mine and now is yours.
I favor the succession; for you know
Far more than many doctors, though your doubt
Is your peculiar poison. I foresaw
Long since, and I have latterly been told
What moves in this commotion down below
To show men what it means. It means the end—
If men whose tongues had less to say to me
Than had their shoulders are adept enough
To know; and you may pray for me or not,
Sir Friend, Sir Dagonet."

                        "Sir fool, you mean,"
Dagonet said, and gazed on Merlin sadly:
"I'll never pray again for anything,
And last of all for this that you behold—
The smouldering faggot of unlovely bones
That God has given to me to call Myself.
When Merlin comes to Dagonet for prayer,
It is indeed the end."

                        "And in the end
Are more beginnings, Dagonet, than men
Shall name or know today. It was the end
Of Arthur's insubstantial majesty
When to him and his knights the Grail foreshowed
The quest of life that was to be the death
Of many, and the slow discouraging
Of many more. Or do I err in this?"

"No," Dagonet replied; "there was a Light;
And Galahad, in the Siege Perilous,
Alone of all on whom it fell, was calm;
There was a Light wherein men saw themselves
In one another as they might become—
Or so they dreamed. There was a long to-do,
And Gawaine, of all forlorn ineligibles,
Rose up the first, and cried more lustily
Than any after him that he should find
The Grail, or die for it,—though he did neither;
For he came back as living and as fit
For new and old iniquity as ever.
Then Lancelot came back, and Bors came back,—
Like men who had seen more than men should see,
And still come back. They told of Percival
Who saw too much to make of this worn life
A long necessity, and of Galahad,
Who died and is alive. They all saw Something.
God knows the meaning or the end of it,
But they saw Something. And if I've an eye,
Small joy has the Queen been to Lancelot
Since he came back from seeing what he saw;
For though his passion hold him like hot claws,
He's neither in the world nor out of it.
Gawaine is king, though Arthur wears the crown;
And Gawaine's hate for Lancelot is the sword
That hangs by one of Merlin's fragile hairs
Above the world. Were you to see the King,
The frenzy that has overthrown his wisdom,
Instead of him and his upheaving empire,
Might have an end."

                              "I came to see the King,"
Said Merlin, like a man who labors hard
And long with an importunate confession.

"No, Dagonet, you cannot tell me why,
Although your tongue is eager with wild hope
To tell me more than I may tell myself
About myself. All this that was to be
Might show to man how vain it were to wreck
The world for self if it were all in vain.
When I began with Arthur I could see
In each bewildered man who dots the earth
A moment with his days a groping thought
Of an eternal will, strangely endowed
With merciful illusions whereby self
Becomes the will itself and each man swells
In fond accordance with his agency.
Now Arthur, Modred, Lancelot, and Gawaine
Are swollen thoughts of this eternal will
Which have no other way to find the way
That leads them on to their inheritance
Than by the time-infuriating flame
Of a wrecked empire, lighted by the torch
Of woman, who, together with the light
That Galahad found, is yet to light the world."

A wan smile crept across the weary face
Of Dagonet the fool: "If you knew that
Before your burial in Broceliande,
No wonder your eternal will accords
With all your dreams of what the world requires.
My master, I may say this unto you
Because I am a fool, and fear no man;
My fear is that I've been a groping thought
That never swelled enough. You say the torch
Of woman and the light that Galahad found
Are some day to illuminate the world?
I'll meditate on that. The world is done
For me; and I have been. to make men laugh,

A lean thing of no shape and many capers.
I made them laugh, and I could laugh anor
Myself to see them killing one another
Because a woman with corn-colored hair
Has pranked a man with horns. 'Twas but a flash
Of chance, and Lancelot, the other day
That saved this pleasing sinner from the fire
That she may spread for thousands. Were she now
The cinder the King willed, or were you now
To see the King, the fire might yet go out;
But the eternal will says otherwise.
So be it; I'll assemble certain gold
That I may say is mine and get myself
Away from this accurst unhappy court,
And in some quiet place where shepherd clowns
And cowherds may have more respondent ears
Than kings and kingdom-builders, I shall troll
Old men to easy graves and be a child
Again among the children of the earth.
I'll have no more kings, even though I loved
King Arthur, who is mad, as I could love
No other man save Merlin, who is dead."

"Not wholly dead, but old. Merlin is old."
The wizard shivered as he spoke, and stared
Away into the sunset where he saw
Once more, as through a cracked and cloudy glass,
A crumbling sky that held a crimson cloud
Wherein there was a town of many towers
All swayed and shaken, in a woman's hand
This time, till out of it there spilled and flashed
And tumbled, like loose jewels, town, towers, and walls,
And there was nothing but a crumbling sky
That made anon of black and red and ruin
A wild and final rain on Camelot.

He bowed, and pressed his eyes: "Now by my soul,
I have seen this before—all black and red—
Like that—like that—like Vivian—black and red;
Like Vivian, when her eyes looked into mine
Across the cups of gold. A flute was playing—
Then all was black and red."

                              Another smile
Crept over the wan face of Dagonet,
Who shivered in his turn. "The torch of woman,"
He muttered, "and the light that Galahad found,
Will some day save us all, as they saved Merlin.
Forgive my shivering wits, but I am cold,
And it will soon be dark. Will you go down
With me to see the King, or will you not?
If not, I go tomorrow to the shepherds.
The world is mad, and I'm a groping thought
Of your eternal will; the world and I
Are strangers, and I'll have no more of it—
Except you go with me to see the King."

"No, Dagonet, you cannot leave me now,"
Said Merlin, sadly. "You and I are old;
And, as you say, we fear no man. God knows
I would not have the love that once you had
For me be fear of me, for I am past
All fearing now. But Fate may send a fly
Sometimes, and he may sting us to the grave.
So driven to test our faith in what we see.
Are you, now I am coming to an end,
As Arthur's days are coming to an end,
To sting me like a fly? I do not ask
Of you to say that you see what I see,
Where you see nothing; nor do I require
Of any man more vision than is his;

Yet I could wish for you a larger part
For your last entrance here than this you play
Tonight of a sad insect stinging Merlin.
The more you sting, the more he pities you;
And you were never overfond of pity.
Had you been so, I doubt if Arthur's love,
Or Gawaine's, would have made of you a knight.
No, Dagonet, you cannot leave me now,
Nor would you if you could. You call yourself
A fool, because the world and you are strangers.
You are a proud man, Dagonet; you have suffered
What I alone have seen. You are no fool;
And surely you are not a fly to sting
My love to last regret. Believe or not
What I have seen, or what I say to you,
But say no more to me that I am dead
Because the King is mad, and you are old,
And I am older. In Broceliande
Time overtook me as I knew he must;
And I, with a fond overplus of words,
Had warned the lady Vivian already,
Before these wrinkles and this hesitancy
Inhibiting my joints oppressed her sight
With age and dissolution. She said once
That she was cold and cruel; but she meant
That she was warm and kind, and over-wise
For woman in a world where men see not
Beyond themselves. She saw beyond them all,
As I did; and she waited, as I did,
The coming of a day when cherry-blossoms
Were to fall down all over me like snow
In springtime. I was far from Camelot
That afternoon; and I am farther now
From her. I see no more for me to do
Than to leave her and Arthur and the world

Behind me, and to pray that all be well
With Vivian, whose unquiet heart is hungry
For what is not, and what shall never be
Without her, in a world that men are making,
Knowing not how, nor caring yet to know
How slowly and how grievously they do it,—
Though Vivian, in her golden shell of exile,
Knows now and cares, not knowing that she cares,
Nor caring that she knows. In time to be,
The like of her shall have another name
Than Vivian, and her laugh shall be a fire,
Not shining only to consume itself
With what it burns. She knows not yet the name
Of what she is, for now there is no name;
Some day there shall be. Time has many names,
Unwritten yet, for what we say is old
Because we are so young that it seems old.
And this is all a part of what I saw
Before you saw King Arthur. When we parted.
I told her I should see the King again,
And, having seen him, might go back again
To see her face once more. But I shall see
No more the lady Vivian. Let her love
What man she may, no other love than mine
Shall be an index of her memories.
I fear no man who may come after me,
And I see none. I see her, still in green,
Beside the fountain. I shall not go back.
We pay for going back; and all we get
Is one more needless ounce of weary wisdom
To bring away with us. If I come not,
The lady Vivian will remember me,
And say: 'I knew him when his heart was young,
Though I have lost him now. Time called him home,

And that was as it was; for much is lost
Between Broceliande and Camelot.'"

He stared away into the west again,
Where now no crimson cloud or phantom town
Deceived his eyes. Above a living town
There were gray clouds and ultimate suspense,
And a cold wind was coming. Dagonet,
Now crouched at Merlin's feet in his dejection,
Saw multiplying lights far down below,
Where lay the fevered streets. At length he felt
On his lean shoulder Merlin's tragic hand
And trembled, knowing that a few more days
Would see the last of Arthur and the first
Of Modred, whose dark patience had attained
To one precarious half of what he sought:
"And even the Queen herself may fall to him,"
Dagonet murmured.—"The Queen fall to Modred?
Is that your only fear tonight?" said Merlin;
"She may, but not for long."—"No, not my fear;
For I fear nothing. But I wish no fate
Like that for any woman the King loves,
Although she be the scourge and the end of him
That you saw coming, as I see it now."
Dagonet shook, but he would have no tears,
He swore, for any king, queen, knave, or wizard—
Albeit he was a stranger among those
Who laughed at him because he was a fool.
"You said the truth, I cannot leave you now,"
He stammered, and was angry for the tears
That mocked his will and choked him.

                                    Merlin smiled,
Faintly, and for the moment: "Dagonet,
I need your word as one of Arthur's knights

That you will go on with me to the end
Of my short way, and say unto no man
Or woman that you found or saw me here.
No good would follow, for a doubt would live
Unstifled of my loyalty to him
Whose deeds are wrought for those who are to come;
And many who see not what I have seen,
Or what you see tonight, would prattle on
For ever, and their children after them,
Of what might once have been had I gone down
With you to Camelot to see the King.
I came to see the King,—but why see kings?
All this that was to be is what I saw
Before there was an Arthur to be king,
And so to be a mirror wherein men
May see themselves, and pause. If they see not,
Or if they do see and they ponder not,—
I saw; but I was neither Fate nor God.
I saw too much; and this would be the end,
Were there to be an end. I saw myself—
A sight no other man has ever seen;
And through the dark that lay beyond myself
I saw two fires that are to light the world."

On Dagonet the silent hand of Merlin
Weighed now as living iron that held him down
With a primeval power. Doubt, wonderment,
Impatience, and a self-accusing sorrow
Born of an ancient love, possessed and held him
Until his love was more than he could name,
And he was Merlin's fool, not Arthur's now:
"Say what you will, I say that I'm the fool
Of Merlin, King of Nowhere; which is Here.
With you for king and me for court, what else
Have we to sigh for but a place to sleep?

I know a tavern that will take us in;
And on the morrow I shall follow you
Until I die for you. And when I die . . ."—
"Well, Dagonet, the King is listening."—
And Dagonet answered, hearing in the words
Of Merlin a grave humor and a sound
Of graver pity, "I shall die a fool."
He heard what might have been a father's laugh,
Faintly behind him; and the living weight
Of Merlin's hand was lifted. They arose,
And, saying nothing, found a groping way
Down through the gloom together. Fiercer now,
The wind was like a flying animal
That beat the two of them incessantly
With icy wings, and bit them as they went.
The rock above them was an empty place
Where neither seer nor fool should view again
The stricken city. Colder blew the wind
Across the world, and on it heavier lay
The shadow and the burden of the night;
And there was darkness over Camelot.

LANCELOT

I

GAWAINE, aware again of Lancelot
In the King's garden, coughed and followed him;
Whereat he turned and stood with folded arms
And weary-waiting eyes, cold and half-closed—
Hard eyes, where doubts at war with memories
Fanned a sad wrath. "Why frown upon a friend?
Few live that have too many," Gawaine said,
And wished unsaid, so thinly came the light
Between the narrowing lids at which he gazed.
"And who of us are they that name their friends?"
Lancelot said. "They live that have not any.
Why do they live, Gawaine? Ask why, and answer."

Two men of an elected eminence,
They stood for a time silent. Then Gawaine,
Acknowledging the ghost of what was gone,
Put out his hand: "Rather, I say, why ask?
If I be not the friend of Lancelot,
May I be nailed alive along the ground
And emmets eat me dead. If I be not
The friend of Lancelot, may I be fried
With other liars in the pans of hell.
What item otherwise of immolation
Your Darkness may invent, be it mine to endure
And yours to gloat on. For the time between,
Consider this thing you see that is my hand.
If once, it has been yours a thousand times;

Why not again? Gawaine has never lied
To Lancelot; and this, of all wrong days—
This day before the day when you go south
To God knows what accomplishment of exile—
Were surely an ill day for lies to find
An issue or a cause or an occasion.
King Ban your father and King Lot my father,
Were they alive, would shake their heads in sorrow
To see us as we are, and I shake mine
In wonder. Will you take my hand, or no?
Strong as I am, I do not hold it out
For ever and on air. You see—my hand."
Lancelot gave his hand there to Gawaine,
Who took it, held it, and then let it go,
Chagrined with its indifference.

                    "Yes, Gawaine,
I go tomorrow, and I wish you well;
You and your brothers, Gareth, Gaheris,—
And Agravaine; yes, even Agravaine,
Whose tongue has told all Camelot and all Britain
More lies than yet have hatched of Modred's envy.
You say that you have never lied to me,
And I believe it so. Let it be so.
For now and always. Gawaine, I wish you well.
Tomorrow I go south, as Merlin went,
But not for Merlin's end. I go, Gawaine,
And leave you to your ways. There are ways left."

"There are three ways I know, three famous ways,
And all in Holy Writ," Gawaine said, smiling:
"The snake's way and the eagle's way are two,
And then we have a man's way with a maid—
Or with a woman who is not a maid.
Your late way is to send all women scudding,
To the last flash of the last cramoisy,

While you go south to find the fires of God.
Since we came back again to Camelot
From our immortal Quest—I came back first—
No man has known you for the man you were
Before you saw whatever 't was you saw,
To make so little of kings and queens and friends
Thereafter. Modred? Agravaine? My brothers?
And what if they be brothers? What are brothers,
If they be not our friends, your friends and mine?
You turn away, and my words are no mark
On you affection or your memory?
So be it then, if so it is to be.
God save you, Lancelot; for by Saint Stephen,
You are no more than man to save yourself."

"Gawaine, I do not say that you are wrong,
Or that you are ill-seasoned in your lightness;
You say that all you know is what you saw,
And on your own averment you saw nothing.
Your spoken word, Gawaine, I have not weighed
In those unhappy scales of inference
That have no beam but one made out of hates
And fears, and venomous conjecturings;
Your tongue is not the sword that urges me
Now out of Camelot. Two other swords
There are that are awake, and in their scabbards
Are parching for the blood of Lancelot.
Yet I go not away for fear of them,
But for a sharper care. You say the truth,
But not when you contend the fires of God
Are my one fear,—for there is one fear more.
Therefore I go. Gawaine, I wish you well."

"Well-wishing in a way is well enough;
So, in a way, is caution; so, in a way,

Are leeches, neatherds, and astrologers.
Lancelot, listen. Sit you down and listen:
You talk of swords and fears and banishment.
Two swords, you say; Modred and Agravaine,
You mean. Had you meant Gaheris and Gareth,
Or willed an evil on them, I should welcome
And hasten your farewell. But Agravaine
Hears little what I say; his ears are Modred's.
The King is Modred's father, and the Queen
A prepossession of Modred's lunacy.
So much for my two brothers whom you fear,
Not fearing for yourself. I say to you,
Fear not for anything—and so be wise
And amiable again as heretofore;
Let Modred have his humor, and Agravaine
His tongue. The two of them have done their worst,
And having done their worst, what have they done?
A whisper now and then, a chirrup or so
In corners,—and what else? Ask what, and answer."

Still with a frown that had no faith in it,
Lancelot, pitying Gawaine's lost endeavour
To make an evil jest of evidence,
Sat fronting him with a remote forbearance—
Whether for Gawaine blind or Gawaine false,
Or both, or neither, he could not say yet,
If ever; and to himself he said no more
Than he said now aloud: "What else, Gawaine?
What else, am I to say? Then ruin, I say;
Destruction, dissolution, desolation,
I say,—should I compound with jeopardy now.
For there are more than whispers here, Gawaine:
The way that we have gone so long together
Has underneath our feet, without our will,
Become a twofold faring. Yours, I trust,

May lead you always on, as it has led you,
To praise and to much joy. Mine, I believe,
Leads off to battles that are not yet fought,
And to the Light that once had blinded me.
When I came back from seeing what I saw,
I saw no place for me in Camelot.
There is no place for me in Camelot.
There is no place for me save where the Light
May lead me; and to that place I shall go.
Meanwhile I lay upon your soul no load
Of counsel or of empty admonition;
Only I ask of you, should strife arise
In Camelot, to remember, if you may,
That you've an ardor that outruns your reason,
Also a glamour that outshines your guile;
And you are a strange hater. I know that;
And I'm in fortune that you hate not me.
Yet while we have our sins to dream about,
Time has done worse for time than in our making;
Albeit there may be sundry falterings
And falls against us in the Book of Man."

"Praise Adam, you are mellowing at last!
I've always liked this world, and would so still;
And if it is your new Light leads you on
To such an admirable gait, for God's sake,
Follow it, follow it, follow it, Lancelot;
Follow it as you never followed glory.
Once I believed that I was on the way
That you call yours, but I came home again
To Camelot—and Camelot was right,
For the world knows its own that knows not you;
You are a thing too vaporous to be sharing
The carnal feast of life. You mow down men
Like elder-stems, and you leave women sighing

For one more sight of you; but they do wrong.
You are a man of mist, and have no shadow.
God save you, Lancelot. If I laugh at you,
I laugh in envy and in admiration."

The joyless evanescence of a smile,
Discovered on the face of Lancelot
By Gawaine's unrelenting vigilance,
Wavered, and with a sullen change went out;
And then there was the music of a woman
Laughing behind them, and a woman spoke:
"Gawaine, you said 'God save you, Lancelot.'
Why should He save him any more to-day
Than on another day? What has he done,
Gawaine, that God should save him?" Guinevere,
With many questions in her dark blue eyes
And one gay jewel in her golden hair,
Had come upon the two of them unseen,
Till now she was a russet apparition
At which the two arose—one with a dash
Of easy leisure in his courtliness,
One with a stately calm that might have pleased
The Queen of a strange land indifferently.
The firm incisive languor of her speech,
Heard once, was heard through battles: "Lancelot,
What have you done to-day that God should save you?
What has he done, Gawaine, that God should save him?
I grieve that you two pinks of chivalry
Should be so near me in my desolation,
And I, poor soul alone, know nothing of it.
What has he done, Gawaine?"

                              With all her poise,
To Gawaine's undeceived urbanity
She was less queen than woman for the nonce,

And in her eyes there was a flickering
Of a still fear that would not be veiled wholly
With any mask of mannered nonchalance.
"What has he done? Madam, attend your nephew;
And learn from him, in your incertitude,
That this inordinate man Lancelot,
This engine of renown, this hewer down daily
Of potent men by scores in our late warfare,
Has now inside his head a foreign fever
That urges him away to the last edge
Of everything, there to efface himself
In ecstasy, and so be done with us.
Hereafter, peradventure certain birds
Will perch in meditation on his bones,
Quite as if they were some poor sailor's bones,
Or felon's jettisoned, or fisherman's,
Or fowler's bones, or Mark of Cornwall's bones.
In fine, this flower of men that was our comrade
Shall be for us no more, from this day on,
Than a much remembered Frenchman far away.
Magnanimously I leave you now to prize
Your final sight of him; and leaving you,
I leave the sun to shine for him alone,
Whiles I grope on to gloom. Madam, farewell;
And you, contrarious Lancelot, farewell."

II

THE flash of oak leaves over Guinevere
That afternoon, with the sun going down,
Made memories there for Lancelot, although
The woman who in silence looked at him
Now seemed his inventory of the world
That he must lose, or suffer to be lost
For love of her who sat there in the shade,

With oak leaves flashing in a golden light
Over her face and over her golden hair.
"Gawaine has all the graces, yet he knows;
He knows enough to be the end of us,
If so he would," she said. "He knows and laughs
And we are at the mercy of a man
Who, if the stars went out, would only laugh."
She looked away at a small swinging blossom,
And then she looked intently at her fingers,
While a frown gathered slowly round her eyes,
And wrinkled her white forehead.

                        Lancelot,
Scarce knowing whether to himself he spoke
Or to the Queen, said emptily: "As for Gawaine,
My question is, if any curious hind
Or knight that is alive in Britain breathing,
Or prince, or king, knows more of us, or less,
Than Gawaine, in his gay complacency,
Knows or believes he knows. There's over mucl
Of knowing in this realm of many tongues,
Where deeds are less to those who tell of them
Than are the words they sow; and you and I
Are like to yield a granary of such words,
For God knows what next harvesting. Gawain
I fear no more than Gareth, or Colgrevance;
So far as it is his to be the friend
Of any man, so far is he my friend—
Till I have crossed him in some enterprise
Unlikely and unborn. So fear not Gawaine
But let your primal care be now for one
Whose name is yours."

                  The Queen, with her blue eyes
Too bright for joy, still gazed on Lancelot,

Who stared as if in ongry malediction
Upon the shorn grass growing at his feet.
"Why do you speak as if the grass had ears
And I had none? What are you saying now,
So darkly to the grass, of knights and hinds?
Are you the Lancelot who rode, long since,
Away from me on that unearthly Quest,
Which left no man the same who followed it—
Or none save Gawaine, who came back so soon
That we had hardly missed him?" Faintly then
She smiled a little, more in her defence,
He knew, than for misprision of a man
Whom yet she feared: "Why do you set this day—
This golden day, when all are not so golden—
To tell me, with your eyes upon the ground,
That idle words have been for idle tongues
And ears a moment's idle entertainment?
Have I become, and all at once, a thing
So new to courts, and to the buzz they make,
That I should hear no murmur, see no sign?
Where malice and ambition dwell with envy,
They go the farthest who believe the least;
So let them,—while I ask of you again,
Why this day for all this? Was yesterday
A day of ouphes and omens? Was it Friday?
I don't remember. Days are all alike
When I have you to look on; when you go,
There are no days but hours. You might say now
What Gawaine said, and say it in our language."
The sharp light still was in her eyes, alive
And anxious with a reminiscent fear.

Lancelot, like a strong man stricken hard
With pain, looked up at her unhappily;
And slowly, on a low and final note,

Said: "Gawaine laughs alike at what he knows,
And at the loose convenience of his fancy;
He sees in others what his humor needs
To nourish it, and lives a merry life.
Sometimes a random shaft of his will hit
Nearer the mark than one a wise man aims
With infinite address and reservation;
So has it come to pass this afternoon."

Blood left the quivering cheeks of Guinevere
As color leaves a cloud; and where white was
Before, there was a ghostliness not white,
But gray; and over it her shining hair
Coiled heavily its mocking weight of gold.
The pride of her forlorn light-heartedness
Fled like a storm-blown feather; and her fear,
Possessing her, was all that she possessed.
She sought for Lancelot, but he seemed gone.
There was a strong man glowering in a chair
Before her, but he was not Lancelot,
Or he would look at her and say to her
That Gawaine's words were less than chaff in the wind—
A nonsense about exile, birds, and bones,
Born of an indolence of empty breath.
"Say what has come to pass this afternoon,"
She said, "or I shall hear you all my life,
Not hearing what it was you might have told."

He felt the trembling of her slow last words,
And his were trembling as he answered them:
"Why this day, why no other? So you ask,
And so must I in honor tell you more—
For what end, I have yet no braver guess
Than Modred has of immortality,
Or you of Gawaine. Could I have him alone

Between me and the peace I cannot know,
My life were like the sound of golden bells
Over still fields at sunset, where no storm
Should ever blast the sky with fire again,
Or thunder follow ruin for you and me,—
As like it will, if I for one more day,
Assume that I see not what I have seen,
See now, and shall see. There are no more lies
Left anywhere now for me to tell myself
That I have not already told myself,
And overtold, until today I seem
To taste them as I might the poisoned fruit
That Patrise had of Mador, and so died.
And that same apple of death was to be food
For Gawaine; but he left it and lives on,
To make his joy of living your confusion.
His life is his religion; he loves life
With such a manifold exuberance
That poison shuns him and seeks out a way
To wreak its evil upon innocence.
There may be chance in this, there may be '
Be what there be, I do not fear Gawaine."

The Queen, with an indignant little foot,
Struck viciously the unoffending grass
And said: "Why not let Gawaine go his way?
I'll think of him no more, fear him no more,
And hear of him no more. I'll hear no more
Of any now save one who is, or was,
All men to me. And he said once to me
That he would say why this day, of all days,
Was more mysteriously felicitous
For solemn commination than another."
Again she smiled, but her blue eyes were telling
No more their story of old happiness.

"For me today is not as other days,"
He said, "because it is the first, I find,
That has empowered my will to say to you
What most it is that you must hear and heed.
When Arthur, with a faith unfortified,
Sent me alone, of all he might have sent,
That May-day to Leodogran your father,
I went away from him with a sore heart;
For in my heart I knew that I should fail
My King, who trusted me too far beyond
The mortal outpost of experience.
And this was after Merlin's admonition,
Which Arthur, in his passion, took for less
Than his inviolable majesty.
When I rode in between your father's guards
And heard his trumpets blown for my loud honor,
I sent my memory back to Camelot,
And said once to myself, 'God save the king!'
But the words tore my throat and were like blood
Upon my tongue. Then a great shout went up
From shining men around me everywhere;
And I remember more fair women's eyes
Than there are stars in autumn, all of them
Thrown on me for a glimpse of that high knight
Sir Lancelot—Sir Lancelot of the Lake.
I saw their faces and I saw not one
To sever a tendril of my integrity;
But I thought once again, to make myself
Believe a silent lie, 'God save the King' . . .
I saw your face, and there were no more kings."

The sharp light softened in the Queen's blue eyes,
And for a moment there was joy in them:
"Was I so menacing to the peace, I wonder,
Of anyone else alive? But why go back?

I tell you that I fear Gawaine no more;
And if you fear him not, and I fear not
What you fear not, what have we then to fear?"
Fatigued a little with her reasoning,
She waited longer than a woman waits,
Without a cloudy sign, for Lancelot's
Unhurried answer: "Whether or not you fear,
Know always that I fear for me no stroke
Maturing for the joy of any knave
Who sees the world, with me alive in it,
A place too crowded for the furtherance
Of his inflammatory preparations.
But Lot of Orkney had a wife, a dark one;
And rumor says no man who gazed at her,
Attentively, might say his prayers again
Without a penance or an absolution.
I know not about that; but the world knows
That Arthur prayed in vain once, if he prayed,
Or we should have no Modred watching us.
Know then that what you fear to call my fear
Is all for you; and what is all for you
Is all for love, which were the same to me
As life—had I not seen what I have seen.
But first I am to tell you what I see,
And what I mean by fear. It is yourself
That I see now; and if I saw you only,
I might forego again all other service,
And leave to Time, who is Love's almoner,
The benefaction of what years or days
Remaining might be found unchronicled
For two that have not always watched or seen
The sands of gold that flow for golden hours.
If I saw you alone! But I know now
That you are never more to be alone.
The shape of one infernal foul attendant

Will be for ever prowling after you,
To leer at me like a damned thing whipped out
Of the last cave in hell. You know his name.
Over your shoulder I could see him now,
Adventuring his misbegotten patience
For one destroying word in the King's ear—
The word he cannot whisper there quite yet,
Not having it yet to say. If he should say it,
Then all this would be over, and our days
Of life, your days and mine, be over with it.
No day of mine that were to be for you
Your last, would light for me a longer span
Than for yourself; and there would be no twilight."

The Queen's implacable calm eyes betrayed
The doubt that had as yet for what he said
No healing answer: "If I fear no more
Gawaine, I fear your Modred even less.
Your fear, you say, is for an end outside
Your safety; and as much as that I grant you.
And I believe in your belief, moreover,
That some far-off unheard-of retribution
Hangs over Camelot, even as this oak-bough,
That I may almost reach, hangs overhead,
All dark now. Only a small time ago
The light was falling through it, and on me.
Another light, a longer time ago,
Was living in your eyes, and we were happy.
Yet there was Modred then as he is now,
As much a danger then as he is now,
And quite as much a nuisance. Let his eyes
Have all the darkness in them they may hold,
And there will be less left of it outside
For fear to grope and thrive in. Lancelot,
I say the dark is not what you fear most.

There is a Light that you fear more today
Than all the darkness that has ever been;
Yet I doubt not that your Light will burn on
For some time yet without your ministration.
I'm glad for Modred,—though I hate his eyes,—
That he should hold me nearer to your thoughts
Than I should hold myself, I fear, without him;
I'm glad for Gawaine, also,—who, you tell me,
Misled my fancy with his joy of living."

Incredulous of her voice and of her lightness,
He saw now in the patience of her smile
A shining quiet of expectancy
That made as much of his determination
As he had made of giants and Sir Peris.
"But I have more to say than you have heard,"
He faltered—"though God knows what you have heard
Should be enough."

    "I see it now," she said;
"I see it now as always women must
Who cannot hold what holds them any more.
If Modred's hate were now the only hazard—
The only shadow between you and me—
How long should I be saying all this to you,
Or you be listening? No, Lancelot,—no.
I knew it coming for a longer time
Than you fared for the Grail. You told yourself,
When first that wild light came to make men mad
Round Arthur's Table—as Gawaine told himself,
And many another tired man told himself—
That it was God, not something new, that called you.
Well, God was something new to most of them,
And so they went away. But you were changing
Long before you, or Bors, or Percival,

Or Galahad rode away—or poor Gawaine,
Who came back presently; and for a time
Before you went—albeit for no long time—
I may have made for your too loyal patience
A jealous exhibition of my folly—
All for those two Elaines; and one of them
Is dead, poor child, for you. How do you feel,
You men, when women die for you? They do,
Sometimes, you know. Not often, but sometimes."

Discomfiture, beginning with a scowl
And ending in a melancholy smile,
Crept over Lancelot's face the while he stared,
More like a child than like the man he was,
At Guinevere's demure serenity
Before him in the shadow, soon to change
Into the darkness of a darker night
Than yet had been since Arthur was a king.
"What seizure of an unrelated rambling
Do you suppose it was that had you then?"
He said; and with a frown that had no smile
Behind it, he sat brooding.

                    The Queen laughed,
And looked at him again with lucent eyes
That had no sharpness in them; they were soft now,
And a blue light, made wet with happiness,
Distilled from pain into abandonment,
Shone out of them and held him while she smiled,
Although they trembled with a questioning
Of what his gloom foretold: "All that I saw
Was true, and I have paid for what I saw—
More than a man may know. Hear me, and listen:
You cannot put me or the truth aside,
With half-told words that I could only wish

No man had said to me; not you, of all men.
If there were only Modred in the way,
Should I see now, from here and in this light,
So many furrows over your changed eyes?
Why do you fear for me when all my fears
Are for the needless burden you take on?
To put me far away, and your fears with me,
Were surely no long toil, had you the will
To say what you have known and I have known
Longer than I dare guess. Have little fear:
Never shall I become for you a curse
Laid on your conscience to be borne for ever;
Nor shall I be a weight for you to drag
On always after you, as a poor slave
Drags iron at his heels. Therefore, today,
These ominous reassurances of mine
Would seem to me to be a waste of life,
And more than life."

                                Lancelot's memory wandered
Into the blue and wistful distances
That her soft eyes unveiled. He knew their trick,
As he knew the great love that fostered it,
And the wild passionate fate that hid itself
In all the perilous calm of white and gold
That was her face and hair, and might as well
Have been of gold and marble for the world,
And for the King. Before he knew, she stood
Behind him with her warm hands on his cheeks,
And her lips on his lips; and though he heard
Not half of what she told, he heard enough
To make as much of it, or so it seemed,
As man was ever told, or should be told,
Or need be, until everything was told,
And all the mystic silence of the stars

Had nothing more to keep or to reveal.
"If there were only Modred in the way,"
She murmured, "would you come to me tonight?
The King goes to Carleon or Carlisle,
Or some place where there's hunting. Would you come,
If there were only Modred in the way?"
She felt his hand on hers and laid her cheek
Upon his forehead, where the furrows were:
"All these must go away, and so must I—
Before there are more shadows. You will come,
And you may tell me everything you must
That I must hear you tell me—if I must—
Of bones and horrors and of horrid waves
That break for ever on the world's last edge."

III

LANCELOT looked about him, but he saw
No Guinevere. The place where she had sat
Was now an empty chair that might have been
The shadowy throne of an abandoned world,
But for the living fragrance of a kiss
That he remembered, and a living voice
That hovered when he saw that she was gone.
There was too much remembering while he felt
Upon his cheek the warm sound of her words;
There was too much regret; there was too much
Remorse. Regret was there for what had gone,
Remorse for what had come. Yet there was time,
That had not wholly come. There was time enough
Between him and the night—as there were shoals
Enough, no doubt, that in the sea somewhere
Were not yet hidden by the drowning tide.
"So there is here between me and the dark
Some twilight left," he said. He sighed, and said

Again, "Time, tide, and twilight—and the dark;
And then, for me, the Light. But what for her?
I do not think of anything but life
That I may give to her by going now;
And if I look into her eyes again,
Or feel her breath upon my face again,
God knows if I may give so much as life;
Or if the durance of her loneliness
Would have it for the asking. What am I?
What have I seen that I must leave behind
So much of heaven and earth to burn itself
Away in white and gold, until in time
There shall be no more white and no more gold?
I cannot think of such a time as that;
I cannot—yet I must; for I am he
That shall have hastened it and hurried on
To dissolution all that wonderment—
That envy of all women who have said
She was a child of ice and ivory;
And of all men, save one. And who is he?
Who is this Lancelot that has betrayed
His King, and served him with a cankered honor?
Who is this Lancelot that sees the Light
And waits now in the shadow for the dark?
Who is this King, this Arthur, who believes
That what has been, and is, will be for ever,—
Who has no eye for what he will not see,
And will see nothing but what's passing here
In Camelot, which is passing? Why are we here?
What are we doing—kings, queens, Camelots,
And Lancelots? And what is this dim world
That I would leave, and cannot leave tonight
Because a Queen is in it and a King
Has gone away to some place where there's hunting—
Carleon or Carlisle! Who is this Queen,

This pale witch-wonder of white fire and gold,
This Guinevere that I brought back with me
From Cameliard for Arthur, who knew then
What Merlin told, as he forgets it now
And rides away from her—God watch the world!—
To some place where there's hunting! What are kings?
And how much longer are there to be kings?
When are the millions who are now like worms
To know that kings are worms, if they are worms?
When are the women who make toys of men
To know that they themselves are less than toys
When Time has laid upon their skins the touch
Of his all-shrivelling fingers? When are they
To know that men must have an end of them
When men have seen the Light and left the world
That I am leaving now. Yet, here I am,
And all because a king has gone a-hunting. . . .
Carleon or Carlisle!"

                                        So Lancelot
Fed with a sullen rancor, which he knew
To be as false as he was to the King,
The passion and the fear that now in him
Were burning like two slow infernal fires
That only flight and exile far away
From Camelot should ever cool again.
"Yet here I am," he said,—"and here I am.
Time, tide, and twilight; and there is no twilight—
And there is not much time. But there's enough
To eat and drink in; and there may be time
For me to frame a jest or two to prove
How merry a man may be who sees the Light.
And I must get me up and go along,
Before the shadows blot out everything,
And leave me stumbling among skeletons.

God, what a rain of ashes falls on him
Who sees the new and cannot leave the old!"

He rose and looked away into the south
Where a gate was, by which he might go out,
Now, if he would, while Time was yet there with him—
Time that was tearing minutes out of life
While he stood shivering in his loneliness,
And while the silver lights of memory
Shone faintly on a far-off eastern shore
Where he had seen on earth for the last time
The triumph and the sadness in the face
Of Galahad, for whom the Light was waiting.
Now he could see the face of him again,
He fancied; and his flickering will adjured him
To follow it and be free. He followed it
Until it faded and there was no face,
And there was no more light. Yet there was time
That had not come, though he could hear it now
Like ruining feet of marching conquerors
That would be coming soon and were not men.
Forlornly and unwillingly he came back
To find the two dim chairs. In one of them
Was Guinevere, and on her phantom face
There fell a golden light that might have been
The changing gleam of an unchanging gold
That was her golden hair. He sprang to touch
The wonder of it, but she too was gone,
Like Galahad; he was alone again
With shadows, and one face that he still saw.
The world had no more faces now than one
That for a moment, with a flash of pain,
Had shown him what it is that may be seen
In embers that break slowly into dust,
Where for a time was fire. He saw it there

Before him, and he knew it was not good
That he should learn so late, and of this hour,
What men may leave behind them in the eyes
Of women who have nothing more to give,
And may not follow after. Once again
He gazed away to southward, but the face
Of Galahad was not there. He turned, and saw
Before him, in the distance, many lights
In Arthur's palace; for the dark had come
To Camelot, while Time had come and gone.

IV

Not having viewed Carleon or Carlisle,
The King came home to Camelot after midnight,
Feigning an ill not feigned; and his return
Brought Bedivere, and after him Gawaine,
To the King's inner chamber, where they waited
Through the grim light of dawn. Sir Bedivere,
By nature stern to see, though not so bleak
Within as to be frozen out of mercy,
Sat with arms crossed and with his head weighed low
In heavy meditation. Once or twice
His eyes were lifted for a careful glimpse
Of Gawaine at the window, where he stood
Twisting his fingers feverishly behind him,
Like one distinguishing indignantly,
For swift eclipse and for offence not his,
The towers and roofs and the sad majesty
Of Camelot in the dawn, for the last time.

Sir Bedivere, at last, with a long sigh
That said less of his pain than of his pity,
Addressed the younger knight who turned and heard
His elder, but with no large eagerness:

"So it has come, Gawaine; and we are here.
I find when I see backward something farther,
By grace of time, than you are given to see—
Though you, past any doubt, see much that I
See not—I find that what the colder speech
Of reason most repeated says to us
Of what is in a way to come to us
Is like enough to come. And we are here.
Before the unseeing sun is here to mock us,
Or the King here to prove us, we are here.
We are the two, it seems, that are to make
Of words and of our presences a veil
Between him and the sight of what he does.
Little have I to say that I may tell him:
For what I know is what the city knows,
Not what it says,—for it says everything.
The city says the first of all who met
The sword of Lancelot was Colgrevance,
Who fell dead while he wept—a brave machine,
Cranked only for the rudiments of war.
But some of us are born to serve and shift,
And that's not well. The city says, also,
That you and Lancelot were in the garden,
Before the sun went down."

                        "Yes," Gawaine groaned;
"Yes, we were there together in the garden,
Before the sun went down; and I conceive
A place among the possibilities
For me with other causes unforeseen
Of what may shake down soon to grief and ashes
This kingdom and this empire. Bedivere,
Could I have given a decent seriousness
To Lancelot while he said things to me
That pulled his heart half out of him by the roots,

And left him, I see now, half sick with pity
For my poor uselessness to serve a need
That I had never known, we might be now
Asleep and easy in our beds at home,
And we might hear no murmurs after sunrise
Of what we are to hear. A few right words
Of mine, if said well, might have been enough.
That shall I never know. I shall know only
That it was I who laughed at Lancelot
When he said what lay heaviest on his heart.
By now he might be far away from here,
And farther from the world. But the Queen came;
The Queen came, and I left them there together;
And I laughed as I left them. After dark
I met with Modred and said what I could,
When I had heard him, to discourage him.
His mother was my mother. I told Bors,
And he told Lancelot; though as for that,
My story would have been the same as his,
And would have had the same acknowledgment:
'Thanks, but no matter'—or to that effect.
The Queen, of course, had fished him for his word,
And had it on the hook when she went home;
And after that, an army of red devils
Could not have held the man away from her.
And I'm to live as long as I'm to wonder
What might have been, had I not been—myself.
I heard him, and I laughed. Then the Queen came."

"Recriminations are not remedies,
Gawaine; and though you cast them at yourself,
And hurt yourself, you cannot end or swerve
The flowing of these minutes that leave hours
Behind us, as we leave our faded selves
And yesterdays. The surest-visioned of us

Are creatures of our dreams and inferences,
And though it look to us a few go far
For seeing far, the fewest and the farthest
Of all we know go not beyond themselves.
No, Gawaine, you are not the cause of this;
And I have many doubts if all you said,
Or in your lightness may have left unsaid,
Would have unarmed the Queen. The Queen was
    there."—
Gawaine looked up, and then looked down again:
"Good God, if I had only said—said something!"

"Say nothing now, Gawaine." Bedivere sighed,
And shook his head: "Morning is not in the west.
The sun is rising and the King is coming;
Now you may hear him in the corridor,
Like a sick landlord shuffling to the light
For one last look-out on his mortgaged hills.
But hills and valleys are not what he sees;
He sees with us the fire—the sign—the law.
The King that is the father of the law
Is weaker than his child, except he slay it.
Not long ago, Gawaine, I had a dream
Of a sword over kings, and of a world
Without them."—"Dreams, dreams."—"Hush, Gawaine."

                                    King Arthur
Came slowly on till in the darkened entrance
He stared and shivered like a sleep-walker,
Brought suddenly awake where a cliff's edge
Is all he sees between another step
And his annihilation. Bedivere rose,
And Gawaine rose; and with instinctive arms
They partly guided, partly carried him,
To the King's chair.

                              "I thank you, gentlemen,
Though I am not so shaken, I dare say,
As you would have me. This is not the hour
When kings who do not sleep are at their best;
And had I slept this night that now is over,
No man should ever call me King again."
He pulled his heavy robe around him closer,
And laid upon his forehead a cold hand
That came down warm and wet. "You, Bedivere,
And you, Gawaine, are shaken with events
Incredible yesterday,—but kings are men.
Take off their crowns and tear away their colors
And let them see with my eyes what I see—
Yes, they are men, indeed! If there's a slave
In Britain with a reptile at his heart
Like mine that with his claws of ice and fire
Tears out of me the fevered roots of mercy,
Find him, and I will make a king of him!
And then, so that his happiness may swell
Tenfold, I'll sift the beauty of all courts
And capitals, to fetch the fairest woman
That evil has in hiding; after that,
That he may know the sovran one man living
To be his friend, I'll prune all chivalry
To one sure knight. In this wise our new king
Will have his queen to love, as I had mine,—
His friend that he may trust, as I had mine,—
And he will be as gay, if all goes well,
As I have been: as fortunate in his love,
And in his friend as fortunate—as I am!
And what am I? . . . And what are you—you two!
If you are men, why don't you say I'm dreaming?
I know men when I see them, I know daylight;
And I see now the gray shine of our dreams.
I tell you I'm asleep and in my bed! . . .

But no—no . . . I remember. You are men.
You are no dreams—but God, God, if you were!
If I were strong enough to make you vanish
And have you back again with yesterday—
Before I lent myself to that false hunting,
Which yet may stalk the hours of many more
Than Lancelot's unhappy twelve who died,—
With a misguided Colgrevance to lead them,
And Agravaine to follow and fall next,—
Then should I know at last that I was King,
And I should then be King. But kings are men,
And I have gleaned enough these two years gone
To know that queens are women. Merlin told me:
'The love that never was.' Two years ago
He told me that: 'The love that never was!'
I saw—but I saw nothing. Like the bird
That hides his head, I made myself see nothing.
But yesterday I saw—and I saw fire.
I think I saw it first in Modred's eyes;
Yet he said only truth—and fire is right.
It is—it must be fire. The law says fire.
And I, the King who made the law, say fire!
What have I done—what folly have I said,
Since I came here, of dreaming? Dreaming? Ha!
I wonder if the Queen and Lancelot
Are dreaming! . . . Lancelot! Have they found him
    yet?
He slashed a way into the outer night—
Somewhere with Bors. We'll have him here anon,
And we shall feed him also to the fire.
There are too many faggots lying cold
That might as well be cleansing, for our good,
A few deferred infections of our state
That honor should no longer look upon.
Thank heaven, I man my drifting wits again!

Gawaine, your brothers, Gareth and Gaheris,
Are by our royal order there to see
And to report. They went unwillingly,
For they are new to law and young to justice;
But what they are to see will harden them
With wholesome admiration of a realm
Where treason's end is ashes. Ashes. Ashes!
Now this is better. I am King again.
Forget, I pray, my drowsy temporizing,
For I was not then properly awake. . . .
What? Hark! Whose crass insanity is that!
If I be King, go find the fellow and hang him
Who beats into the morning on that bell
Before there is a morning! This is dawn!
What! Bedivere? Gawaine? You shake your heads?
I tell you this is dawn! . . . What have I done?
What have I said so lately that I flinch
To think on! What have I sent those boys to see?
I'll put clouts on my eyes, and I'll not see it!
Her face, and hands, and little small white feet,
And all her shining hair and her warm body—
No—for the love of God, no!—it's alive!
She's all alive, and they are burning her—
The Queen—the love—the love that never was!
Gawaine! Bedivere! Gawaine!—Where is Gawaine!
Is he there in the shadow? Is he dead?
Are we all dead? Are we in hell?—Gawaine! . . .
I cannot see her now in the smoke. Her eyes
Are what I see—and her white body is burning!
She never did enough to make me see her
Like that—to make her look at me like that!
There's not room in the world for so much evil
As I see clamoring in her poor white face
For pity. Pity her, God! God! . . . Lancelot!"

V

GAWAINE, his body trembling and his heart
Pounding as if he were a boy in battle,
Sat crouched as far away from everything
As walls would give him distance. Bedivere
Stood like a man of stone with folded arms,
And wept in stony silence. The King moved
His pallid lips and uttered fitfully
Low fragments of a prayer that was half sad,
Half savage, and was ended in a crash
Of distant sound that anguish lifted near
To those who heard it. Gawaine sprang again
To the same casement where the towers and roofs
Had glimmered faintly a long hour ago,
But saw no terrors yet—though now he heard
A fiercer discord than allegiance rings
To rouse a mourning city: blows, groans, cries,
Loud iron struck on iron, horses trampling,
Death-yells and imprecations, and at last
A moaning silence. Then a murmuring
Of eager fearfulness, which had a note
Of exultation and astonishment,
Came nearer, till a tumult of hard feet
Filled the long corridor where late the King
Had made a softer progress.

                    "Well then, Lucan,"
The King said, urging an indignity
To qualify suspense: "For what arrears
Of grace are we in debt for this attention?
Why all this early stirring of our sentries,
And their somewhat unseasoned innovation,
To bring you at this unappointed hour?

Are we at war with someone or another,
Without our sanction or intelligence?
Are Lucius and the Romans here to greet us,
Or was it Lucius we saw dead?"

                                   Sir Lucan
Bowed humbly in amazed acknowledgment
Of his intrusion, meanwhile having scanned
What three grief-harrowed faces were revealing:
"Praise God, sir, there are tears in the King's eyes,
And in his friends'. Having regarded them,
And having ventured an abrupt appraisal
Of what I translate. . . ."

                              "Lucan," the King said,
"No matter what procedure or persuasion
Gave you an entrance—tell us what it is
That you have come to tell us, and no more.
There was a most uncivil sound abroad
Before you came. Who riots in the city?"

"Sir, will your patience with a clement ear,
Attend the confirmation of events,
I will, with all available precision,
Say what this morning has inaugurated.
No preface or prolonged exordium
Need aggravate the narrative, I venture.
The man of God, requiring of the Queen
A last assoiling prayer for her salvation,
Heard what none else did hear save God the Father.
Then a great hush descended on a scene
Where stronger men than I fell on their knees,
And wet with tears their mail of shining iron
That soon was to be cleft unconscionably
Beneath a blast of anguish as intense
And fabulous in ardor and effect

As Jove's is in his lightning. To be short,
They led the Queen—and she went bravely to it,
Or so she was configured in the picture—
A brief way more; and we who did see that,
Believed we saw the last of all her sharing
In this conglomerate and perplexed existence.
But no—and here the prodigy comes in—
The penal flame had hardly bit the faggot,
When, like an onslaught out of Erebus,
There came a crash of horses, and a flash
Of axes, and a hewing down of heroes,
Not like to any in its harsh, profound,
Unholy, and uneven execution.
I felt the breath of one horse on my neck,
And of a sword that all but left a chasm
Where still, praise be to God, I have intact
A face, if not a fair one. I achieved
My flight, I trust, with honorable zeal,
Not having arms, or mail, or preservation
In any phase of necessary iron.
I found a refuge; and there saw the Queen,
All white, and in a swound of woe uplifted
By Lionel, while a dozen fought about him,
And Lancelot, who seized her while he struck,
And with his insane army galloped away,
Before the living, whom he left amazed,
Were sure they were alive among the dead.
Not even in the legendary mist
Of wars that none today may verify,
Did ever men annihilate their kind
With a more vicious inhumanity,
Or a more skilful frenzy. Lancelot
And all his heated adjuncts are by now
Too far, I fear, for such immediate
Reprisal as your majesty perchance . . ."

"O' God's name, Lucan," the King cried, "be still!"
He gripped with either sodden hand an arm
Of his unyielding chair, while his eyes blazed
In anger, wonder, and fierce hesitation.
Then with a sigh that may have told unheard
Of an unwilling gratitude, he gazed
Upon his friends who gazed again at him;
But neither King nor friend said anything
Until the King turned once more to Sir Lucan:
"Be still, or publish with a shorter tongue
The names of our companions who are dead.
Well, were you there? Or did you run so fast
That you were never there? You must have eyes,
Or you could not have run to find us here."

Then Lucan, with a melancholy glance
At Gawaine, who stood glaring his impatience,
Addressed again the King: "I will be short, sir;
Too brief to measure with finality
The scope of what I saw with indistinct
Amazement and incredulous concern.
Sir Tor, Sir Griflet, and Sir Aglovale
Are dead. Sir Gillimer, he is dead. Sir—Sir—
But should a living error be detailed
In my account, how should I meet your wrath
For such a false addition to your sorrow?"
He turned again to Gawaine, who shook now
As if the fear in him were more than fury.—
The King, observing Gawaine, beat his foot
In fearful hesitancy on the floor:
"No, Lucan; if so kind an error lives
In your dead record, you need have no fear.
My sorrow has already, in the weight
Of this you tell, too gross a task for that."

"Then I must offer you cold naked words,
Without the covering warmth of even one
Forlorn alternative," said Lucan, slowly:
"Sir Gareth, and Sir Gaheris—are dead."

The rage of a fulfilled expectancy,
Long tortured on a rack of endless moments,
Flashed out of Gawaine's overflowing eyes
While he flew forward, seizing Lucan's arms,
And hurled him while he held him.—"Stop, Gawaine,"
The King said grimly. "Now is no time for that.
If Lucan, in a too bewildered heat
Of observation or sad reckoning,
Has added life to death, our joy therefor
Will be the larger. You have lost yourself."

"More than myself it is that I have lost,"
Gawaine said, with a choking voice that faltered:
"Forgive me, Lucan; I was a little mad.
Gareth?—and Gaheris? Do you say their names,
And then say they are dead! They had no arms—
No armor. They were like you—and you live!
Why do you live when they are dead! You ran,
You say? Well, why were they not running—
If they ran only for a pike to die with?
I knew my brothers, and I know your tale
Is not all told. Gareth?—and Gaheris?
Would they stay there to die like silly children?
Did they believe the King would have them die
For nothing? There are dregs of reason, Lucan,
In lunacy itself. My brothers, Lucan,
Were murdered like two dogs. Who murdered them?"

Lucan looked helplessly at Bedivere,
The changeless man of stone, and then at Gawaine:

"I cannot use the word that you have used,
Though yours must have an answer. Your two brothers
Would not have squandered or destroyed themselves
In a vain show of action. I pronounce it,
If only for their known obedience
To the King's instant wish. Know then your brothers
Were caught and crowded, this way and then that,
With men and horses raging all around them;
And there were swords and axes everywhere
That heads of men were. Armored and unarmored,
They knew the iron alike. In so great press,
Discrimination would have had no pause
To name itself; and therefore Lancelot
Saw not—or seeing, he may have seen too late—
On whom his axes fell."

                              "Why do you flood
The name of Lancelot with words enough
To drown him and his army—and his axes! . . .
His axes?—or his axe! Which, Lucan? Speak!
Speak, or by God you'll never speak again! . . .
Forgive me, Lucan; I was a little mad.
You, sir, forgive me; and you, Bedivere.
There are too many currents in this ocean
Where I'm adrift, and I see no land yet.
Men tell of a great whirlpool in the north
Where ships go round until the men aboard
Go dizzy, and are dizzy when they're drowning.
But whether I'm to drown or find the shore,
There is one thing—and only one thing now—
For me to know. . . . His axes? or his axe!
Say, Lucan, or I—O Lucan, speak—speak—speak!
Lucan, did Lancelot kill my two brothers?"

"I say again that in all human chance
He knew not upon whom his axe was falling."

"So! Then it was his axe and not his axes.
It was his hell-begotten self that did it,
And it was not his men. Gareth! Gaheris!
You came too soon. There was no place for you
Where there was Lancelot. My folly it was,
Not yours, to take for true the inhuman glamour
Of his high-shining fame for that which most
Was not the man. The truth we see too late
Hides half its evil in our stupidity;
And we gape while we groan for what we learn.
An hour ago and I was all but eager
To mourn with Bedivere for grief I had
That I did not say something to this villain—
To this true, gracious, murderous friend of mine—
To comfort him and urge him out of this,
While I was half a fool and half believed
That he was going. Well, there is this to say:
The world that has him will not have him long.
You see how calm I am, now I have said it?
And you, sir, do you see how calm I am?
And it was I who told of shipwrecks—whirlpools—
Drowning! I must have been a little mad,
Not having occupation. Now I have one.
And I have now a tongue as many-phrased
As Lucan's. Gauge it, Lucan, if you will;
Or take my word. It's all one thing to me—
All one, all one! There's only one thing left . . .
Gareth and Gaheris! Gareth! . . . Lancelot!"

"Look, Bedivere," the King said: "look to Gawaine.
Now lead him, you and Lucan, to a chair—
As you and Gawaine led me to this chair
Where I am sitting. We may all be led,
If there be coming on for Camelot
Another day like this. Now leave me here,

Alone with Gawaine. When a strong man goes
Like that, it makes him sick to see his friends
Around him. Leave us, and go now. Sometimes
I'll scarce remember that he's not my son,
So near he seems. I thank you, gentlemen."

The King, alone with Gawaine, who said nothing,
Had yet no heart for news of Lancelot
Or Guinevere. He saw them on their way
To Joyous Gard, where Tristram and Isolt
Had islanded of old their stolen love,
While Mark of Cornwall entertained a vengeance
Envisaging an ending of all that;
And he could see the two of them together
As Mark had seen Isolt there, and her knight,—
Though not, like Mark, with murder in his eyes.
He saw them as if they were there already,
And he were a lost thought long out of mind;
He saw them lying in each other's arms,
Oblivious of the living and the dead
They left in Camelot. Then he saw the dead
That lay so quiet outside the city walls,
And wept, and left the Queen to Lancelot—
Or would have left her, had the will been his
To leave or take; for now he could acknowledge
An inrush of a desolate thanksgiving
That she, with death around her, had not died.
The vision of a peace that humbled him,
And yet might save the world that he had won,
Came slowly into view like something soft
And ominous on all-fours, without a spirit
To make it stand upright. "Better be that,
Even that, than blood," he sighed, "if that be peace."
But looking down on Gawaine, who said nothing,
He shook his head: "The King has had his world,

And he shall have no peace. With Modred here,
And Agravaine with Gareth, who is dead
With Gaheris, Gawaine will have no peace.
Gawaine or Modred—Gawaine with his hate,
Or Modred with his anger for his birth,
And the black malady of his ambition—
Will make of my Round Table, where was drawn
The circle of a world, a thing of wreck
And yesterday—a furniture forgotten;
And I, who loved the world as Merlin did,
May lose it as he lost it, for a love
That was not peace, and therefore was not love."

VI

THE dark of Modred's hour not yet availing,
Gawaine it was who gave the King no peace;
Gawaine it was who goaded him and drove him
To Joyous Gard, where now for long his army,
Disheartened with unprofitable slaughter,
Fought for their weary King and wearily ·
Died fighting. Only Gawaine's hate it was
That held the King's knights and his warrior slaves
Close-hived in exile, dreaming of old scenes
Where Sorrow, and her demon sister Fear,
Now shared the dusty food of loneliness,
From Orkney to Cornwall. There was no peace,
Nor could there be, so Gawaine told the King,
And so the King in anguish told himself,
Until there was an end of one of them—
Of Gawaine or the King, or Lancelot,
Who might have had an end, as either knew,
Long since of Arthur and of Gawaine with him.
One evening in the moonlight Lancelot
And Bors, his kinsman, and the loyalest,

If least assured, of all who followed him,
Sat gazing from an ivy-cornered casement
In angry silence upon Arthur's horde,
Who in the silver distance, without sound,
Were dimly burying dead men. Sir Bors,
Reiterating vainly what was told
As wholesome hearing for unhearing ears,
Said now to Lancelot: "And though it be
For no more now than always, let me speak:
You have a pity for the King, you say,
That is not hate; and for Gawaine you have
A grief that is not hate. Pity and grief!
And the Queen all but shrieking out her soul
That morning when we snatched her from the faggots
That were already crackling when we came!
Why, Lancelot, if in you is an answer,
Have you so vast a charity for the King,
And so enlarged a grief for his gay nephew,
Whose tireless hate for you has only one
Disastrous appetite? You know for what—
For your slow blood. I knew you, Lancelot,
When all this would have been a merry fable
For smiling men to yawn at and forget,
As they forget their physic. Pity and grief
Are in your eyes. I see them well enough;
And I saw once with you, in a far land,
The glimmering of a Light that you saw nearer—
Too near for your salvation or advantage,
If you be what you seem. What I saw then
Made life a wilder mystery than ever,
And earth a new illusion. You, maybe,
Saw pity and grief. What I saw was a Gleam,
To fight for or to die for—till we know
Too much to fight or die. Tonight you turn
A page whereon your deeds are to engross

Inexorably their story of tomorrow;
And then tomorrow. How many of these tomorrows
Are coming to ask unanswered why this war
Was fought and fought for the vain sake of slaughter?
Why carve a compost of a multitude,
When only two, discriminately despatched,
Would sum the end of what you know is ending
And leave to you the scorch of no more blood
Upon your blistered soul? The Light you saw
Was not for this poor crumbling realm of Arthur,
Nor more for Rome; but for another state
That shall be neither Rome nor Camelot,
Nor one that we may name. Why longer, then,
Are you and Gawaine to anoint with war,
That even in hell would be superfluous,
A reign already dying, and ripe to die?
I leave you to your last interpretation
Of what may be the pleasure of your madness."

Meanwhile a mist was hiding the dim work
Of Arthur's men; and like another mist,
All gray, came Guinevere to Lancelot,
Whom Bors had left, not having had of him
The largess of a word. She laid her hands
Upon his hair, vexing him to brief speech:
"And you—are you like Bors?"

                              "I may be so,"
She said; and she saw faintly where she gazed,
Like distant insects of a shadowy world,
Dim clusters here and there of shadowy men
Whose occupation was her long abhorrence:
"If he came here and went away again,
And all for nothing, I may be like Bors.
Be glad, at least, that I am not like Mark

Of Cornwall, who stood once behind a man
And slew him without saying he was there.
Not Arthur, I believe, nor yet Gawaine,
Would have done quite like that; though only God
May say what there's to come before this war
Shall have an end—unless you are to see,
As I have seen so long, a way to end it."

He frowned, and watched again the coming mist
That hid with a cold veil of augury
The stillness of an empire that was dying:
"And are you here to say that if I kill
Gawaine and Arthur we shall both be happy?"

"Is there still such a word as happiness?
I come to tell you nothing, Lancelot,
That folly and waste have not already told you.
Were you another man than Lancelot,
I might say folly and fear. But no,—no fear,
As I know fear, was yet composed and wrought,
By man, for your delay and your undoing.
God knows how cruelly and how truly now
You might say, that of all who breathe and suffer
There may be others who are not so near
To you as I am, and so might say better
What I say only with a tongue not apt
Or guarded for much argument. A woman,
As men have known since Adam heard the first
Of Eve's interpreting of how it was
In Paradise, may see but one side only—
Where maybe there are two, to say no more.
Yet here, for you and me, and so for all
Caught with us in this lamentable net,
I see but one deliverance: I see none,
Unless you cut for us a clean way out,

So rending these hate-woven webs of horror
Before they mesh the world. And if the world
Or Arthur's name be now a dying glory,
Why bleed it for the sparing of a man
Who hates you, and a King that hates himself?
If war be war—and I make only blood
Of your red writing—why dishonor Time
For torture longer drawn in your slow game
Of empty slaughter? Tomorrow it will be
The King's move, I suppose, and we shall have
One more magnificent waste of nameless pawns,
And of a few more knights. God, how you love
This game!—to make so loud a shambles of it,
When you have only twice to lift your finger
To signal peace, and give to this poor drenched
And clotted earth a time to heal itself.
Twice over I say to you, if war be war,
Why play with it? Why look a thousand ways
Away from what it is, only to find
A few stale memories left that would requite
Your tears with your destruction? Tears, I say,
For I have seen your tears; I see them now,
Although the moon is dimmer than it was
Before I came. I wonder if I dimmed it.
I wonder if I brought this fog here with me
To make you chillier even than you are
When I am not so near you. . . . Lancelot,
There must be glimmering yet somewhere within you
The last spark of a little willingness
To tell me why it is this war goes on.
Once I believed you told me everything;
And what you may have hidden was no matter,
For what you told was all I needed then.
But crumbs that are a festival for joy
Make a dry fare for sorrow; and the few

Spared words that were enough to nourish faith,
Are for our lonely fears a frugal poison.
So, Lancelot, if only to bring back
For once the ghost of a forgotten mercy,
Say now, even though you strike me to the floor
When you have said it, for what untold end
All this goes on. Am I not anything now?
Is Gawaine, who would feed you to wild swine,
And laugh to see them tear you, more than I am?
Is Arthur, at whose word I was dragged out
To wear for you the fiery crown itself
Of human torture, more to you than I am?
Am I, because you saw death touch me once,
Too gross a trifle to be longer prized?
Not many days ago, when you lay hurt
And aching on your bed, and I cried out
Aloud on heaven that I should bring you there,
You said you would have paid the price of hell
To save me that foul morning from the fire.
You paid enough: yet when you told me that,
With death going on outside the while you said it,
I heard the woman in me asking why.
Nor do I wholly find an answer now
In any shine of any far-off Light
You may have seen. Knowing the world, you know
How surely and how indifferently that Light
Shall burn through many a war that is to be,
To which this war were no more than a smear
On circumstance. The world has not begun.
The Light you saw was not the Light of Rome,
Or Time, though you seem battling here for time,
While you are still at war with Arthur's host
And Gawaine's hate. How many thousand men
Are going to their death before Gawaine
And Arthur go to theirs—and I to mine?"

Lancelot, looking off into the fog,
In which his fancy found the watery light
Of a dissolving moon, sighed without hope
Of saying what the Queen would have him say:
"I fear, my lady, my fair nephew Bors,
Whose tongue affords a random wealth of sound,
May lately have been scattering on the air
For you a music less oracular
Than to your liking. . . . Say, then, you had split
The uncovered heads of two men with an axe,
Not knowing whose heads—if that's a palliation—
And seen their brains fly out and splash the ground
As they were common offal, and then learned
That you had butchered Gaheris and Gareth—
Gareth, who had for me a greater love
Than any that has ever trod the ways
Of a gross world that early would have crushed him,—
Even you, in your quick fever of dispatch,
Might hesitate before you drew the blood
Of him that was their brother, and my friend.
Yes, he was more my friend, was I to know,
Than I had said or guessed; for it was Gawaine
Who gave to Bors the word that might have saved us,
And Arthur's fading empire, for the time
Till Modred had in his dark wormy way
Crawled into light again with a new ruin
At work in that occult snake's brain of his.
And even in your prompt obliteration
Of Arthur from a changing world that rocks
Itself into a dizziness around him,
A moment of attendant reminiscence
Were possible, if not likely. Had he made
A knight of you, scrolling your name with his
Among the first of men—and in his love
Inveterately the first—and had you then

Betrayed his fame and honor to the dust
That now is choking him, you might in time—
You might, I say—to my degree succumb.
Forgive me, if my lean words are for yours
Too bare an answer, and ascribe to them
No tinge of allegation or reproach.
What I said once to you I said for ever—
That I would pay the price of hell to save you.
As for the Light, leave that for me alone;
Or leave as much of it as yet for me
May shine. Should I, through any unforeseen
Remote effect of awkwardness or chance,
Be done to death or durance by the King,
I leave some writing wherein I beseech
For you the clemency of afterthought.
Were I to die and he to see me dead,
My living prayer, surviving the cold hand
That wrote, would leave you in his larger prudence,
If I have known the King, free and secure
To bide the summoning of another King
More great than Arthur. But all this is language;
And I know more than words have yet the scope
To show of what's to come. Go now to rest;
And sleep, if there be sleep. There was a moon;
And now there is no sky where the moon was.
Sometimes I wonder if this be the world
We live in, or the world that lives in us."

The new day, with a cleansing crash of rain
That washed and sluiced the soiled and hoof-torn field
Of Joyous Gard, prepared for Lancelot
And his wet men the not unwelcome scene
Of a drenched emptiness without an army.
"Our friend the foe is given to dry fighting,"
Said Lionel, advancing with a shrug,

To Lancelot, who saw beyond the rain.
And later Lionel said, "What fellows are they,
Who are so thirsty for their morning ride
That swimming horses would have hardly time
To eat before they swam? You, Lancelot,
If I see rather better than a blind man,
Are waiting on three pilgrims who must love you,
To voyage a flood like this. No friend have I,
To whisper not of three, on whom to count
For such a loyal wash. The King himself
Would entertain a kindly qualm or so,
Before he suffered such a burst of heaven
To splash even three musicians."

                              "Good Lionel,
I thank you, but you need afflict your fancy
No longer for my sake. For these who come,
If I be not immoderately deceived,
Are bearing with them the white flower of peace—
Which I could hope might never parch or wither,
Were I a stranger to this ravening world
Where we have mostly a few rags and tags
Between our skins and those that wrap the flesh
Of less familiar brutes we feed upon
That we may feed the more on one another."

"Well, now that we have had your morning grace
Before our morning meat, pray tell to me
The why and whence of this anomalous
Horse-riding offspring of the Fates. Who are they?"

"I do not read their features or their names;
But if I read the King, they are from Rome,
Spurred here by the King's prayer for no delay;

And I pray God aloud that I say true."
And after a long watching, neither speaking,
"You do," said Lionel; "for by my soul,
I see no other than my lord the Bishop,
Who does God's holy work in Rochester.
Since you are here, you may as well abide here,
While I go foraging."

        Now in the gateway,
The Bishop, who rode something heavily,
Was glad for rest though grim in his refusal
At once of entertainment or refection:
"What else you do, Sir Lancelot, receive me
As one among the honest when I say
That my voluminous thanks were less by cantos
Than my damp manner feels. Nay, hear my voice:
If once I'm off this royal animal,
How o' God's name shall I get on again?
Moreover, the King waits. With your accord,
Sir Lancelot, I'll dry my rainy face,
While you attend what's herein written down,
In language of portentous brevity,
For the King's gracious pleasure and for yours,
Whereof the burden is the word of Rome,
Requiring your deliverance of the Queen
Not more than seven days hence. The King returns
Anon to Camelot; and I go with him,
Praise God, if what he waits now is your will
To end an endless war. No recrudescence,
As you may soon remark, of what is past
Awaits the Queen, or any doubt soever
Of the King's mercy. Have you more to say
Than Rome has written, or do I perceive
Your tranquil acquiescence? Is it so?
Then be it so! Venite. Pax vobiscum."

"To end an endless war with 'pax vobiscum'
Would seem a ready schedule for a bishop;
Would God that I might see the end of it!"
Lancelot, like a statue in the gateway,
Regarded with a qualified rejoicing   .
The fading out of his three visitors
Into the cold and swallowing wall of storm
Between him and the battle-wearied King
And the unwearying hatred of Gawaine.
To Bors his nephew, and to Lionel,
He glossed a tale of Roman intercession,
Knowing that for a time, and a long time,
The sweetest fare that he might lay before them
Would hold an evil taste of compromise.
To Guinevere, who questioned him at noon
Of what by then had made of Joyous Gard
A shaken hive of legend-heavy wonder,
He said what most it was the undying Devil,
Who ruled him when he might, would have him say:
"Your confident arrangement of the board
For this day's game was notably not to be;
Today was not for the King's move or mine,
But for the Bishop's; and the board is empty.
The words that I have waited for more days
Than are to now my tallage of gray hairs
Have come at last, and at last you are free.
So, for a time, there will be no more war;
And you are going home to Camelot."

"To Camelot?" . . .

                    "To Camelot." But his words
Were said for no queen's hearing. In his arms
He caught her when she fell; and in his arms
He carried her away. The word of Rome
Was in the rain. There was no other sound.

VII

All day the rain came down on Joyous Gard,
Where now there was no joy, and all that night
The rain came down. Shut in for none to find him
Where an unheeded log-fire fought the storm
With upward swords that flashed along the wall
Faint hieroglyphs of doom not his to read,
Lancelot found a refuge where at last
He might see nothing. Glad for sight of nothing,
He saw no more. Now and again he buried
A lonely thought among the coals and ashes
Outside the reaching flame and left it there,
Quite as he left outside in rainy graves
The sacrificial hundreds who had filled them.
"They died, Gawaine," he said, "and you live on,
You and the King, as if there were no dying;
And it was I, Gawaine, who let you live—
You and the King. For what more length of time,
I wonder, may there still be found on earth
Foot-room for four of us? We are too many
For one world, Gawaine; and there may be soon,
For one or other of us, a way out.
As men are listed, we are men for men
To fear; and I fear Modred more than any.
But even the ghost of Modred at the door—
The ghost I should have made him—would employ
For time as hard as this a louder knuckle,
Assuredly now, than that. And I would see
No mortal face till morning. . . . Well, are you well
Again? Are you as well again as ever?"

He led her slowly on with a cold show
Of care that was less heartening for the Queen

Than anger would have been, into the firelight,
And there he gave her cushions. "Are you warm?"
He said; and she said nothing. "Are you afraid?"
He said again; "are you still afraid of Gawaine?
As often as you think of him and hate him,
Remember too that he betrayed his brothers
To us that he might save us. Well, he saved us;
And Rome, whose name to you was never music,
Saves you again, with heaven alone may tell
What others who might have their time to sleep
In earth out there, with the rain falling on them,
And with no more to fear of wars tonight
Than you need fear of Gawaine or of Arthur.
The way before you is a safer way
For you to follow than when I was in it.
We children who forget the whips of Time,
To live within the hour, are slow to see
That all such hours are passing. They were past
When you came here with me."

                              She looked away,
Seeming to read the firelight on the walls
Before she spoke: "When I came here with you,
And found those eyes of yours, I could have wished
And prayed it were the end of hours, and years.
What was it made you save me from the fire,
If only out of memories and forebodings
To build around my life another fire
Of slower faggots? If you had let me die,
Those other faggots would be ashes now,
And all of me that you have ever loved
Would be a few more ashes. If I read
The past as well as you have read the future
You need say nothing of ingratitude,
For I say only lies. My soul, of course,

It was you loved. You told me so yourself.
And that same precious blue-veined cream-white soul
Will soon be safer, if I understand you,
In Camelot, where the King is, than elsewhere
On earth. What more, in faith, have I to ask
Of earth or heaven than that! Although I fell
When you said Camelot, are you to know,
Surely, the stroke you gave me then was not
The measure itself of ecstasy? We women
Are such adept inveterates in our swooning
That we fall down for joy as easily
As we eat one another to show our love.
Even horses, seeing again their absent masters,
Have wept for joy; great dogs have died of it."
Having said as much as that, she frowned and held
Her small white hands out for the fire to warm them.
Forward she leaned, and forward her thoughts went—
To Camelot. But they were not there long,
Her thoughts; for soon she flashed her eyes again,
And he found in them what he wished were tears
Of angry sorrow for what she had said.
"What are you going to do with me?" she asked;
And all her old incisiveness came back,
With a new thrust of malice, which he felt
And feared. "What are you going to do with me?
What does a child do with a worn-out doll?
I was a child once; and I had a father.
He was a king; and, having royal ways,
He made a queen of me—King Arthur's queen.
And if that happened, once upon a time,
Why may it not as well be happening now
That I am not a queen? Was I a queen
When first you brought me here with one torn rag
To cover me? Was I overmuch a queen
When I sat up at last, and in a gear

That would have made a bishop dance to Cardiff
To see me wearing it? Was I Queen then?"

"You were the Queen of Christendom," he said,
Not smiling at her, "whether now or not
You deem it an unchristian exercise
To vilipend the wearing of the vanished.
The women may have reasoned, insecurely,
That what one queen had worn would please another.
I left them to their ingenuities."

Once more he frowned away a threatening smile,
But soon forgot the memory of all smiling
While he gazed on the glimmering face and hair
Of Guinevere—the glory of white and gold
That had been his, and were, for taking of it,
Still his, to cloud, with an insidious gleam
Of earth, another that was not of earth,
And so to make of him a thing of night—
A moth between a window and a star,
Not wholly lured by one or led by the other.
The more he gazed upon her beauty there,
The longer was he living in two kingdoms,
Not owning in his heart the king of either,
And ruling not himself. There was an end
Of hours, he told her silent face again,
In silence. On the morning when his fury
Wrenched her from that foul fire in Camelot,
Where blood paid irretrievably the toll
Of her release, the whips of Time had fallen
Upon them both. All this to Guinevere
He told in silence and he told in vain.

Observing her ten fingers variously,
She sighed, as in equivocal assent,
"No two queens are alike."

Is never more to ask me if my life
Be one that I could wish had not been lived—
And that you never torture it again,
To make it bleed and ache as you do now,
Past all indulgence or necessity.
Were you to give a lonely child who loved you
One living thing to keep—a bird, may be—
Before you went away from her forever,
Would you, for surety not to be forgotten,
Maim it and leave it bleeding on her fingers?
And would you leave the child alone with it—
Alone, and too bewildered even to cry,
Till you were out of sight? Are you men never
To know what words are? Do you doubt sometimes
A Vision that lets you see so far away
That you forget so lightly who it was
You must have cared for once to be so kind—
Or seem so kind—when she, and for that only,
Had that been all, would throw down crowns and glories
To share with you the last part of the world?
And even the queen in me would hardly go
So far off as to vanish. If I were patched
And scrapped in what the sorriest fisher-wife
In Orkney might give mumbling to a beggar,
I doubt if oafs and yokels would annoy me
More than I willed they should. Am I so old
And dull, so lean and waning, or what not,
That you must hurry away to grasp and hoard
The small effect of time I might have stolen
From you and from a Light that where it lives
Must live for ever? Where does history tell you
The Lord himself would seem in so great haste
As you for your perfection? If our world—
Your world and mine and Arthur's, as you say—
Is going out now to make way for another,

Why not before it goes, and I go with it,
Have yet one morsel more of life together,
Before death sweeps the table and our few crumbs
Of love are a few last ashes on a fire
That cannot hurt your Vision, or burn long?
You cannot warm your lonely fingers at it
For a great waste of time when I am dead:
When I am dead you will be on your way,
With maybe not so much as one remembrance
Of all I was, to follow you and torment you.
Some word of Bors may once have given color
To some few that I said, but they were true—
Whether Bors told them first to me, or whether
I told them first to Bors. The Light you saw
Was not the Light of Rome; the word you had
Of Rome was not the word of God—though Rome
Has refuge for the weary and heavy-laden.
Were I to live too long I might seek Rome
Myself, and be the happier when I found it.
Meanwhile, am I to be no more to you
Than a moon-shadow of a lonely stranger
Somewhere in Camelot? And is there no region
In this poor fading world of Arthur's now
Where I may be again what I was once—
Before I die? Should I live to be old,
I shall have been long since too far away
For you to hate me then; and I shall know
How old I am by seeing it in your eyes."
Her misery told itself in a sad laugh,
And in a rueful twisting of her face
That only beauty's perilous privilege
Of injury would have yielded or suborned
As hope's infirm accessory while she prayed
Through Lancelot to heaven for Lancelot.
She looked away: "If I were God," she said,

                       "Is that the flower
Of all your veiled invention?" Lancelot said,
Smiling at last: "If you say, saying all that,
You are not like Isolt—well, you are not.
Isolt was a physician, who cured men
Their wounds, and sent them rowelling for more;
Isolt was too dark, and too versatile;
She was too dark for Mark, if not for Tristram.
Forgive me; I was saying that to myself,
And not to make you shiver. No two queens—
Was that it?—are alike? A longer story
Might have a longer telling and tell less.
Your tale's as brief as Pelleas with his vengeance
On Gawaine, whom he swore that he would slay
At once for stealing of the lady Ettard."

"Treasure my scantling wits, if you enjoy them;
Wonder a little, too, that I conserve them
Through the eternal memory of one morning,
And in these years of days that are the death
Of men who die for me. I should have died.
I should have died for them."

                      "You are wrong," he said;
"They died because Gawaine went mad with hate
For loss of his two brothers and set the King
On fire with fear, the two of them believing
His fear was vengeance when it was in fact
A royal desperation. They died because
Your world, my world, and Arthur's world is dying,
As Merlin said it would. No blame is yours;
For it was I who led you from the King—
Or rather, to say truth, it was your glory
That led my love to lead you from the King—
By flowery ways, that always end somewhere,

To fire and fright and exile, and release.
And if you bid your memory now to blot
Your story from the book of what has been,
Your phantom happiness were a ghost indeed,
And I the least of weasels among men,—
Too false to manhood and your sacrifice
To merit a niche in hell. If that were so,
I'd swear there was no light for me to follow,
Save your eyes to the grave; and to the last
I might not know that all hours have an end;
I might be one of those who feed themselves
By grace of God, on hopes dryer than hay,
Enjoying not what they eat, yet always eating.
The Vision shattered, a man's love of living
Becomes at last a trap and a sad habit,
More like an ailing dotard's love of liquor
That ails him, than a man's right love of woman,
Or of his God. There are men enough like that,
And I might come to that. Though I see far
Before me now, could I see, looking back,
A life that you could wish had not been lived,
I might be such a man. Could I believe
Our love was nothing mightier then than we were,
I might be such a man—a living dead man,
One of these days."

                    Guinevere looked at him,
And all that any woman has not said
Was in one look: "Why do you stab me now
With such a needless 'then'? If I am going—
And I suppose I am—are the words all lost
That men have said before to dogs and children
To make them go away? Why use a knife,
When there are words enough without your 'then'
To cut as deep as need be? What I ask you

"I should say, 'Let them be as they have been.
A few more years will heap no vast account
Against eternity, and all their love
Was what I gave them. They brought on the end
Of Arthur's empire, which I wrought through Merlin
For the world's knowing of what kings and queens
Are made for; but they knew not what they did—
Save as a price, and as a fear that love
Might end in fear. It need not end that way,
And they need fear no more for what I gave them;
For it was I who gave them to each other.'
If I were God, I should say that to you."
He saw tears quivering in her pleading eyes,
But through them she could see, with a wild hope,
That he was fighting. When he spoke, he smiled—
Much as he might have smiled at her, she thought,
Had she been Gawaine, Gawaine having given
To Lancelot, who yet would have him live,
An obscure wound that would not heal or kill.

"My life was living backward for the moment,"
He said, still burying in the coals and ashes
Thoughts that he would not think. His tongue was dry,
And each dry word he said was choking him
As he said on: "I cannot ask of you
That you be kind to me, but there's a kindness
That is your proper debt. Would you cajole
Your reason with a weary picturing
On walls or on vain air of what your fancy,
Like firelight, makes of nothing but itself?
Do you not see that I go from you only
Because you go from me?—because our path
Led where at last it had an end in havoc,
As long we knew it must—as Arthur too,
And Merlin knew it must?—as God knew it must?

A power that I should not have said was mine—
That was not mine, and is not mine—avails me
Strangely tonight, although you are here with me;
And I see much in what has come to pass
That is to be. The Light that I have seen,
As you say true, is not the light of Rome,
Albeit the word of Rome that set you free
Was more than mine or the King's. To flout that word
Would sound the preparation of a terror
To which a late small war on our account
Were a king's pastime and a queen's annoyance;
And that, for the good fortune of a world
As yet not over-fortuned, may not be.
There may be war to come when you are gone,
For I doubt yet Gawaine; but Rome will hold you,
Hold you in Camelot. If there be more war,
No fire of mine shall feed it, nor shall you
Be with me to endure it. You are free;
And free, you are going home to Camelot.
There is no other way than one for you,
Nor is there more than one for me. We have lived,
And we shall die. I thank you for my life.
Forgive me if I say no more tonight."
He rose, half blind with pity that was no longer
The servant of his purpose or his will,
To grope away somewhere among the shadows
For wine to drench his throat and his dry tongue,
That had been saying he knew not what to her
For whom his life-devouring love was now
A scourge of mercy.

                    Like a blue-eyed Medea
Of white and gold, broken with grief and fear
And fury that shook her speechless while she waited,
Yet left her calm enough for Lancelot

To see her without seeing, she stood up
To breathe and suffer. Fury could not live long,
With grief and fear like hers and love like hers,
When speech came back: "No other way now than one?
Free? Do you call me free? Do you mean by that
There was never woman alive freer to live
Than I am free to die? Do you call me free
Because you are driven so near to death yourself
With weariness of me, and the sight of me,
That you must use a crueller knife than ever,
And this time at my heart, for me to watch
Before you drive it home? For God's sake, drive it!
Drive it as often as you have the others,
And let the picture of each wound it makes
On me be shown to women and men for ever;
And the good few that know—let them reward you.
I hear them, in such low and pitying words
As only those who know, and are not many,
Are used to say: 'The good knight Lancelot
It was who drove the knife home to her heart,
Rather than drive her home to Camelot.'
Home! Free! Would you let me go there again—
To be at home?—be free? To be his wife?
To live in his arms always, and so hate him
That I could heap around him the same faggots
That you put out with blood? Go home, you say?
Home?—where I saw the black post waiting for me
That morning?—saw those good men die for me—
Gareth and Gaheris, Lamorak's brother Tor,
And all the rest? Are men to die for me
For ever? Is there water enough, do you think,
Between this place and that for me to drown in?"

"There is time enough, I think, between this hour
And some wise hour tomorrow, for you to sleep in.

When you are safe again in Camelot,
The King will not molest you or pursue you;
The King will be a suave and chastened man.
In Camelot you shall have no more to dread
Than you shall hear then of this rain that roars
Tonight as if it would be roaring always.
I do not ask you to forgive the faggots,
Though I would have you do so for your peace.
Only the wise who know may do so much,
And they, as you say truly, are not many.
And I would say no more of this tonight."

"Then do not ask me for the one last thing
That I shall give to God! I thought I died
That morning. Why am I alive again,
To die again? Are you all done with me?
Is there no longer something left of me
That made you need me? Have I lost myself
So fast that what a mirror says I am
Is not what is, but only what was once?
Does half a year do that with us, I wonder,
Or do I still have something that was mine
That afternoon when I was in the sunset,
Under the oak, and you were looking at me?
Your look was not all sorrow for your going
To find the Light and leave me in the dark—
But I am the daughter of Leodogran,
And you are Lancelot,—and have a tongue
To say what I may not. . . . Why must I go
To Camelot when your kinsmen hold all France?
Why is there not some nook in some old house
Where I might hide myself—with you or not?
Is there no castle, or cabin, or cave in the woods?
Yes, I could love the bats and owls, in France,
A lifetime sooner than I could the King

That I shall see in Camelot, waiting there
For me to cringe and beg of him again
The dust of mercy, calling it holy bread.
I wronged him, but he bought me with a name
Too large for my king-father to relinquish—
Though I prayed him, and I prayed God aloud,
To spare that crown. I called it crown enough
To be my father's child—until you came.
And then there were no crowns or kings or fathers
Under the sky. I saw nothing but you.
And you would whip me back to bury myself
In Camelot, with a few slave maids and lackeys
To be my grovelling court; and even their faces
Would not hide half the story. Take me to France—
To France or Egypt,—anywhere else on earth
Than Camelot! Is there not room in France
For two more dots of mortals?—or for one?—
For me alone? Let Lionel go with me—
Or Bors. Let Bors go with me into France,
And leave me there. And when you think of me,
Say Guinevere is in France, where she is happy;
And you may say no more of her than that . . .
Why do you not say something to me now—
Before I go? Why do you look—and look?
Why do you frown as if you thought me mad?
I am not mad—but I shall soon be mad,
If I go back to Camelot where the King is.
Lancelot! . . . Is there nothing left of me?
Nothing of what you called your white and gold,
And made so much of? Has it all gone by?
He must have been a lonely God who made
Man in his image and then made only a woman!
Poor fool she was! Poor Queen! Poor Guinevere!
There were kings and bishops once, under her window
Like children, and all scrambling for a flower.

Time was!—God help me, what am I saying now!
Does a Queen's memory wither away to that?
Am I so dry as that? Am I a shell?
Have I become so cheap as this? . . . I wonder
Why the King cared!" She fell down on her knees
Crying, and held his knees with hungry fear.

Over his folded arms, as over the ledge
Of a storm-shaken parapet, he could see,
Below him, like a tumbling flood of gold,
The Queen's hair with a crumpled foam of white
Around it: "Do you ask, as a child would,
For France because it has a name? How long
Do you conceive the Queen of the Christian world
Would hide herself in France were she to go there?
How long should Rome require to find her there?
And how long, Rome or not, would such a flower
As you survive the unrooting and transplanting
That you commend so ingenuously tonight?
And if we shared your cave together, how long,
And in the joy of what obscure seclusion,
If I may say it, were Lancelot of the Lake
And Guinevere an unknown man and woman,
For no eye to see twice? There are ways to France,
But why pursue them for Rome's interdict,
And for a longer war? Your path is now
As open as mine is dark—or would be dark,
Without the Light that once had blinded me
To death, had I seen more. I shall see more,
And I shall not be blind. I pray, moreover,
That you be not so now. You are a Queen,
And you may be no other. You are too brave
And kind and fair for men to cheer with lies.
We cannot make one world of two, nor may we
Count one life more than one. Could we go back

To the old garden, we should not stay long;
The fruit that we should find would all be fallen,
And have the taste of earth."

                              When she looked up,
A tear fell on her forehead. "Take me away!"
She cried. "Why do you do this? Why do you say this?
If you are sorry for me, take me away
From Camelot! Send me away—drive me away—
Only away from there! The King is there—
And I may kill him if I see him there.
Take me away—take me away to France!
And if I cannot hide myself in France,
Then let me die in France!"

                              He shook his head,
Slowly, and raised her slowly in his arms,
Holding her there; and they stood long together.
And there was no sound then of anything,
Save a low moaning of a broken woman,
And the cold roaring down of that long rain.

All night the rain came down on Joyous Gard;
And all night, there before the crumbling embers
That faded into feathery death-like dust,
Lancelot sat and heard it. He saw not
The fire that died, but he heard rain that fell
On all those graves around him and those years
Behind him; and when dawn came, he was cold.
At last he rose, and for a tim stood seeing
The place where she had been. She was not there;
He was not sure that she had ever been there;
He was not sure there was a Queen, or a King,
Or a world with kingdoms on it. He was cold.
He was not sure of anything but the Light—

The Light he saw not. "And I shall not see it,"
He thought, "so long as I kill men for Gawaine.
If I kill him, I may as well kill myself;
And I have killed his brothers." He tried to sleep,
But rain had washed the sleep out of his life,
And there was no more sleep. When he awoke,
He did not know that he had been asleep;
And the same rain was falling. At some strange hour
It ceased, and there was light. And seven days after,
With a cavalcade of silent men and women,
The Queen rode into Camelot, where the King was,
And Lancelot rode grimly at her side.

When he rode home again to Joyous Gard,
The storm in Gawaine's eyes and the King's word
Of banishment attended him. "Gawaine
Will give the King no peace," Lionel said;
And Lancelot said after him, "Therefore
The King will have no peace."—And so it was
That Lancelot, with many of Arthur's knights
That were not Arthur's now, sailed out one day
From Cardiff to Bayonne, where soon Gawaine,
The King, and the King's army followed them,
For longer sorrow and for longer war.

VIII

For longer war they came, and with a fury
That only Modred's opportunity,
Seized in the dark of Britain, could have hushed
And ended in a night. For Lancelot,
When he was hurried amazed out of his rest
Of a gray morning to the scarred gray wall
Of Benwick, where he slept and fought, and saw
Not yet the termination of a strife

That irked him out of utterance, found again
Before him a still plain without an army.
What the mist hid between him and the distance
He knew not, but a multitude of doubts
And hopes awoke in him, and one black fear,
At sight of a truce-waving messenger
In whose approach he read, as by the Light
Itself, the last of Arthur. The man reined
His horse outside the gate, and Lancelot,
Above him on the wall, with a sick heart,
Listened: "Sir Gawaine to Sir Lancelot
Sends greeting; and this with it, in his hand.
The King has raised the siege, and you in France
He counts no longer with his enemies.
His toil is now for Britain, and this war
With you, Sir Lancelot, is an old war,
If you will have it so."—"Bring the man in,"
Said Lancelot, "and see that he fares well."

All through the sunrise, and alone, he sat
With Gawaine's letter, looking toward the sea
That flowed somewhere between him and the land
That waited Arthur's coming, but not his.
"King Arthur's war with me is an old war,
If I will have it so," he pondered slowly;
"And Gawaine's hate for me is an old hate,
If I will have it so. But Gawaine's wound
Is not a wound that heals; and there is Modred—
Inevitable as ruin after flood.
The cloud that has been darkening Arthur's empire
May now have burst, with Arthur still in France,
Many hours away from Britain, and a world
Away from me. But I read this in my heart.
If in the blot of Modred's evil shadow,
Conjecture views a cloudier world than is,

So much the better, then, for clouds and worlds,
And kings. Gawaine says nothing yet of this,
But when he tells me nothing he tells all.
Now he is here, fordone and left behind,
Pursuant of his wish; and there are words
That he would say to me. Had I not struck him
Twice to the earth, unwillingly, for my life,
My best eye then, I fear, were best at work
On what he has not written. As it is,
If I go seek him now, and in good faith,
My faith may dig my grave. If so, then so.
If I know only with my eyes and ears,
I may as well not know."

                    Gawaine, having scanned
His words and sent them, found a way to sleep—
And sleeping, to forget. But he remembered
Quickly enough when he woke up to meet
With his the shining gaze of Lancelot
Above him in a shuttered morning gloom,
Seeming at first a darkness that had eyes.
Fear for a moment seized him, and his heart,
Long whipped and driven with fever, paused and flickered,
As like to fail too soon. Fearing to move,
He waited; fearing to speak, he waited; fearing
To see too clearly or too much, he waited;
For what, he wondered—even the while he knew
It was for Lancelot to say something.
And soon he did: "Gawaine, I thought at first
No man was here."

                    "No man was, till you came.
Sit down; and for the love of God who made you,
Say nothing to me now of my three brothers.
Gareth and Gaheris and Agravaine

Are gone; and I am going after them;
Of such is our election. When you gave
That ultimate knock on my revengeful head,
You did a piece of work."

                                "May God forgive,"
Lancelot said, "I did it for my life,
Not yours."

                        "I know, but I was after yours;
Had I been Lancelot, and you Gawaine,
You might be dead."

                        "Had you been Lancelot,
And I Gawaine, my life had not been yours—
Not willingly. Your brothers are my debt
That I shall owe to sorrow and to God,
For whatsoever payment there may be.
What I have paid is not a little, Gawaine."

"Why leave me out? A brother more or less
Would hardly be the difference of a shaving.
My loose head would assure you, saying this,
That I have no more venom in me now
On their account than mine, which is not much.
There was a madness feeding on us all,
As we fed on the world. When the world sees,
The world will have in turn another madness;
And so, as I've a glimpse, *ad infinitum*.
But I'm not of the seers: Merlin it was
Who turned a sort of ominous early glimmer
On my profane young life. And after that
He falls himself, so far that he becomes
One of our most potential benefits—
Like Vivian, or the mortal end of Modred.

Why could you not have taken Modred also,
And had the five of us? You did your best,
We know, yet he's more poisonously alive
Than ever; and he's a brother, of a sort,
Or half of one, and you should not have missed him.
A gloomy curiosity was our Modred,
From his first intimation of existence.
God made him as He made the crocodile,
To prove He was omnipotent. Having done so,
And seeing then that Camelot, of all places
Ripe for annihilation, most required him,
He put him there at once, and there he grew.
And there the King would sit with him for hours,
Admiring Modred's growth; and all the time
His evil it was that grew, the King not seeing
In Modred the Almighty's instrument
Of a world's overthrow. You, Lancelot,
And I, have rendered each a contribution;
And your last hard attention on my skull
Might once have been a benison on the realm,
As I shall be, too late, when I'm laid out
With a clean shroud on—though I'd liefer stay
A while alive with you to see what's coming.
But I was not for that; I may have been
For something, but not that. The King, my uncle,
Has had for all his life so brave a diet
Of miracles, that his new fare before him
Of late has ailed him strangely; and of all
Who loved him once he needs you now the most—
Though he would not so much as whisper this
To me or to my shadow. He goes alone
To Britain, with an army brisk as lead,
To battle with his Modred for a throne
That waits, I fear, for Modred—should your France
Not have it otherwise. And the Queen's in this,

For Modred's game and prey. God save the Queen,
If not the King! I've always liked this world;
And I would a deal rather live in it
Than leave it in the middle of all this music.
If you are listening, give me some cold water."

Lancelot, seeing by now in dim detail
What little was around him to be seen,
Found what he sought and held a cooling cup
To Gawaine, who, with both hands clutching it,
Drank like a child. "I should have had that first,"
He said, with a loud breath, "before my tongue
Began to talk. What was it saying? Modred?
All through the growing pains of his ambition
I've watched him; and I might have this and that
To say about him, if my hours were days.
Well, if you love the King and hope to save him,
Remember his many infirmities of virtue—
Considering always what you have in Modred,
For ever unique in his iniquity.
My truth might have a prejudicial savor
To strangers, but we are not strangers now.
Though I have only one spoiled eye that sees,
I see in yours we are not strangers now.
I tell you, as I told you long ago—
When the Queen came to put my candles out
With her gold head and her propinquity—
That all your doubts that you had then of me,
When they were more than various imps and harpies
Of your inflamed invention, were sick doubts:
King Arthur was my uncle, as he is now;
But my Queen-aunt, who loved him something less
Than cats love rain, was not my only care.
Had all the women who came to Camelot
Been aunts of mine, I should have been, long since,

The chilliest of all unwashed eremites
In a far land alone. For my dead brothers,
Though I would leave them where I go to them,
I read their story as I read my own,
And yours, and—were I given the eyes of God—
As I might yet read Modred's. For the Queen,
May she be safe in London where she's hiding
Now in the Tower. For the King, you only—
And you but hardly—may deliver him yet
From that which Merlin's vision long ago,
If I made anything of Merlin's words,
Foretold of Arthur's end. And for ourselves,
And all who died for us, or now are dying
Like rats around us of their numerous wounds
And ills and evils, only this do I know—
And this you know: The world has paid enough
For Camelot. It is the world's turn now—
Or so it would be if the world were not
The world. 'Another Camelot,' Bedivere says;
'Another Camelot and another King'—
Whatever he means by that. With a lineal twist,
I might be king myself; and then, my lord,
Time would have sung my reign—I say not how.
Had I gone on with you, and seen with you
Your Gleam, and had some ray of it been mine,
I might be seeing more and saying less.
Meanwhile, I liked this world; and what was on
The Lord's mind when He made it is no matter.
Be lenient, Lancelot; I've a light head.
Merlin appraised it once when I was young,
Telling me then that I should have the world
To play with. Well, I've had it, and played with it;
And here I'm with you now where you have sent me
Neatly to bed, with a towel over one eye;
And we were two of the world's ornaments.

Praise all you are that Arthur was your King;
You might have had no Gleam had I been King,
Or had the Queen been like some queens I knew.
King Lot, my father—"

                  Lancelot laid a finger
On Gawaine's lips: "You are too tired for that."—
"Not yet," said Gawaine, "though I may be soon.
Think you that I forget this Modred's mother
Was mine as well as Modred's? When I meet
My mother's ghost, what shall I do—forgive?
When I'm a ghost, I'll forgive everything . . .
It makes me cold to think what a ghost knows.
Put out the bonfire burning in my head,
And light one at my feet. When the King thought
The Queen was in the flames, he called on you:
'God, God,' he said, and 'Lancelot.' I was there,
And so I heard him. That was a bad morning
For kings and queens, and there are to be worse.
Bedivere had a dream, once on a time:
'Another Camelot and another King,'
He says when he's awake; but when he dreams,
There are no kings. Tell Bedivere, some day,
That he saw best awake. Say to the King
That I saw nothing vaster than my shadow,
Until it was too late for me to see;
Say that I loved him well, but served him ill—
If you two meet again. Say to the Queen . . .
Say what you may say best. Remember me
To Pelleas, too, and tell him that his lady
Was a vain serpent. He was dying once
For love of her, and had me in his eye
For company along the dusky road
Before me now. But Pelleas lived, and married.
Lord God, how much we know!—What have I done?

Why do you scowl? Well, well,—so the earth clings
To sons of earth; and it will soon be clinging,
To this one son of earth you deprecate,
Closer than heretofore. I say too much,
Who should be thinking all a man may think
When he has no machine. I say too much—
Always. If I persuade the devil again
That I'm asleep, will you espouse the notion
For a small hour or so? I might be glad—
Not to be here alone." He gave his hand
Slowly, in hesitation. Lancelot shivered,
Knowing the chill of it. "Yes, you say too much,"
He told him, trying to smile. "Now go to sleep;
And if you may, forget what you forgive."

Lancelot, for slow hours that were as long
As leagues were to the King and his worn army,
Sat waiting,—though not long enough to know
From any word of Gawaine, who slept on,
That he was glad not to be there alone.—
"Peace to your soul, Gawaine," Lancelot said,
And would have closed his eyes. But they were closed.

IX

So Lancelot, with a world's weight upon him,
Went heavily to that heaviest of all toil,
Which of itself tells hard in the beginning
Of what the end shall be. He found an army
That would have razed all Britain, and found kings
For generals; and they all went to Dover,
Where the white cliffs were ghostlike in the dawn,
And after dawn were deathlike. For the word
Of the dead King's last battle chilled the sea
Before a sail was down; and all who came

With Lancelot heard soon from little men,
Who clambered overside with larger news,
How ill had fared the great. Arthur was dead,
And Modred with him, each by the other slain;
And there was no knight left of all who fought
On Salisbury field save one, Sir Bedivere,
Of whom the tale was told that he had gone
Darkly away to some far hermitage,
To think and die. There were tales told of a ship.

Anon, by further sounding of more men,
Each with a more delirious involution
Than his before him, he believed at last
The Queen was yet alive—if it were life
To draw now the Queen's breath, or to see Britain
With the Queen's eyes—and that she fared somewhere
To westward out of London, where the Tower
Had held her, as once Joyous Gard had held her,
For dolorous weeks and months a prisoner there,
With Modred not far off, his eyes afire
For her and for the King's avenging throne,
That neither King nor son should see again.
" 'The world had paid enough for Camelot,'
Gawaine said; and the Queen had paid enough,
God knows," said Lancelot. He saw Bors again
And found him angry—angry with his tears,
And with his fate that was a reason for them:
"Could I have died with Modred on my soul,
And had the King lived on, then had I lived
On with him; and this played-out world of ours
Might not be for the dead."

                              "A played-out world,
Although that world be ours, had best be dead,"
Said Lancelot: "There are worlds enough to follow.

'Another Camelot and another King,'
Bedivere said. And where is Bedivere now?
And Camelot?"

                    "There is no Camelot,"
Bors answered. "Are we going back to France,
Or are we to tent here and feed our souls
On memories and on ruins till even our souls
Are dead? Or are we to set free for sport
An idle army for what comes of it?"

"Be idle till you hear from me again,
Or for a fortnight. Then, if you have no word,
Go back; and I may follow you alone,
In my own time, in my own way."

                            "Your way
Of late, I fear, has been too much your own;
But what has been, has been, and I say nothing.
For there is more than men at work in this;
And I have not your eyes to find the Light,
Here in the dark—though some day I may see it."

"We shall all see it, Bors," Lancelot said,
With his eyes on the earth. He said no more.
Then with a sad farewell, he rode away,
Somewhere into the west. He knew not where.

"We shall all see it, Bors," he said again.
Over and over he said it, still as he rode,
And rode, away to the west, he knew not where,
Until at last he smiled unhappily
At the vain sound of it. "Once I had gone
Where the Light guided me, but the Queen came.
And then there was no Light. We shall all see—"

He bit the words off short, snapping his teeth,
And rode on with his memories before him,
Before him and behind. They were a cloud
For no Light now to pierce. They were a cloud
Made out of what was gone; and what was gone
Had now another lure than once it had,
Before it went so far away from him—
To Camelot. And there was no Camelot now—
Now that no Queen was there, all white and gold,
Under an oaktree with another sunlight
Sifting itself in silence on her glory
Through the dark leaves above her where she sat,
Smiling at what she feared, and fearing least
What most there was to fear. Ages ago
That must have been; for a king's world had faded
Since then, and a king with it. Ages ago,
And yesterday, surely it must have been
That he had held her moaning in the firelight
And heard the roaring down of that long rain,
As if to wash away the walls that held them
Then for that hour together. Ages ago,
And always, it had been that he had seen her,
As now she was, floating along before him,
Too far to touch and too fair not to follow,
Even though to touch her were to die. He closed
His eyes, only to see what he had seen
When they were open; and he found it nearer,
Seeing nothing now but the still white and gold
In a wide field of sable, smiling at him,
But with a smile not hers until today—
A smile to drive no votary from the world
To find the Light. "She is not what it is
That I see now," he said: "No woman alive
And out of hell was ever like that to me.
What have I done to her since I have lost her?

What have I done to change her? No, it is I—
I who have changed. She is not one who changes.
The Light came, and I did not follow it;
Then she came, knowing not what thing she did,
And she it was I followed. The gods play
Like that, sometimes; and when the gods are playing,
Great men are not so great as the great gods
Had led them once to dream. I see her now
Where now she is alone. We are all alone,
We that are left; and if I look too long
Into her eyes . . . I shall not look too long.
Yet look I must. Into the west, they say,
She went for refuge. I see nuns around her;
But she, with so much history tenanting
Her eyes, and all that gold over her eyes,
Were not yet, I should augur, out of them.
If I do ill to see her, then may God
Forgive me one more trespass. I would leave
The world and not the shadow of it behind me."

Time brought his weary search to a dusty end
One afternoon in Almesbury, where he left,
With a glad sigh, his horse in an innyard;
And while he ate his food and drank his wine,
Thrushes, indifferent in their loyalty
To Arthur dead and to Pan never dead,
Sang as if all were now as all had been.
Lancelot heard them till his thoughts came back
To freeze his heart again under the flood
Of all his icy fears. What should he find?
And what if he should not find anything?
"Words, after all," he said, "are only words;
And I have heard so many in these few days
That half my wits are sick."

He found the queen,
But she was not the Queen of white and gold
That he had seen before him for so long.
There was no gold; there was no gold anywhere.
The black hood, and the white face under it,
And the blue frightened eyes, were all he saw—
Until he saw more black, and then more white.
Black was a foreign foe to Guinevere;
And in the glimmering stillness where he found her
Now, it was death; and she Alcestis-like,
Had waited unaware for the one hand
Availing, so he thought, that would have torn
Off and away the last fell shred of doom
That was destroying and dishonoring
All the world held of beauty. His eyes burned
With a sad anger as he gazed at hers
That shone with a sad pity. "No," she said;
"You have not come for this. We are done with this.
For there are no queens here; there is a Mother.
The Queen that was is only a child now,
And you are strong. Remember you are strong,
And that your fingers hurt when they forget
How strong they are."

He let her go from him
And while he gazed around him, he frowned hard
And long at the cold walls: "Is this the end
Of Arthur's kingdom and of Camelot?"—
She told him with a motion of her shoulders
All that she knew of Camelot or of kingdoms;
And then said: "We are told of oth_ı States
Where there are palaces, if we should need them,
That are not made with hands. I thought you knew."

Dumb, like a man twice banished, Lancelot
Stood gazing down upon the cold stone floor;

And she, demurely, with a calm regard
That he met once and parried, stood apart,
Appraising him with eyes that were no longer
Those he had seen when first they had seen his.
They were kind eyes, but they were not the eyes
Of his desire; and they were not the eyes
That he had followed all the way from Dover.
"I feared the Light was leading you," she said,
"So far by now from any place like this
That I should have your memory, but no more.
Might not that way have been the wiser way?
There is no Arthur now, no Modred now,—
No Guinevere." She paused, and her voice wandered
Away from her own name: "There is nothing now
That I can see between you and the Light
That I have dimmed so long. If you forgive me,
And I believe you do—though I know all
That I have cost, when I was worth so little—
There is no hazard that I see between you
And all you sought so long, and would have found
Had I not always hindered you. Forgive me—
I could not let you go. God pity men
When women love too much—and women more."
He scowled and with an iron shrug he said:
"Yes, there is that between me and the light."
He glared at her black hood as if to seize it;
Their eyes met, and she smiled: "No, Lancelot;
We are going by two roads to the same end;
Or let us hope, at least, what knowledge hides,
And so believe it. We are going somewhere.
Why the new world is not for you and me,
I cannot say; but only one was ours.
I think we must have lived in our one world
All that earth had for us. You are good to me,
Coming to find me here for the last time;

For I should have been lonely many a night,
Not knowing if you cared. I do know now;
And there is not much else for me to know
That earth may tell me. I found in the Tower,
With Modred watching me, that all you said
That rainy night was true. There was time there
To find out everything. There were long days,
And there were nights that I should not have said
God would have made a woman to endure.
I wonder if a woman lives who knows
All she may do."

                              "I wonder if one woman
Knows one thing she may do," Lancelot said,
With a sad passion shining out of him
While he gazed on her beauty, palled with black
That hurt him like a sword. The full blue eyes
And the white face were there, and the red lips
Were there, but there was no gold anywhere.
"What have you done with your gold hair?" he said;
"I saw it shining all the way from Dover,
But here I do not see it. Shall I see it?"—
Faintly again she smiled: "Yes, you may see it
All the way back to Dover; but not here.
There's not much of it here, and what there is
Is not for you to see."

                              "Well, if not here,"
He said at last, in a low voice that shook,
"Is there no other place left in the world?"

"There is not even the world left, Lancelot,
For you and me."

                              "There is France left," he said.
His face flushed like a boy's, but he stood firm
As a peak in the sea and waited.

"How many lives
Must a man have in one to make him happy?"
She asked, with a wan smile of recollection
That only made the black that was around
Her calm face more funereal: "Was it you,
Or was it Gawaine who said once to me,
'We cannot make one world of two, nor may we
Count one life more than one. Could we go back
To the old garden' . . . Was it you who said it,
Or was it Bors? He was always saying something.
It may have been Bors." She was not looking then
At Lancelot; she was looking at her fingers
In her old way, as to be sure again
How many of them she had.

                        He looked at her,
Without the power to smile, and for the time
Forgot that he was Lancelot: "Is it fair
For you to drag that back, out of its grave,
And hold it up like this for the small feast
Of a small pride?"

                        "Yes, fair enough for a woman,"
Guinevere said, not seeing his eyes. "How long
Do you conceive the Queen of the Christian world
Would hide herself in France . . ."

                        "Why do you pause?
I said it; I remember when I said it;
And it was not today. Why in the name
Of grief should we hide anywhere? Bells and banners
Are not for our occasion, but in France
There may be sights and silences more fair
Than pageants. There are seas of difference
Between this land and France, albeit to cross them

Were no immortal voyage, had you an eye
For France that you had once."

                      "I have no eye
Today for France, I shall have none tomorrow;
And you will have no eye for France tomorrow.
Fatigue and loneliness, and your poor dream
Of what I was, have led you to forget.
When you have had your time to think and see
A little more, then you will see as I do;
And if you see France, I shall not be there,
Save as a memory there. We are done, you and I,
With what we were. 'Could we go back again,
The fruit that we should find'—but you know best
What we should find. I am sorry for what I said;
But a light word, though it cut one we love,
May save ourselves the pain of a worse wound.
We are all women. When you see one woman—
When you see me—before you in your fancy,
See me all white and gold, as I was once.
I shall not harm you then; I shall not come
Between you and the Gleam that you must follow,
Whether you will or not. There is no place
For me but where I am; there is no place
For you save where it is that you are going.
If I knew everything as I know that,
I should know more than Merlin, who knew all,
And long ago, that we are to know now.
What more he knew he may not then have told
The King, or anyone,—maybe not even himself;
Though Vivian may know something by this time
That he has told her. Have you wished, I wonder,
That I was more like Vivian, or Isolt?
The dark ones are more devious and more famous,

And men fall down more numerously before them—
Although I think more men get up again,
And go away again, than away from us.
If I were dark, I might say otherwise.
Try to be glad, even if you are sorry,
That I was not born dark; for I was not.
For me there was no dark until it came
When the King came, and with his heavy shadow
Put out the sun that you made shine again
Before I was to die. So I forgive
The faggots; I can do no more than that—
For you, or God." She looked away from him
And in the casement saw the sunshine dying:
"The time that we have left will soon be gone;
When the bell rings, it rings for you to go,
But not for me to go. It rings for me
To stay—and pray. I, who have not prayed much,
May as well pray now. I have not what you have
To make me see, though I shall have, sometime,
A new light of my own. I saw in the Tower,
When all was darkest and I may have dreamed,
A light that gave to men the eyes of Time
To read themselves in silence. Then it faded,
And the men faded. I was there alone.
I shall not have what you have, or much else—
In this place. I shall see in other places
What is not here. I shall not be alone.
And I shall tell myself that you are seeing
All that I cannot see. For the time now,
What most I see is that I had no choice,
And that you came to me. How many years
Of purgatory shall I pay God for saying
This to you here?" Her words came slowly out,
And her mouth shook.

                                                He took her two small hands
That were so pale and empty, and so cold:
"Poor child, I said too much and heard too little
Of what I said. But when I found you here,
So different, so alone, I would have given
My soul to be a chattel and a gage
For dicing fiends to play for, could so doing
Have brought one summer back."

                                        "When they are gone,"
She said, with grateful sadness in her eyes,
"We do not bring them back, or buy them back,
Even with our souls. I see now it is best
We do not buy them back, even with our souls."

A slow and hollow bell began to sound
Somewhere above them, and the world became
For Lancelot one wan face—Guinevere's face.
"When the bell rings, it rings for you to go,"
She said; "and you are going . . . I am not.
Think of me always as I used to be,
All white and gold—for that was what you called me.
You may see gold again when you are gone;
And I shall not be there."—He drew her nearer
To kiss the quivering lips that were before him
For the last time. "No, not again," she said;
"I might forget that I am not alone . . .
I shall not see you in this world again,
But I am not alone. No, . . . not alone.
We have had all there was, and you were kind—
Even when you tried so hard once to be cruel.
I knew it then . . . or now I do. Good-bye."
He crushed her cold white hands and saw them falling
Away from him like flowers into a grave.

When she looked up to see him, he was gone;
And that was all she saw till she awoke
In her white cell, where the nuns carried her
With many tears and many whisperings.
"She was the Queen, and he was Lancelot,"
One said. "They were great lovers. It is not good
To know too much of love. We who love God
Alone are happiest. Is it not so, Mother?"—
"We who love God alone, my child, are safest,"
The Mother replied; "and we are not all safe
Until we are all dead. We watch, and pray."

Outside again, Lancelot heard the sound
Of reapers he had seen. With lighter tread
He walked away to them to see them nearer;
He walked and heard again the sound of thrushes
Far off. He saw below him, stilled with yellow,
A world that was not Arthur's, and he saw
The convent roof; and then he could see nothing
But a wan face and two dim lonely hands
That he had left behind. They were down there,
Somewhere, her poor white face and hands, alone.
"No man was ever alone like that," he thought,
Not knowing what last havoc pity and love
Had still to wreak on wisdom. Gradually,
In one long wave it whelmed him, and then broke—
Leaving him like a lone man on a reef,
Staring for what had been with him, but now
Was gone and was a white face under the sea,
Alive there, and alone—always alone.
He closed his eyes, and the white face was there,
But not the gold. The gold would not come back.
There were gold fields of corn that lay around him,
But they were not the gold of Guinevere—
Though men had once, for sake of saying words,

Prattled of corn about it. The still face
Was there, and the blue eyes that looked at him
Through all the stillness of all distances;
And he could see her lips, trying to say
Again, "I am not alone." And that was all
His life had said to him that he remembered
While he sat there with his hands over his eyes,
And his heart aching. When he rose again
The reapers had gone home. Over the land
Around him in the twilight there was rest.
There was rest everywhere; and there was none
That found his heart. "Why should I look for peace
When I have made the world a ruin of war?"
He muttered; and a Voice within him said:
"Where the Light falls, death falls; a world has died
For you, that a world may live. There is no peace.
Be glad no man or woman bears for ever
The burden of first days. There is no peace."

A word stronger than his willed him away
From Almesbury. All alone he rode that night,
Under the stars, led by the living Voice
That would not give him peace. Into the dark
He rode, but not for Dover. Under the stars,
Alone, all night he rode, out of a world
That was not his, or the King's; and in the night
He felt a burden lifted as he rode,
While he prayed he might bear it for the sake
Of a still face before him that was fading,
Away in a white loneliness. He made,
Once, with groping hand as if to touch it,
But a black branch of leaves was all he found.

Now the still face was dimmer than before,
And it was not so near him. He gazed hard,

But through his tears he could not see it now;
And when the tears were gone he could see only
That all he saw was fading, always fading;
And she was there alone. She was the world
That he was losing; and the world he sought
Was all a tale for those who had been living,
And had not lived. Once even he turned his horse,
And would have brought his army back with him
To make her free. They should be free together.
But the Voice within him said: "You are not free.
You have come to the world's end, and it is best
You are not free. Where the Light falls, death falls;
And in the darkness comes the Light." He turned
Again; and he rode on, under the stars,
Out of the world, into he knew not what,
Until a vision chilled him and he saw,
Now as in Camelot, long ago in the garden,
The face of Galahad who had seen and died,
And was alive, now in a mist of gold.
He rode on into the dark, under the stars,
And there were no more faces. There was nothing.
But always in the darkness he rode on,
Alone; and in the darkness came the Light.

TRISTRAM

I

Isolt of the white hands, in Brittany,
Could see no longer northward anywhere
A picture more alive or less familiar
Than a blank ocean and the same white birds
Flying, and always flying, and still flying,
Yet never bringing any news of him
That she remembered, who had sailed away
The spring before—saying he would come back,
Although not saying when.   Not one of them,
For all their flying, she thought, had heard the name
Of Tristram, or of him beside her there
That was the King, her father.   The last ship
Was out of sight, and there was nothing now
For her to see before the night came down
Except her father's face.   She looked at him
And found him smiling in the way she feared,

And loved the while she feared it. The King took
One of her small still hands in one of his
That were so large and hard to be so kind,
And weighed a question, not for the first time:

"Why should it be that I must have a child
Whose eyes are wandering always to the north?
The north is a bad region full of wolves
And bears and hairy men that have no manners.
Why should her eyes be always on the north,
I wonder, when all's here that one requires
Of comfort, love, and of expediency?
You are not cheered, I see, or satisfied
Entirely by the sound of what I say.
You are too young, may be, to make yourself
A nest of comfort and expediency."

"I may be that," she said, and a quick flush
Made a pink forage of her laughing face,
At which he smiled again. "But not so young
As to be told for ever how young I am.
I have been growing for these eighteen years,
And waiting here, for one thing and another.

Besides, his manners are as good as yours,
And he's not half so hairy as you are,
Even though you be the King of Brittany,
Or the great Jove himself, and then my father."
With that she threw her arms around his neck,
Throbbing as if she were a child indeed.

"You are no heavier than a cat," said he,
"But otherwise you are somewhat like a tiger.
Relinquish your commendable affection
A little, and tell me why it is you dream
Of someone coming always from the north.
Are there no proper knights or princes else
Than one whose eyes, wherever they may be fixed,
Are surely not fixed hard on Brittany?
You are a sort of child, or many sorts,
Yet also are too high and too essential
To be much longer the quaint sport and food
Of shadowy fancies. For a time I've laughed
And let you dream, but I may not laugh always.
Because he praised you as a child one day,
And may have liked you as a child one day,
Why do you stare for ever into the north,

Over that water, where the good God placed
A land known only to your small white ears?"

"Only because the good God, I suppose,
Placed England somewhere north of Brittany—
Though not so far but one may come and go
As many a time as twice before he dies.
I know that's true, having been told about it.
I have been told so much about this world
That I have wondered why men stay in it.
I have been told of devils that are in it,
And some right here in Brittany.   Griffon
Is one of them; and if he ever gets me,
I'll pray for the best way to kill myself."

King Howel held his daughter closer to him,
As if a buried and forgotten fear
Had come to life and was confronting him
With a new face.   "Never you mind the devils,"
He said, "be they in Brittany or elsewhere.
They are for my attention, if need be.
You will affright me and amuse me less
By saying, if you are ready, how much longer

You are to starve yourself with your delusion
Of Tristram coming back. He may come back,
Or Mark, his uncle, who tonight is making
Another Isolt his queen—the dark Isolt,
Isolt of Ireland—may be coming back,
Though I'd as lief he would remain at home
In Cornwall, with his new queen—if he keeps her."

"And who is this far-off Isolt of Ireland?"
She said, like a thing waiting to be hurt:
"A creature that one hears of constantly,
And one that no man sees, or none to say so,
Must be unusual—if she be at all."

"The few men who have told of her to me
Have told of silence and of Irish pride,
Inhabiting too much beauty for one woman.
My eyes have never seen her; and as for beauty,
My eyes would rather look on yours, my child.
And as for Tristram coming back, what then—
One of these days?   Any one may come back.
King Arthur may come back; and as for that,
Our Lord and Saviour may come back some time,

Though hardly all for you.   Have you kept hid
Some promise or protestation heretofore,
That you may shape a thought into a reason
For making always of a distant wish
A dim belief?   You are too old for that—
If it will make you happy to be told so.
You have been told so much."   King Howel smiled,
And waited, holding her white hands in his.

"I have been told that Tristram will come back,"
She said; "and it was he who told me so.
Also I have this agate that he gave me;
And I believe his eyes."

                         "Believe his agate,"
The king said, "for as long as you may save it.
An agate's a fair plaything for a child,
Though not so boundless and immovable
In magnitude but that a child may lose it.
Since you esteem it such an acquisition,
Treasure it more securely, and believe it
As a bright piece of earth, and nothing more.
Believe his agate, and forget his eyes;

And go to bed. You are not young enough,
I see, to stay awake and entertain
Much longer your exaggerated fancies.
And if he should come back? Would you prepare
Upon the ruinous day of his departure
To drown yourself, and with yourself his agate?"

Isolt, now on a cushion at his feet,
Finding the King's hard knees a meagre pillow,
Sat upright, thinking. "No I should not do that;
Though I should never trust another man
So far that I should go away with him.
King's daughters, I suppose, are bought and sold,
But you would not sell me."

                              "You seize a question
As if it were an agate—or a fact,"
The King said, laughing at the calm gray eyes
That were so large in the small face before him.
"I might sell you, perhaps, at a fair bargain.
To play with an illustrious example,
If Modred were to overthrow King Arthur—
And there are prophets who see Arthur's end
In Modred, who's an able sort of reptile—

And come for you to go away with him,
And to be Queen of Britain, I might sell you,
Perhaps.   You might say prayers that you be sold."

"I may say prayers that you be reasonable
And serious, and that you believe me so."
There was a light now in his daughter's eyes
Like none that he remembered having seen
In eyes before, whereat he paused and heard,
Not all amused.   "He will come back," she said,
"And I shall wait.   If he should not come back,
I shall have been but one poor woman more
Whose punishment for being born a woman
Was to believe and wait.   You are my King,
My father, and of all men anywhere,
Save one, you are the world of men to me.
When I say this of him you must believe me,
As I believe his eyes.   He will come back;
And what comes then I leave to him, and God."

Slowly the King arose, and with his hands
He lifted up Isolt, so frail, so light,
And yet, with all, mysteriously so strong.
He raised her patient face between his hands,

Observing it as if it were some white
And foreign flower, not certain in his garden
To thrive, nor like to die. Then with a vague
And wavering effect of shaking her
Affectionately back to his own world,
Which never would be hers, he smiled once more
And set her free. "You should have gone to bed
When first I told you. You had best go now,
And while you are still dreaming. In the morning
Your dreams, if you remember them, will all
Be less than one bird singing in a tree."

Isolt of the white hands, unchangeable,
Half childlike and half womanly, looked up
Into her father's eyes and shook her head,
Smiling, but less for joy than certainty:
"There's a bird then that I have never seen
In Brittany; and I have never heard him.
Good night, my father." She went slowly out,
Leaving him in the gloom.

                              "Good night, my child,
Good night," he said, scarce hearing his own voice
For crowded thoughts that were unseizable

And unforeseen within him.   Like Isolt,
He stood now in the window looking north
Over the misty sea.   A seven days' moon
Was in the sky, and there were a few stars
That had no fire.   " I have no more a child,"
He thought, " and what she is I do not know.
It may be fancy and fantastic youth
That ails her now; it may be the sick touch
Of prophecy concealing disillusion.
If there were not inwoven so much power
And poise of sense with all her seeming folly,
I might assume a concord with her faith
As that of one elected soon to die.
But surely no infringement of the grave
In her conceits and her appearances
Encourages a fear that still is fear;
And what she is to know, I cannot say.
A changeling down from one of those white stars
Were more like her than like a child of mine."

Nothing in the cold glimmer of a moon
Over a still, cold ocean there before him
Would answer for him in the silent voice

Of time an idle question. So the King,
With only time for company, stood waiting
Alone there in the window, looking off
At the still sea between his eyes and England.

II

The moon that glimmered cold on Brittany
Glimmered as cold on Cornwall, where King Mark,
Only by kingly circumstance endowed
With friends enough to make a festival,
On this dim night had married and made Queen—
Of all fair women in the world by fate
The most forgotten in her loveliness
Till now—Isolt of Ireland, who had flamed
And fought so long with love that she called hate,
Inimical to Tristram for the stroke
That felled Morhaus her kinsman. Tristram, blind
With angry beauty, or in honor blind,
Or in obscure obedience unawakened,
Had given his insane promise to his uncle
Of intercession with the Irish King
And so drawn out of him a slow assent,
Not fathoming or distinguishing aright

Within himself a passion that was death,
Nor gauging with a timely recognition
The warfare of a woman's enmity
With love without love's name. He knew too late
How one word then would have made arras-rats
For her of all his uncles, and all kings
That he might serve with cloudy promises,
Not weighed until redeemed. Now there was time
For him to weigh them, and to weigh them well,
To the last scorching ounce of desperation,
Searing his wits and flesh like heated mail
Amidst the fiery downfall of a palace,
Where there was no one left except himself
To save, and no way out except through fire.

Partly to balk his rage, partly to curse
Unhindered an abject ineptitude
That like a drug had held him and withheld him
In seizing once from love's imperial garden
The flower of all things there, now Tristram leaned
Alone upon a parapet below
The lights of high Tintagel, where gay music
Had whipped him as a lash and driven him out

Into the misty night, which might have held
A premonition and a probing chill
For one more tranquil and less exigent,
And not so much on fire. Down through the gloom
He gazed at nothing, save a moving blur
Where foamed eternally on Cornish rocks
The moan of Cornish water; and he asked,
With a malignant inward voice of envy,
How many scarred cold things that once had laughed
And loved and wept and sung, and had been men,
Might have been knocked and washed indifferently
On that hard shore, and eaten gradually
By competent quick fishes and large crabs
And larger birds, not caring a wink which
Might be employed on their spent images,
No longer tortured there, if God was good,
By memories of the fools and royal pimps
That once unwittingly they might have been—
Like Tristram, who could wish himself as far
As they were from a wearing out of life
On a racked length of days. Now and again
A louder fanfare of malicious horns
Would sing down from the festival above him,

Smiting his angry face like a wet clout
That some invisible scullion might have swung,
Too shadowy and too agile to be seized
And flung down on those rocks. Now and again
Came over him a cold soul-retching wave
Of recognition past reality,
Recurrent, vile, and always culminating
In a forbidden vision thrice unholy
Of Mark, his uncle, like a man-shaped goat
Appraising with a small salacious eye,
And slowly forcing into his gaunt arms,
And all now in a few impossible hours
That were as possible as pain and death,
The shuddering unreal miracle of Isolt,
Which was as real as torture to the damned
In hell, or in Cornwall. Before long now
That music and that wordless murmuring
Of distant men and women, who divined
As much or little as they might, would cease;
The mocking lights above him would go out;
There would be silence; and the King would hold
Isolt—Isolt of the dark eyes—Isolt
Of the patrician passionate helplessness—

Isolt of the soft waving blue-black hair—
Isolt of Ireland—in his vicious arms
And crush the bloom of her resisting life
On his hot, watery mouth, and overcome
The protest of her suffering silk skin
With his crude senile claws. And it was he,
Tristram, the loud-accredited strong warrior,
Tristram, the loved of women, the harp-player,
Tristram, the learned Nimrod among hunters,
Tristram, the most obedient imbecile
And humble servant of King Mark his uncle,
Who had achieved all this. For lack of sight
And sense of self, and imperturbably,
He had achieved all this and might do more,
No doubt, if given the time. Whereat he cursed
Himself again, and his complacent years
Of easy blindness. Time had saved for him
The flower that he had not the wit to seize
And carry a few leagues across the water,
Till when he did so it was his no more,
And body and soul were sick to think of it.
Why should he not be sick? "Good God in heaven,"
He groaned aloud, "why should I not be sick!"

"No God will answer you to say why not,"
Said one descending heavily but unheard,
And slowly, down the stairs. "And one like me,
Having seen more seasons out than you have seen,
Would say it was tonight your prime intention
To make yourself the sickest man in Cornwall."
Gouvernail frowned and shivered as he spoke,
And waited as a stranger waits in vain
Outside a door that none within will open.

"I may be that already," Tristram said,
"But I'm not cold. For I'm a seer tonight,
And consequently full of starry thoughts.
The stars are not so numerous as they were,
But there's a brotherly white moon up there,
Such as it is. Well, Gouvernail, what word
Has my illustrious and most amorous
And most imperious Uncle Mark prepared
For you to say to me that you come scowling
So far down here to say it? You are next
To nearest, not being my father, of all men
Of whom I am unworthy. What's the word?"

"Tristram, I left the King annoyed and anxious
On your account, and for the nonce not pleased."

"What most annoys my uncle, for the nonce?
God knows that I have done for him of late
More than an army, made of nephews only,
Shall ever be fools enough to do again.
When tired of feasting and of too much talk,
And too much wine and too much happy music,
May not his royal nephew have some air,
Even though his annoyed uncle be a king?
My father is a king, in Lyonesse;
And that's about as much as being a king
In Cornwall is—or one here now might say so."

"Forgive me Tristram, but I'm old for this.
The King knows well what you have done for him,
And owns a gratitude beyond the gift
Of utterance for the service of your word.
But the King does not know, and cannot know,
Your purpose in an act ungenerous,
If not unseemly. What shall I say to him
If I go back to him alone? Tristram,
There are some treasured moments I remember
When you have made me loyal to you always
For saying good words of me, and with no care

Whether or not they came back to my ears.
Surely, if past attention and tuition
Are not forgotten, you will not forget
This present emptiness of my confusion.
If I go back alone, what shall I say?"

"Say to the King that if the King command
Implacably my presence, I will come.
But say as an addition that I'm sick,
And that another joyful hour with him
This night might have eventful influences.
Nothing could be more courteous, if said well,
Or more consistent with infirm allegiance.
Say to the King I'm sick. If he doubts that,
Or takes it ill, say to the King I'm drunk.
His comprehensions and remembrances
Will compass and envisage, peradventure,
The last deplorable profundity
Of my defection if you say, for me,
That in my joy my caution crept away
Like an unfaithful hound and went to sleep.
Gouvernail, you are cold."

                              Gouvernail sighed
And fixed an eye calm with experience,

And with affection kind, on Tristram, sadly.
"Yes, I am cold," he said. "Here at my heart
I feel a blasting chill. Will you not come
With me to see the King and Queen together?
Or must I mumble as I may to them,
Alone, this weary jest of your complaint?"

"God's love, have I not seen the two together!
And as for my complaint, mumble or not.
Mumble or shriek it; or, as you see fit,
Call for my harp and sing it." Tristram laid
His hands on Gouvernail's enduring shoulders
Which many a time had carried him for sport
In a far vanished childhood, and looked off
Where patient skill had made of shrubs and rocks
Together a wild garden half way down
To the dusk-hidden shore. "Believe my word,
My loyal and observing Gouvernail,"
He said, and met the older man's regard
With all that he could muster of a smile.
"Believe my word, and say what I have said,
Or something as much better as you may.
Believe my word no less that I am sick,

And that I'd feed a sick toad to my brother
If in my place he were not sick without it."

Gouvernail sighed, and with a deeper sigh
Looked off across the sea. "Tristram," he said,
"I can see no good coming out of this,
But I will give your message as I can,
And with as light misgiving as I may.
Yet where there is no love, too often I find
As perilous a constriction in our judgment
As where there is too much."

                                    Tristram pursued
The mentor of his childhood and his youth
With no more words, and only made of him
In the returning toil of his departure
A climbing silence that would soon be met
By sound and light, and by King Mark again,
And by Isolt again. Isolt of Ireland!
Isolt, so soon to be the bartered prey
Of an unholy sacrifice, by rites
Of Rome made holy. Tristram groaned and wept,
And heard once more the changeless moan below

Of an insensate ocean on those rocks
Whereon he had a mind to throw himself.
"My God! If I were dreaming this," he said,
"My sleep would be a penance for a year.
But I am neither dead nor dreaming now,
I'm living and awake. If this be life,
What a soul-healing difference death must be,
Being something else . . . Isolt! Isolt of Ireland!"

Gazing at emptiness for a long time
He looked away from life, and scarcely heard,
Coming down slowly towards him from above,
A troubling sound of cloth. "Good evening, sir,
Perhaps you do not know me, or remember
That once you gave a lady so much honor
As to acknowledge her obscure existence.
From late accounts you are not here to know
Your friends on this especial famous evening.
Why do you stay away from history
Like this? Kings are not married every night."

Perceiving there beside him a slim figure
Provisionally cloaked against the cold,

He bowed as in a weary deference
To childish fate. "Surely I know you, Madam;
You are among the creatures of distinction
Whose quality may be seen even in the dark.
You are Queen Morgan, a most famous lady,
And one that only kings in holy joy
Could ask or dream to be their messenger.
What new persuasion has the King conceived
Beyond this inspiration of your presence?"

"It is not dark," she said; "or not so dark
But that a woman sees—if she be careful
Not to fall down these memorable stairs
And break her necessary little neck
At Tristram's feet. And you might make of that
Only another small familiar triumph
Hardly worth sighing for. Well then, the King
Is vexed and vicious. Your man Gouvernail
Says you are sick with wine. Was that the best
That your two heads together could accomplish?
Will you not for the King's sake, or the Queen's,
Be more compliant, and not freeze to death?"

"Madam, say to the King that if the King
Command me, I will come. Having said that,

It would be gracious of you to be merry—
Malicious, if you must—and say, also,
You found in me a melancholy warning
For all who dim their wits obliviously.
Say it as delicately or as directly
As humors your imperial preference."

Queen Morgan, coming closer, put a small
And cat-like hand on Tristram: "In this world
Of lies, you lay a burden on my virtue
When you would teach me a new alphabet.
I'll turn my poor wits inside out, of course,
Telling an angry king how sick you are—
With wine or whatsoever. Though I shall know
The one right reason why you are not merry,
I'll never scatter it, not for the King's life—
Though I might for the Queen's. Isolt should live,
If only to be sorry she came here—
With you—away from Ireland to be married
To a man old enough to bury himself.
But kings are kings, and by contriving find
Ways over many walls. This being their fate,
It was a clever forethought of the Lord

That there should be a woman or two left
With even Isolt no longer possible.
A school of prudence would establish you
Among the many whose hearts have bled and healed."

"Madam, you are a woman and a queen;
Wherefore a man, by force of courtesy,
Will hardly choose but listen. No doubt your words
Have a significance in their disguise;
Yet having none for me, they might be uttered
As well in a lost language found on ruins
As in our northern manner. If kings are kings
In your report, queens, I perceive, are queens,
And have their ways also."

                              "A sort of queen."
She laughed, showing her teeth and shining eyes,
And shrugged herself a little nearer to him,
Having not far to come: "But not the sort
That makes a noise where now there are so many.
If silly men pursue me and make songs
About me, it may be because they've heard
Some legend that I'm strange. I am not strange—
Not half so strange as you are."

Tristram saw

Before him a white neck and a white bosom
Beneath a fair and feline face whereon
Demure determination was engraved
As on a piece of moonlit living marble,
And could at once have smiled and sighed to see
So much premeditated danger wasted
On his despair and wrath. "Yes, you are strange,"
He said, "and a sagacious peril to men—
Wherefore they must pursue you and make songs.
You are an altogether perilous lady,
And you had best go back now to the King,
Saying that I'm not well. I would conserve
The few shreds left of my integrity
From your displeasure and for wiser vision.
Say to the King I feasted over much
In recognition of his happiness—
An error that apology too soon
Might qualify too late. Tell the King so,
And I am your obedient slave for ever.

A wry twist, all but imperceptible
Disfigured for an instant her small mouth

Before she smiled and said: "We are the slaves,
Not you.   Not even when most we are in power
Are women else than slaves to men they honor.
Men worthy of their reverence know this well,
And honor them sometimes to humor them.
We are their slaves and their impediments,
And there is much in us to be forgiven."

He drew the fringes of her cloak together,
Smiling as one who suffers to escape
Through silence to familiar misery.
"Madam, I fear that you are taking cold,"
He said.   "Say to the King that I'm not well."
She laughed, and having mounted a few steps
Paused and looked down at him inscrutably:
"'An error that apology too soon
May qualify too late?'   Was it like that?
England is not so large as the wide sky
That holds the stars, and we may meet again.
Good night, Sir Tristram, Prince of Lyonesse."

III

Lost in a gulf of time where time was lost,
And heedless of a light queen's light last words
That were to be remembered, he saw now

Before him in the gloom a ghostly ship
Cleaving a way to Cornwall silently
From Ireland, with himself on board and one
That with her eyes told him intolerably
How little of his blind self a crowded youth,
With a sight error-flecked and pleasure-flawed,
Had made him see till on that silent voyage
There was no more to see than faith betrayed
Or life disowned. The sorrow in his name
Came out, and he was Tristram, born for sorrow
Of an unguarded and forgotten mother,
Who may have seen as those who are to die
Are like to see. A king's son, he had given
Himself in honor unto another king
For gratitude, not knowing what he had given,
Or seeing what he had done. Now he could see,
And there was no need left of a ship's ghost,
Or ghost of anything else than life before him,
To make him feel, though he might not yet hear it,
The nearness of a doom that was descending
Upon him, and anon should hold him fast—
If he were not already held fast enough
To please the will of fate.

                                "Brangwaine!" he said,
Turning and trembling.   For a softer voice
Than Morgan's now had spoken; a truer voice,
Which had not come alone to plead with him
In the King's name for courtesy.

                                "Sir Tristram! . . ."
Brangwaine began, and ended.   Then she seized
His hands and held them quickly to her lips
In fealty that he felt was his for ever.
"Brangwaine, for this you make a friend of me
Until I die.   If there were more for one
To say . . ."   He said no more, for some one else
Than Brangwaine was above him on the stairs.
Coming down slowly and without a sound
She moved, and like a shadow saying nothing
Said nothing while she came.   Isolt of Ireland,
With all her dark young majesty unshaken
By grief and shame and fear that made her shake
Till to go further would have been to fall,
Came nearer still to him and still said nothing,
Till terror born of passion became passion
Reborn of terror while his lips and hers

Put speech out like a flame put out by fire.
The music poured unheard, Brangwaine had vanished,
And there were these two in the world alone,
Under the cloudy light of a cold moon
That glimmered now as cold on Brittany
As on Cornwall.

        Time was aware of them,
And would beat soon upon his empty bell
Release from such a fettered ecstasy
As fate would not endure. But until then
There was no room for time between their souls
And bodies, or between their silences,
Which were for them no less than heaven and hell,
Fused cruelly out of older silences
That once a word from either might have ended,
And so annihilated into life
Instead of death—could her pride then have spoken,
And his duped eyes have seen, before his oath
Was given to make them see. But silences
By time are slain, and death, or more than death,
May come when silence dies. At last Isolt
Released herself enough to look at him.

With a world burning for him in her eyes,
And two worlds crumbling for him in her words:
"What have I done to you, Tristram!" she said;
"What have you done to me! What have we done
To Fate, that she should hate us and destroy us,
Waiting for us to speak. What have we done
So false or foul as to be burned alive
And then be buried alive—as we shall be—
As I shall be!"

    He gazed upon a face
Where all there was of beauty and of love
That was alive for him, and not for him,
Was his while it was there. "I shall have burned
And buried us both," he said. "Your pride would not
Have healed my blindness then, even had you prayed
For God to let you speak. When a man sues
The fairest of all women for her love,
He does not cleave the skull first of her kinsman
To mark himself a man. That was my way;
And it was not the wisest—if your eyes
Had any truth in them for a long time.
Your pride would not have let me tell them more—
Had you prayed God, I say."

"I did do that,
Tristram, but he was then too far from heaven
To hear so little a thing as I was, praying
For you on earth. You had not seen my eyes
Before you fought with Morhaus; and for that,
There was your side and ours. All history sings
Of two sides, and will do so till all men
Are quiet; and then there will be no men left,
Or women alive to hear them. It was long
Before I learned so little as that; and you
It was who taught me while I nursed and healed
Your wound, only to see you go away."

"And once having seen me go away from you,
You saw me coming back to you again,
Cheerful and healed, as Mark's ambassador.
Would God foresee such folly alive as that
In any thing he had made, and still make more?
If so, his ways are darker than divines
Have drawn them for our best bewilderments.
Be it so or not, my share in this is clear.
I have prepared a way for us to take,
Because a king was not so much a devil

When I was young as not to be a friend,
An uncle, and an easy counsellor.
Later, when love was yet no more for me
Than a gay folly glancing everywhere
For triumph easier sometimes than defeat,
Having made sure that I was blind enough,
He sealed me with an oath to make you his
Before I had my eyes, or my heart woke
From pleasure in a dream of other faces
That now are nothing else than silly skulls
Covered with skin and hair. The right was his
To make of me a shining knight at arms,
By fortune may be not the least adept
And emulous. But God! for seizing you,
And having you here tonight, and all his life
Having you here, by the blind means of me,
I could tear all the cords out of his neck
To make a rope, and hang the rest of him.
Isolt, forgive me! This is only sound
That I am making with a tongue gone mad
That you should be so near me as to hear me
Saying how far away you are to go
When you go back to him, driven by—me!

A fool may die with no great noise or loss;
And whether a fool should always live or not . . ."

Isolt, almost as with a frightened leap
Muffled his mouth with hers in a long kiss,
Blending in their catastrophe two fires
That made one fire.   When she could look at him
Again, her tears, unwilling still to flow,
Made of her eyes two shining lakes of pain
With moonlight living in them; and she said
"There is no time for you to tell me this;
And you are younger than time says you are,
Or you would not be losing it, saying over
All that I know too well, or for my sake
Giving yourself these names that are worth nothing.
It was our curse that you were not to see
Until you saw too late.   No scourge of names
That you may lay for me upon yourself
Will have more consequence for me, or you,
Than beating with a leaf would have on horses;
So give yourself no more of them tonight.
The King says you are coming back with me.
How can you come?   And how can you not come!

It will be cruel enough for me without you,
But with you there alive in the same walls
I shall be hardly worthy of life tonight
If I stay there alive—although I shall,
For this may not be all. This thing has come
For us, and you are not to see the end
Through any such fog of honor and self-hate
As you may seek to throw around yourself
For being yourself. Had you been someone else,
You might have been one like your cousin Andred,
Who looks at me as if he were a snake
That has heard something. Had you been someone else,
You might have been like Modred, or like Mark.
God—you like Mark! You might have been a slave.
We cannot say what either of us had been
Had we been something else. All we can say
Is that this thing has come to us tonight.
You can do nothing more unless you kill him.
And that would be the end of you and me.
Time on our side, this may not be the end."

"I might have been a slave, by you unseen,"
He answered, "and you still Isolt of Ireland,

To me unknown.   That would have been for **you**
The better way.   But that was not the way."

"No it was not," she said, trying to smile;
And weary then for trying, held him closer.
"But I can feel the hands of time on me,
And they will soon be tearing me away.
Tristram, say to me once before I go,
What you believe and what you see for us
Before you.   Are you sure that a word given
Is always worth more than a world forsaken?
Who knows there may not be a lonely place
In heaven for souls that are ashamed and sorry
For fearing hell?"

        "It is not hell tonight,
Isolt," he said, "or any beyond the grave,
That I fear most for you or for myself.
Fate has adjusted and made sure of that
Where we are now—though we see not the end,
And time be on our side.   Praise God for time,
And for such hope of what may come of it
As time like this may grant.   I could be strong,

But to be over-strong now at this hour
Would only be destruction. The King's ways
Are not those of one man against another,
And you must live, and I must live—for you.
If there were not an army of guards below us
To bring you back to fruitless ignominy,
There would soon be an end of this offense
To God and the long insult of this marriage.
But to be twice a fool is not the least
Insane of ways to cure a first affliction.
God!—is it so—that you are going back
To be up there with him—with Mark—tonight?
Before you came, I had been staring down
On those eternal rocks and the white foam
Around them; and I thought how sound and long
A sleep would soon begin for us down there
If we were there together—before you came.
That was a fancy, born of circumstance,
And I was only visioning some such thing
As that. The moon may have been part of it.
I think there was a demon born with me
And in the malediction of my name,
And that his work is to make others suffer—

Which is the worst of burdens for a man
Whose death tonight were nothing, could the death
Of one be the best end of this for two."

"If that was to be said," Isolt replied,
"It will at least not have to be said over.
For since the death of one would only give
The other a twofold weight of wretchedness
To bear, why do you pour these frozen words
On one who cannot be so confident
As you that we may not be nearer life,
Even here tonight, than we are near to death?
I must know more than you have told me yet
Before I see, so clearly as you see it,
The sword that must for ever be between us.
Something in you was always in my father:
A darkness always was around my father,
Since my first eyes remembered him. He saw
Nothing, but he would see the shadow of it
Before he saw the color or shape it had,
Or where the sun was. Tristram, fair things yet
Will have a shadow black as night before them,
And soon will have a shadow black as night

Behind them. And all this may be a shadow,
Sometime, that we may live to see behind us—
Wishing that we had not been all so sure
Tonight that it was always to be night."

"Your father may have fancied where the sun was
When first he saw the shadow of King Mark
Coming with mine before me. You are brave
Tonight, my love. A bravery like yours now
Would be the summons for a mightier love
Than mine, if there were room for such a love
Among things hidden in the hearts of men.
Isolt! Isolt! . . ."

                    Out of her struggling eyes
There were tears flowing, and withheld in his,
Tears were a veil of pity and desperation
Through which he saw the dim face of Isolt
Before him like a phantom in a mist—
Till to be sure that she was not a phantom,
He clutched and held her fast against his heart,
And through the cloak she wore felt the warm life
Within her trembling to the life in him,

And to the sorrow and the passion there
That would be always there. "Isolt! Isolt!"
Was all the language there was left in him
And she was all that was left anywhere—
She that would soon be so much worse than gone
That if he must have seen her lying still,
Dead where she was, he could have said that fate
Was merciful at least to one of them.
He would have worn through life a living crown
Of death, for memory more to be desired
Than any furtive and forsworn desire,
Or shattered oath of his to serve a King,
His mother's brother, without wilful stain,
Was like to be with all else it might be.
So Tristram, in so far as there was reason
Left in him, would have reasoned—when Isolt
'Drew his face down to hers with all her strength.
Or so it seemed, and kissed his eyes and cheeks
And mouth until there was no reason left
In life but love—love that was not to be,
Save as a wrenching and a separation
Past reason or reprieve. If she forgot
For long enough to smile at him through tears,

He may have read it as a sign that God
Was watching her and all might yet be well;
And if he knew that all might not be well,
Some God might still be watching over her,
With no more power than theirs now against Rome,
Or the pernicious valor of sure ruin,
Or against fate, that like an unseen ogre
Made hungry sport of these two there alone
Above the moaning wash of Cornish water,
Cold upon Cornish rocks.

                            "No bravery, love,"
She said, "or surely none like mine, would hide,
Among things in my heart that are not hidden,
A love larger than all time and all places,
And stronger beyond knowledge than all numbers
Around us that can only make us dead
When they are done with us.   Tristram, believe
That if I die my love will not be dead,
As I believe that yours will not be dead.
If in some after time your will may be
To slay it for the sake of a new face,
It will not die.   Whatever you do to it,

It will not die.   We cannot make it die,
We are not mighty enough to sentence love
Stronger than death to die, though we may die.
I do not think there is much love like ours
Here in this life, or that too much of it
Would make poor men and women who go alone
Into their graves without it more content,
Or more by common sorrow to be envied
Than they are now.   This may be true, or not.
Perhaps I am not old enough to know—
Not having lived always, nor having seen
Much else than everything disorderly
Deformed to order into a small court,
Where love was most a lie.   Might not the world,
If we could sift it into a small picture,
Be more like that than it would be like—this?
No, there is not much like this in the world—
And there may not be this!"

                        Tristram could see
Deep in the dark wet splendor of her eyes,
A terror that he knew was more for him
Than for herself.   "You are still brave enough,"

He said, "and you might look to me for strength,
If I were a magician and a wizard,
To vanquish the invincible.   Destruction
Of such a sort as one here among hundreds
Might wreak upon himself would be a pastime,
If ruin of him would make you free again
Without him."

             "I would not be free without him,"
Isolt said, as if angry: "And you know
That I should not be free if I were free
Without him.   Say no more about destruction
Till we see more, who are not yet destroyed.
O God, if only one of us had spoken—
When there was all that time!"

                  "You mean by that,
If only I had spoken," Tristram said;
And he could say no more till her quick lips
That clung to his again would let him speak.
"You mean, if only I had been awake
In paradise, instead of asleep there,
No jealous angel with a burning sword

Would have had power enough to drive me out,
Though God himself had sent him."

                                  Isolt smiled,
As with a willing pity, and closed her eyes
To keep more tears from coming out of them;
And for a time nothing was to be heard
Except the pounding of two hearts in prison,
The torture of a doom-begotten music
Above them, and the wash of a cold foam
Below them on those cold eternal rocks
Where Tristram and Isolt had yesterday
Come to be wrecked together. When her eyes
Opened again, he saw there, watching him,
An aching light of memory; and his heart
Beat harder for remembering the same light
That he had seen before in the same eyes.

"Alone once in the moonlight on that ship,"
She said, still watching him and clinging warm
Against him, "I believed that you would speak,
For I could hear your silence like a song
Out of the sea. I stood by the ship's rail,

Looking away into the night, with only
You and the ocean and the moon and stars
There with me. I was not seeing where I looked,
For I had waited too long for your step
Behind me to care then if the ship sailed
Or sank, so long as one true word of yours
Went wheresoever the ship went with me.
If these eyes, that were looking off so far
Over the foam, found anything there that night
Worth looking at, they have forgotten it;
And if my ears heard even the waves that night,
Or if my cheeks felt even the wind that night,
They have forgotten waves and wind together,
Remembering only there was you somewhere
On the same ship where I was, all alone
As I was, and alive   When you did come,
At last, and were there with me, and still silent,
You had already made yourself in vain
The loyal counterfeit of someone else
That never was, and I hope never shall be,
To make me sure there was no love for me
To find in you, where love was all I found.
You had not quite the will or quite the wish,

Knowing King Mark, not to reveal yourself,
When revelation was no more the need
Of my far larger need than revelation.
There was enough revealed, but nothing told.
Since I dare say to you how sure I am
Of the one thing that's left me to be sure of,
Know me and love me as I was that night,
As I am now, and as I shall be always—
All yours; and all this means for you and me
Is no small care for you. If you had spoken
There on that ship what most was in your heart
To say—if you had held me close—like this—
If you had kissed me then—like this—I wonder
If there would have been kings and crowns enough
In Cornwall or in England or elsewhere
To make the crowns of all kings everywhere
Shine with a light that would have let me see
No king but you and no crown but our love.
Tristram, believe, whatever the rest may be,
This is all yours—for God to weigh at last,
And as he will. And if it be found wanting,
He will not find what's left so ordinary
As not to say of it, 'This was Isolt—

Isolt who was all love.' He made her so,
And some time he may tell her why it is
So many that are on earth are there to suffer.
I say this now, for time will not wait always,
And we shall not be here when we are old—
If time can see us old. I had not thought
Of that; and will not think of it again.
There must be women who are made for love,
And of it, and are mostly pride and fire
Without it. There would not be much else left
Of them without it than sold animals
That might as well be driven and eating grass
As weaving, riding, hunting, and being queens,
Or not being queens. But when two loves like ours
Wear down the wall of time dividing them,
Two oceans come together and flow over
Time and his evil work. It was too long,
That wall, but there is nothing left of it,
And there is only love where the wall was.
And while you love me you will not forget
That you are all there is in my life now
That I would live for longer. And since nothing
Is left to me but to be sure of nothing

That you have not been sure of and been told,
You can believe me, though you cannot save me.
No, there is only one way to do that. . . .
If I were sure this was to be the end,
I should make this the end . . . Tristram! Tristram!
With you in the same house!"

                              "Do not say that."

He shook, and held her face away from him,
Gazing upon it as a man condemned
To darkness might have gazed for the last time
At all there was of life that he should see
Before his eyes were blinded by white irons.
"Tell me to throw myself over this wall,
Down upon those dead rocks, and I will do it.
Tell me to fall down now upon the point
Of this too restive sword, and you will see
How brief a sting death has. Tell me to drink
Tonight the most efficient mortal poison,
And of all drink that may be poured tomorrow
None shall be poured for me. But do not say,
Or make me say, where I shall be tonight.
All I can say is, I shall not be here.

Something within me is too near to breaking,
And it is not my heart. That will not break,
Nor shall a madness that is in me now
Break time in two—time that is on our side.
Yet I would see as little of Mark tonight
As may be well for my forgetfulness.
That was the best for me to say to you,
For now it has been said, I shall not kill him."

She trembled in his arms, and with a cry
Of stricken love gave all there was of her
That she could give to him in one more kiss
In which the world was melted and was nothing
For them but love—until another cry,
From Brangwaine, all forgotten in the garden,
Made the world firm again. He leapt away,
Leaving Isolt bewildered and heart-sick
With fear for him, and for she knew not what,
And lastly for herself. But soon she felt
A noise that was like one of shadows fighting.
Then she saw Tristram, who was bringing with him
A choking load that he dragged after him;
And then she could see Brangwaine, white as death

Behind those two.   And while she saw them there,
She could hear music from those walls above her,
And waves foaming on the cold rocks below.

When Tristram spoke, his words came hoarse and few.
"I knew the vermin I should find," he said,
And said no more.   He muttered and hurled something
Away from him against the parapet,
Hearing the sound that a skull makes on stone;
And without looking one way or another,
He stood there for a time like a man struck
By doom to an ungovernable silence,
Breathing above the crumpled shape of Andred.

IV

Tristram, like one bereft of all attention,
Saw little and heard nothing until Isolt
Sprang with a gasp and held her lips to his
An instant, and looked once into his eyes
Before she whispered in his ears a name,
And sprang away from him.   But this was not
Before King Mark had seen sufficiently
To find himself a shadow and Tristram

The substance of it in his Queen's cold eyes,
Which were as dark and dead to him as death
And had no answers in them.

                "Gouvernail,"
The King said, after staring angrily
About him, "who is lying there at your feet?
Turn him, and let me see?"

                "You know him, sir,"
Tristram replied, in tones of no address:
"The name of that you see down there is Andred;
And it is manifestly at your service."

"That was an unbecoming jest, I fear,
For you tonight, Tristram," answered the King.
"Do you not see what you have done to him?
Andred is bleeding."

             "I am glad of that, sir.
So long as there is less of that bad blood
In him, there will be so much less of Andred.
Wash him, and he will be as good as ever;

And that will be about as good as warts.
If I had been abrupt with him and drowned him,
I'd pity the sick fishes." Tristram's words,
Coming he knew not whence, fell without life
As from a tongue without it.

                              "Gouvernail,"
The King said, trembling in his desperation,
"The Queen and Brangwaine will go back with you.
Come down again with two men of the guard,
And when you come, take Andred through the garden."

"And through the little window he came out of,"
Said Tristram, in the way of one asleep.
Then, seeing the King as if for the first time,
He turned his head to see Isolt once more,
Vanishing, and to see for many a night
And day the last look in her frightened eyes.
But not inured yet fully to his doom,
He waited for the King to speak.

                              "Tristram,"
He said, in words wherein his pride and fury
Together achieved almost an incoherence,

"My first right is to ask what Andred saw
That you should so mistreat him. Do not hide
Yourself in silence, for I saw enough."

Tristram's initial answer was a shrug
Of reckless hate before he spoke: "Well, sir,
If you have seen enough, what matters it
How little or much this thing here may have seen?
His reptile observation must have gathered
Far less than you prepared him to report.
There was not much to see that I remember."

"There was no preparation on my part,
And Andred's act was of a loyalty
As well intentioned as it was unsought
And unforeseen by me. I swear to this,
Tristram. Is there as much of truth in you
As that, or is there nothing you dare name
Left of you now that may survive an oath?"

"I know these kings' beginnings," Tristram said,
Too furious to be prudent, "and I know
The crafty clutch of their advantages

Over the small who cringe.   And it appears
That a place waits for my apology
To fill for one thing left to thank God for."

"Tomorrow, if occasion shows itself,
Tristram, you may thank God you are alive.
Your plea for pardon has the taint of doubt
Upon it; yet I shall make a minute of it,
Here by the smudge of a sick lamp that smells
Of all I thought was honor."

                              Tristram saw
Confronting him two red and rheumy eyes,
Pouched in a face that nature had made comely,
And in appearance was indulgently
Ordained to wait on lust and wine and riot
For more years yet than leeches might foresee.
, Meeting the crafty sadness always in them,
He found it more than sad and worse than crafty,
And saw that no commingled shame and rage
Like that which he could see in them tonight
Would go out soon.   "Damn such a man," he thought;
And inward pain made sweat upon his forehead.
"I could almost believe that he believed

Himself, if I had never known him better.
Possession has a blade that will go deep
Unless I break it; and if I do that,
I shall break with it everything. Isolt!
Isolt and honor are the swords he'll use,
Leaving me mine that I've sworn not to use.
Honor—from him? If he found Honor walking
Here in Cornwall, he would send men to name it,
And would arrest it as a trespasser.
How does one take a thrust that pierces two,
And still defend the other from destruction?"

"Well, Tristram, knight-at-arms and man of honor,"
Mark said, "what last assay have you for me
Of honor now? If you were not the son
Of my dead sister, I should be oppressed
To say how long the sight of you alive
Would be the living cross that my forbearance
Might have to bear. But no, not quite that, either.
I can at least expunge the sight of you
Henceforth from Cornwall, if you care to live."

"Nowhere among my fancies here tonight, sir,
Is there a wish to live and be a cross

Upon your shoulders. If you find a figure
More salient and germane to my condition,
I might then care to live. Your point of honor,
Reduced obscurely to a nothingness,
Would hardly be a solid resting-place,
Or a safe one, for me. Give me the choice
Of death, or of inflicting more than death,
I would not live from now until tomorrow.
All said, what have I done? What you have seen.
And if there's any man or Andred breathing
Who tells you lies of more than you have seen,
Give me his name, and he'll tell no more lies.
Andred is waking up; and if I've ears,
Here are those guards coming with Gouvernail.
Andred, if you were not my lizard-cousin,
You might not be awake."

                              "I heard that, Tristram,"
Groaned a low voice. "I shall remember that.
I heard the Queen say, 'Tristram, I'm all yours—
All yours!' And then she kissed you till her mouth
Might have been part of yours. 'All yours! All yours!'
Let the King say if I'm a lizard now,

Or if I serve him well." He snarled and spat
At Tristram, who, forgetting, drew his sword,
And after staring at it in the moonlight
Replaced it slowly and reluctantly.

"I cannot kill a worm like that," he said.
Yet a voice tells me I had better do so.
Take him away—or let the King say that.
This is no slave of mine."

                  Gouvernail's men
Stood as if waiting for the moon to fall
Into the sea, but the King only nodded,
Like one bemused; and Andred, with an arm
Thrown over each of them, stumbled away.
The King gave one more nod, and Gouvernail,
Like sorrow in the mould of a bowed man,
Went slowly after him.

                  Then the King said,
"Tristram, I cannot trust myself much longer,
With you before me, to be more than man."
His fury shook him into a long silence

That had an end in tears of helpless rage:
"Why have you come between me and my Queen,
Stealing her love as you might steal my gold!
Honor! Good God in heaven! Is this honor—
And after all that I have done for you?"

"Almost as much as buying her with gold,
Or its equivalent in peace, was honor.
And as for all that you have done for me,
There are some tenuous items on my side.
Did I not, fighting Morhaus in your name,
Rid Cornwall of a tribute that for years
Had sucked away the blood and life of Cornwall,
Like vampires feeding on it in the night?
And have I not in my blind gratitude
For kindness that would never have been yours
If it had cost you even a night's rest,
Brought you for Queen the fairest of all women?
If these two gifts, which are but two, were all,
What more, in the King's name, would the King ask?"

"The casuistries of youth will not go far
With me, Tristram. You brought to me a Queen,

Stealing her love while you were bringing her.
What weakness is it in me lets you live?"

"I beg your pardon, sir, and for one error.
Where there was never any love to steal,
No love was ever stolen.   Honor—oh, yes!
If all the rituals, lies, and jigs and drinking
That make a marriage of an immolation—"

"By heaven, if you say one more word like that,"
The King cried, with his sword half out again,
"One of us will be left here!"   Then he stopped,
As if a bat had flown against his ear
And whispered of the night.   "But I will cease,
Mindful of who you are, with one more question.
You cast a cloud around the name of honor
As if the sight of it were none too sweet
In your remembrance.   If it be not honor
That ails you now and makes a madman of you,
It may be there's a reptile with green eyes
Arrived for a long feeding on your heart—
Biting a bit, who knows?"

                              Tristram could see
In the King's eyes the light of a lewd smile

That angrily deformed his aging face
With an avenging triumph. "Is this your way
To make a madman of me? If it be so,
Before you take my reason, take my life.
But no—you cannot. You have taken that."
He drew his sword as if each gleaming inch
Had come in anguish out of his own flesh,
And would have given it for the King to keep—
Fearing himself, in his malevolence,
Longer to be its keeper. But the King,
Seizing his moment, gave Tristram no time
More than to show the trembling steel, and hear
The doom that he had felt and partly seen
With Isolt's hope to cheer him.

                                        "You have drawn
Your sword against the King, Tristram," he said.
"Now put it back. Your speech to me before
Was nearer your last than you are near to me—
Yet I'll not have your blood. I'll have your life,
Instead—since you are sure your life means only
One woman—and will keep it far from you;
So far that you shall hunger for it always.

When you go down those stairs for the last time,
And that time will be now, you leave Cornwall
Farther behind you than hell's way from heaven
Is told in leagues.   And if the sight of you
Offends again my kingdom and infects it,
I swear by God you will be chained and burned.
And while you burn, her eyes will be held open
To watch your passion cooling in the flames.
Go!—and may all infernal fires attend you—
You and your nights and days, and all your dreams
Of her that you have not, and shall have never!"

"You know that for her sake, and for that only,
You are alive to say this," Tristram said;
And after one look upward at those lights
That soon would all be out, he swayed and trembled,
And slowly disappeared down the long stairs,
Passing the guards who knew him with a word
Of empty cheer, regardless of what thoughts
Of theirs were following him and his departure,
Which had no goal but the pursuing clutch
Of a mad retrospect.

                    He strode along
Until there was no moon but a white blur

Low in a blurred gray sky, and all those lights
That once had shone above him and Isolt,
And all that clamor of infernal joy
That once had shrilled above him and Isolt,
Were somewhere miles away among the ages
That he had walked and counted with his feet,
Which he believed, or dreamed that he believed,
Were taking him through hell to Camelot.
There he would send, or so again he dreamed,
A word to Lancelot or to Gawaine,
But what word he knew not.   There was no word,
Save one, that he could seize and separate
Out of the burning fury and regret
That made a fire of all there was of him
That he could call himself.   And when slow rain
Fell cold upon him as upon hot fuel,
It might as well have been a rain of oil
On faggots round some creature at a stake.
For all the quenching there was in it then
Of a sick sweeping heat consuming him
With anguish of intolerable loss,
Which might be borne if it were only loss.
But there was with it, always and again,

A flame-lit picture of Isolt alone
With Mark, in his embrace, and with that mouth
Of his on hers, and that white body of hers
Unspeakably imprisoned in his arms
For nights and days and years. A time had been
When by the quick destruction of all else
And of himself, he might have spared Isolt
By leaving her alone for lonely pain
To prey on till she died and followed him
To whatsoever the dusk-hidden doors
Of death might hide for such a love as theirs;
And there was nothing there so foul, he thought—
So far as he could think—and out of reason,
As to be meted for a sin like theirs
That was not sin, but fate—which must itself
Be but a monstrous and unholy jest
Of sin stronger than fate, sin that had made
The world for love—so that the stars in heaven
Might laugh at it, and the moon hide from it,
And the rain fall on it, and a King's guile
And lust makes one more shuddering toy of it.
He would not see behind him, yet had eyes
That saw behind him and saw nowhere else.

Before him there was nothing left to see
But lines of rain that he could hardly see,
And shapes that had no shape along a road
That had no sodden end. So on he strode
Without a guiding end in sight or mind,
Save one, if there were such an end somewhere,
That suddenly might lead him off the world
To sink again into the mysteries
From which his love had come, to which his love
Would drag him back again with ropes of fire
Behind him in the rain at which he laughed,
As in his torture he might then have laughed
At heaven from hell. He had seen both tonight—
Two had seen both, and two for one were chosen,
Because a love that was to be fulfilled
Only in death, was for some crumbs of hope,
Which he had shared for mercy with Isolt,
Foredoomed to live—how or how long to live
With him, he knew not. If it lived with him
Tonight, it lived only as things asleep
In the same rain where he was not asleep
Were somewhere living, as tomorrow's light
Would prove they were. Tomorrow's light, he thought,

Might prove also that he was living once,
And that Isolt was living once where lamps
Were shining and where music dinned and shrieked
Above her, and cold waves foaming on rocks
Below her called and hushed and called again
To say where there was peace.

                    There was no peace
For Tristram until after two nights' walking,
And two days' ranging under dripping trees,
No care was left in him to range or walk,
Or to be found alive where finally,
Under an aged oak he cast himself,
Falling and lying as a man half dead
Might shape himself to die. Before he slept,
A shame came over him that he, Tristram,
A man stronger than men stronger than he,
Should now be weaker than a man unmade
By slow infirmity into a child
To be the sport of children. Then his rage
Put shame away and was again a madness,
And then a blank, wherein not even a name
That he remembered would stay long enough

For him to grasp it or to recognize it,
Before the ghost of what had been a name
Would vanish like a moonbeam on a tomb
When a cloud comes. Cloud after cloud came fast,
Obliterating before leaving clear
The word that he had lost. It was a name
Of some one far behind him in the gloom,
Where there were lights above, and music sounding,
And the long wash of a cold sea below.
"Isolt!" He smiled as one who from a dream
Wakes to find he was dreaming and not dying,
And then he slept.

             When he awoke again,
It was to find around him, after fever,
A squalid box of woodland poverty
In which he lay like a decrepit worm
Within an empty shell. Through a small square
Clear sunlight slanted, and there was outside
A scattered sound of life that fitfully
Twittered and shrilled. In time there was a tread
Of heavy steps, and soon a door was open;
Then in from somewhere silently there came

A yokel shape, unsightly and half-clad,
That shambled curiously but not unkindly
Towards the low sodden pallet where Tristram
Lay wondering where he was; and after him
Came one that he remembered with a leap
Of gladness in his heart.

                              "You—Gouvernail?"
He cried; and he fell back into a swoon
Of uselessness too deep for Gouvernail
To call him from by kindly word or touch
Till time was ready. In the afternoon,
Tristram, not asking what had come to pass,
Nor caring much, found himself in a cart,
Dimly aware of motion and low words
And of a dull security. He slept,
And half awoke, and slept again, till stones
Under the wheels and a familiar glimpse
Of unfamiliar walls around a court
Told of a journey done. That night he slept,
And in the morning woke to find himself
In a place strange to him. Whose place it was,
Or why he should be in it, was no matter.

There he could rest, and for a time forget.
So, for a time, he lost the name of life,
And of all else except Isolt. . . . "Isolt!"
That was the only name left in the world,
And that was only a name. "Isolt! Isolt!"

After an endless day of sleep and waking,
With Gouvernail adventuring in and out
Like some industrious and unquiet phantom,
He woke again with low light coming in
Through a red window. Now the room was dim,
But with a dimness that would let him see
That he was not alone. "Isolt!" he said,
And waited, knowing that it was not Isolt.

A crooning voice that had within its guile
A laughing ring of metal said, "Isolt?
Isolt is married. Are you young men never
To know that when a princess weds a king
The young man, if he be a wise young man,
Will never afford himself another fever,
And lie for days on a poor zany's rags,
For all the princesses in Christendom?
Gouvernail found you, I found Gouvernail,

And here you are, my lord.   Forget Isolt,
And care a little for your royal self;
For you may be a king one of these days
And make some other young man as miserable
As Mark makes you. The world appears to be,
Though God knows why, just such a place as that.
Remember you are safe, and say your prayers.
For all you know of this life or the next,
You may be safer here than in your shroud.
Good night, Sir Tristram, Prince of Lyonesse."

Days after, vexed with doubt and indecision,
Queen Morgan, with her knight a captive now,
Sat gazing at him in a coming twilight,
Partly in anger, partly in weary triumph,
And more than all in a dark wonderment
Of what enchantment there was wanting in her
To keep this man so long out of her toll
Of willing remnants and of eager cinders,
Now scattered and forgotten save as names
To make her smile. If she sat smiling now,
It was not yet for contemplated havoc
Of this man's loyalty to a lost dream

Where she was nothing. She had made other men
Dream themselves dead for her, but not this man,
Who sat now glowering with a captive scorn
Before her, waiting grimly for a word
Of weariness or of anger or disdain
To set him free.

        "You are not sound enough,
My lord, for travel yet," she said. "I know,
For I have done more delving into life
And death than you, and into this mid-region
Between them, where you are, and where you sit
So cursed with loneliness and lethargy
That I could weep. Hard as this is for you,
It might be worse. You will go on your way,
While I sit knitting, withering and outworn,
With never a man that looks at me, save you,
So truthful as to tell me so." She laughed
At him again, and he heard metal laughing,
As he had heard it speaking, in her low
And stinging words.

          "You are not withering yet,"
He said; and his eyes ranged forgetfully
Over a studied feline slenderness

Where frugal silk was not frugality.
"I am too ill to see, in your account,
More than how safe I am with you." Isolt,
With her scared violet eyes and blue-black hair
Flew like a spirit driven from a star
Into that room and for a moment stayed
Before him. In his eyes he could feel tears
Of passion, desperation, and remorse,
Compounded with abysmal indignation
At a crude sullen hunger not deceived,
Born of a sloth enforced and of a scorn
Transformed malignly to a slow surrender.
His captor, when she saw them, came to him
And with a mocking croon of mother-comfort
Fondled him like a snake with two warm arms
And a warm mouth; and after long chagrin
Of long imprisonment, and long prisoned hate
For her that in his hatred of himself
He sought now like an animal, he made
No more acknowledgment of her cajoling
Than suddenly to rise without a word
And carry her off laughing in his arms,
Himself in hers half strangled.

Gouvernail,

As heretofore, found waiting him again
The same cold uncommunicating guards,
Past whom there was no word. Another day,
And still another and another day
Found them as mute in their obedience
As things made there of wood. Tristram, within
Meanwhile achieved a sorry composition
Of loyalty and circumstance. "Tomorrow,"
He said, "I must be out and on my way."
And Morgan only said, "Which way is that?"
And so on for a fortnight, when at last,
With anger in her eyes and injuries
Of his indifference envenoming
The venom in her passion and her pride,
She let him go—though not without a laugh
That followed him like steel piercing unseen
His flight away from her with Gouvernail.

"You leave me now," she said, "but Fate has eyes,
You are the only blind one who is here,
As you are still to see. I said before,
Britain is less than the whole firmament,

And we may meet again. Until we meet,
Farewell; and find somewhere a good physician
To draw the poison of a lost Isolt
Out of your sick young heart. Till he do so,
You may as well be rearing you a tomb
That else will hold you—presently. Farewell,
Farewell, Sir Tristram, Prince of Lyonesse,
The once redoubtable and undeceived,
Who now in his defeat would put Fate's eyes out.
Not yet, Sir Prince; and we may meet again."
She smiled; and a smile followed him long after
A sharp laugh was forgotten.

                            Gouvernail,

Riding along with Tristram silently
Till there was no glimpse left of Morgan's prison
Through the still trees behind them, sighed and said,
"Where are we going, Tristram, and what next?"
And through the kindness of his weary grief
There glimmered in his eyes a loyal smile
Unseen by Tristram, though as well divined
As if revealed.

                    "You are the last of men,
And so the last of friends now, Gouvernail,

For me to cleave to in extremities
Beyond the malefactions of this world.
You are apart and indispensable,
Holding me out of madness until doom,
Which I feel waiting now like death in the dark,
Shall follow me and strike, unrecognized,
For the last time. Away from that snake's nest
Behind me, it would be enough to know
It is behind me, were it not for knowledge
That in a serpent that is unsubdued
And spurned, a special venom will be waiting
Its time. And when the serpent is a woman,
Or a thin brained and thinner blooded Andred,
Infirm from birth with a malignant envy,
One may not with one thrust annihilate
The slow disease of evil eating in them
For one that never willed them any evil.
Twice have I heard in helpless recognition
A voice to bid me strike. I have not struck,
And shall not . . . For a time now, Gouvernail,
My memory sees a land where there is peace,
And a good King whose world is in his kingdom
And in his quaint possession of a child

Whose innocence may teach me to be wise
Till I be strong again. I see a face
That once was fond of me, and a white hand
Holding an agate that I left in it.
I see a friendliness of old assured
In Brittany. If anywhere there were peace
For me, it might be there—or for some time
Till I'm awake and am a man again."

"I was not saying all that to you, Tristram,"
Gouvernail answered, looking at his reins,
"But since you say it, I'll not fatigue my tongue
Gainsaying it for no good. Time is a casket
Wherein our days are covered certainties
That we lift out of it, one after one,
For what the day may tell. Your day of doom,
Tristram, may like as not be one for you
To smile at, could you see it where it waits,
Far down, I trust, with many a day between
That shall have gladness in it, and more light
Than this day has. When you are on the sea,
And there are white waves everywhere to catch
The sunlight and dance with it and be glad

The sea was made, you may be glad also.
Youth sees too far to see how near it is
To seeing farther.   You are too blind today,
By dim necessity of circumstance,
More than to guess.   Whether you take your crown
In Lyonesse or not, you will be king
Wherever you are.   Many by chance are crowned
As kings that are born rather to be tinkers,
Or farmers, or philosophers, or farriers,
Or barbers, or almost anything under God
Than to be kings.   Whether you will or not,
You are a king, Tristram, for you are one
Of the time-sifted few that leave the world,
When they are gone, not the same place it was.
Mark what you leave."

                              "There was a good man once,"
Said Tristram, "who fed sunshine to the blind
Until the blind went mad, and the good man
Died of his goodness, and died violently.
If untoward pleasantries are your affection,
Say this was in your casket and not mine.
There's a contentious kingdom in myself

For me to rule before I shall rule others.
If it is not too dark for me to fight
In there for my advantage and advancement,
And if my armor holds itself together
So long as not to be disintegrated
Before it breaks and I am broken with it,
There may be such a king as you foresee;
And failing him, I shall not fail my friend,
Who shall not be forgotten.   Gouvernail,
Be glad that you have no more darkness in you."

They rode along in silence, Gouvernail
Retasting an abridgement undeserved,
And undeserving of another venture,
Or so his unofficial ardor warned him,
Into a darkness and a namelessness
Wherein his worldly and well-meaning eyes
Had never sought a name for the unseen.

V

Griffon, the giant scourge of Brittany,
Threatened while Tristram was appraising it,
In his anticipation, all the peace

Awaiting him across the foaming waves
That were to wash, in Gouvernail's invention,
Time out of life. And there King Howel's child,
Isolt of the white hands, living on hope,
Which in all seeming had itself alone
To live on, was for love and safety now
A prisoner in that castle by the sea
Where Tristram once, not thinking twice of it,
Had said that he would some day come again,
And more as a gay plaything than a pledge
Had left with her an agate which had been
For long her father's jest. It was her heart,
Which she had taken out of her white bosom,
He said, and in the forest or in the sea
Would presently be lost and never found
Again—not even for Tristram when he came.
But when he came there was no time for talk
Of hearts and agates. Welcome and wonderment
Appeased, and the still whiteness of Isolt
Regarded once and then at once forgotten,
Tristram, like one athirst with wine before him,
Heard the King's talk of a marauding host
That neither force nor craft had yet subdued

Or more than scattered, like an obscene flock
Of rooks alert around a living quarry
That might not have a longer while to live
Than a few days would hold, or not so many.

"Praise be to God, I could almost have said
For your ill fortune, sir, and for your danger,"
Was Tristram's answer to the King's grim news.
"I have been groping slowly out of life
Into a slough of darkness and disuse—
A place too far from either for life or death
To share with me. Yes, I have had too much
Of what a fool, not knowing its right name,
Would call the joy of life. If that be joy,
Give me a draught out of your cup of trouble,
And let it be seen then what's left of me
To deal with your bad neighbor. For tonight,
Let me have rest before tomorrow's work,
Which may be early."

                    "Early and late, I fear,"
The King said, and eyed Tristram cautiously,
And with a melancholy questioning

Of much that was for him no more a question.
"If it be God that brings you here today,
I praise him in my thanks given to you,
Tristram, for this.   Sleep, and forget tomorrow
Until tomorrow calls you.   If ill comes
To you for this, I shall not wish to live—
But for my child.   And if ill comes to her,
It will be death to live."

                            "Tomorrow, sir,
These ills may be the dregs in empty cups
With all the bitterness drunk out of them.
No ill shall come to her till you and I
And all your men go down defending her;
And I can figure no such havoc as that.
I'm not a thousand men, or more than one,
Yet a new mind and eye, and a new arm
At work with yours, may not combine for ruin."

Uncertain afterwards in a foreseen
Achievement unachieved, Tristram rejoiced
At last when he saw Griffon at his feet
And saw the last of his pernicious minions

Dispatched or disappearing. And that night,
Having espied Isolt's forgotten harp,
He plucked and sang the shadow of himself,
To her his only self, unwittingly
Into the soul and fabric of her life,
Till death should find it there. So day by day
He fostered in his heart a tenderness
Unrecognized for more than a kind fear
For what imaginable small white pawn
Her candor and her flame-white loveliness
Could yet become for the cold game of kings,
Who might not always, if they would, play quite
Their game as others do.

                              Once by the shore
They lingered while a summer sun went down
Beyond the shining sea; and it was then
That sorrow's witchcraft, long at work in him,
Made pity out of sorrow, and of pity
Made the pale wine of love that is not love,
Yet steals from love a name. And while he felt
Within her candor and her artlessness
The still white fire of her necessity,

He asked in vain if this were the same fate
That for so long had played with him so darkly—
With him and with Isolt, Isolt of Ireland,
Isolt of the wild frightened violet eyes
That once had given him that last look of hers
Above the moaning call of those cold waves
On those cold Cornish rocks. This new Isolt,
This new and white Isolt, was nothing real
To him until he found her in his arms,
And, scarcely knowing how he found her there,
Kissed her and felt the sting of happy tears
On his bewildered lips. Her whiteness burned
Against him till he trembled with regret;
For hope so long unrealized real at last
To her, was perilously real to him.
He knew that while his life was in Cornwall,
Something of this white fire and loneliness
In Brittany must be his whereon to lavish
The comfort of kind lies while he should live.
There were some words that he would have been saying
When her eyes told him with a still reproof
That silence would say more; and Tristram wished
That silence might say all.

For a long time
They sat there, looking off across the water
Between them and Tintagel to the north,
Where Tristram saw himself chained to a stake
With flames around him and Isolt of Ireland
Held horribly to see. King Mark, he knew,
Would in his carnal rage cling to his word
And feast his eyes and hate insatiably
On his fulfilment of it—in itself
The least of Tristram's fear. It was her eyes,
Held open to behold him, that he saw,
More than it was himself, or any torture
That would be only torture worse than his
For her. He turned himself away from that,
And saw beside him two gray silent eyes
Searching in his with quaint solemnity
For some unspoken answer to a thought
Unspoken.

"When I told my father first
That you would come, he only smiled at me,"
She said. "But I believe by saying always
That you were coming, he believed you would,
Just as I knew you would."

                                "And why was that,
My child?" he asked, a captive once again
To her gray eyes and her white need of him.
"You might have told your father I was coming
Till the world's end, and I might not have come."

"You would have come, because I knew you would,"
She said, with a smile shaking on her lips
And fading in her eyes. "And you said that,
Because you knew, or because you knew nothing,
Or cared less than you know. Because you knew,
I like to fancy. It will do no harm."

"Were I so sure of that," he thought, "as you are,
There would be no infection of regret
In my remembrance of a usefulness
That Brittany will say was mine. Isolt
Of Brittany? Why were two names like that
Written for me by fate upon my heart
In red and white? Is this white fire of pity,
If pity it be, to burn deeper than love?"
Isolt of Ireland's dark wild eyes before him
In the moonlight, and that last look of hers,
Appeared in answer. Tristram gazed away

Into the north, and having seen enough,
He turned again to find the same gray light
In the same eyes that searched in his before
For an unspoken answer to a thought
Unspoken. They came silently away,
And Tristram sang again to her that night.

And he sang many a time to her thereafter
Songs of old warriors, and old songs of love
Triumphant over wars that were forgotten;
And many a time he found in her gray eyes,
And in the rose-white warmth of her attention,
Dominion of a sure necessity
Beyond experience and the need of reason,
Which had at first amused him and at last
Had made him wonder why there should be tears
In a man's eyes for such a mild white thing
That had so quaint a wisdom in its mildness,
Unless because he watched it going slowly
Its mild white way out of the world without him.
"Can she see farther into time, by chance,
Than I do?" he would ask, observing her:
'She might do so, and still see little farther

Than to the patient ends of her white fingers
That are so much alive, like all of her."
She found him smiling, but in her large eyes
There was no smile. There was a need of him
That made him cold, as if a ghost had risen
Before him with a wordless admonition
That he must go or stay. And many a time
He would have gone, if he had not perforce
As many a time remained to sing for her
Those old songs over, and as many a time
Found in her gaze that sure necessity
Which held him with a wisdom beyond thought,
Or with an innocence beyond all wisdom,
Until he sang one night for the last time
To the King's child. For she was his child now,
And for as long as there was life in him
Was his to cherish and to wonder at,
That he should have this white wise fiery thing
To call his wife.

          "Magicians might have done it"
He pondered once, alone, "but in so far
As I'm aware of them, there are none left
In Brittany so adept as to achieve it.

Stars may have done it." Then King Howel, pleased,
Though in his pleasure as incredulous
As if he were somehow a little injured,
Appearing out of silence from behind him,
Took Tristram's hands approvingly in his,
And said, "You have a child that was a woman
Before she was a child, and is today
Woman and child, and something not of either,
For you to keep or crush—without a sound
Of pain from her to tell you so. Beware
Somewhat of that, Tristram; and may you both
Be wise enough not to ask more of life
Than to be life, and fate." The last word fell
Like a last coin released unwillingly
By caution giving all. And while the King
Said what he said, Tristram was seeing only
A last look in two dark and frightened eyes
That always in the moonlight would be shining,
Alone above the sound of Cornish waves
That always in the moonlight would be breaking,
Cold upon Cornish rocks.

                    But occupation,
Like a neglected and insistent hound

Leaping upon his master's inattention,
Soon found him wearing on his younger shoulders
The yoke of a too mild and easy-trusting
And easy-futured king. He shaped and trained
An army that in time before would soon
Have made of Griffon a small anecdote
Hardly worth telling over after supper;
He built new ships and wharves, and razed old houses,
And so distressed a realm with renovation
Unsought and frowned on by slow denizens
For decades undisturbed, that many of them,
Viewing the visioned waste of a new hand,
Had wished him dead, or far from Brittany;
And for the flower of his activities,
He built a royal garden for Isolt
Of the white hands to bloom in, a white rose
Fairer than all fair roses in the world
Elsewhere—save one that was not white but dark,
Dark and love-red for ever, and not there,
Where the white rose was queen.

                              So for two years
She reigned and waited, and there in her garden
Let rumor's noise, like thunder heard far off,

Rumble itself to silence and as nigh
To nothing as might be. But near the end
Of a long afternoon, alone with him,
She sat there watching Tristram, who in turn,
Still mystified at having in his care
To keep or crush, even as her father said,
So brave and frail a flower, sat watching her
With eyes that always had at least been kind,
If they had not said always everything
She would have had them say. Staring at him,
Like someone suddenly afraid of life,
She chilled him slowly with a question: "Tristram,"
She said, "what should I do were you to die?"

"Are there no prettier notions in your head
Than that?" said he, and made a task of laughing.
"There are no mortal purposes in me
Today, yet I may say what you would do:
Were I to die, you would live on without me.
But I would rather sing you an old song
Than die, and even for you, this afternoon."

"Yes, presently you will sing me an old song,"
She said. "It was a wonder seized me then

And made me ask like that what I should do
Were you to die. Were you to tire of me,
And go away from me and stay some time,
I should not die, for then you would come back.
You came back once, and you would come again;
For you would learn at last you needed me
More than all other creatures. But if you died,
Then you would not come back. What should I do
If you should go away and never come back?
I see almost a shadow on you sometimes,
As if there were some fearful thing behind you,
Not to be felt or seen—while you are here."

"I can feel only the sun behind me now—
Which is a fearful thing if we consider it
Too long, or look too long into its face."
Saying that, he smiled at her, not happily,
But rather as one who has left something out,
And gazed away over a vine-hung wall,
And over the still ocean where one ship
Was coming slowly in.

                    "If I lost you
For a long time," she said, with her insistence,

"I should not cry for what had come between,
For I should have you here with me again.
I am not one who must have everything.
I was not fated to have everything.
One may be wise enough, not having all,
Still to be found among the fortunate."

She stood beside him now and felt his arm
Closing around her like an arm afraid.
"Little you know, my child," he thought, in anguish
A moment for the fear and innocence
That he was holding and was his to hold,
"What ashes of all this wisdom might be left you
After one blast of sick reality
To tell the wise what words are to the heart."
And then aloud: "There's a ship coming in
From somewhere north of us."

                              "There are no ships
From the north now that are worth looking at,"
She said; and he could feel her trembling warm
Against him till he felt her scorching him
With an unconscious and accusing fire.
"There was a time when I was always gazing

North for a ship, but nothing is there now;
Or ships are all alike that are there now."

"They are not all like this one," Tristram said,
More to himself than to the white Isolt
Arming herself with blindness against fate,
"For there are trumpets blowing, as if a king
Were coming—and there's a dragon on the sail.
One of King Arthur's barges—by the Lord
In heaven, it is!—comes here to Brittany,
And for a cause that lives outside my knowledge.
Were this the King, we should have known of him."

"What does it mean?" she whispered; and her words
Wavered as if a terror not yet revealed
Had flown already inland from that ship.

"God knows," he said, "but it will not be long
Before we shall all know." She followed him
Into her father's castle, where the new
Looked ancient now; and slowly, after silence,
He left her waiting there at the same window
Where she had waited for so long before,
When she was looking always to the north;

And having left her there, alone with wonder,
He went alone with wonder to the shore,
Where a gay ship was coming gaily in,
And saw descending from it soon, and gaily,
As always, Sir Gawaine from Camelot.

VI

Gawaine, in Cornwall once, having seen Isolt
Of Ireland with her pallid mask of pride,
Which may have been as easy a mask as any,
He thought, for prisoned love and scorn to wear,
Had found in her dark way of stateliness
Perfection providentially not his
To die for. He recalled a wish to die,
But only as men healed remember pain;
And here in Tristram's garden, far from Cornwall,
Gawaine, musing upon this white Isolt
Of Brittany, whose beauty had heretofore,
For him, lived rather as that of a white name
Than of a living princess, found himself
Again with a preoccupied perfection
To contemplate. The more he contemplated,
The more he arraigned fate and wondered why
Tristram should be at odds with banishment,

Or why Tristram should care who banished him,
Or for how long, or for what violet eyes
And Irish pride and blue-black Irish hair
Soever. He smiled with injured loyalty
For Tristram in a banishment like this,
With a whole world to shine in save Cornwall,
And Cornwall the whole world; and if he sighed,
He may have sighed apart, and harmlessly,
Perceiving in this Isolt a continence
Too sure for even a fool to ponder twice,
A little for himself. They faced each other
On a stone bench with vine-leaves over them,
And flowers too many for them to see before them,
And trees around them with birds singing in them,
And God's whole gift of summer given in vain
For one who could feel coming in her heart
A longer winter than any Breton sun
Should ever warm away, and with it coming,
Could laugh to hear Gawaine making her laugh.

"I have been seeing you for some hours," he said,
"And I appraise you as all wonderful.
The longer I observe and scrutinize you,

The less do I become a king of words
To bring them into action. They retreat
And hide themselves, leaving me as I may
To make the best of a disordered remnant,
Unworthy of allegiance to your face
And all the rest of you. You are supreme
In a deceit that says fragility
Where there is nothing fragile. You have eyes
That almost weep for grief, seeing from heaven
How trivial and how tragic a small place
This earth is, and so make a sort of heaven
Where they are seen. Your hair, if shorn and woven,
The which may God forbid, would then become
A nameless cloth of gold whiter than gold,
Imprisoning light captured from paradise.
Your small ears are two necessary leaves
Of living alabaster never of earth,
Whereof the flower that is your face is made,
And is a paradisal triumph also—
Along with your gray eyes and your gold hair
That is not gold. Only God knows, who made it,
What color it is exactly. I don't know.
The rest of you I dare not estimate,

Saving your hands and feet, which authorize
A period of some leisure for the Lord
On high for their ineffable execution.
Your low voice tells how bells of singing gold
Would sound through twilight over silent water.
Yourself is a celestial emanation
Compounded of a whiteness and a warmth
Not yet so near to heaven, or far from it,
As not to leave men wiser for their dreams
And distances in apprehending you.
Your signal imperfection, probably,
Is in your peril of having everything,
And thereby overwhelming with perfection
A man who sees so much of it at once,
And says no more of it than I am saying.
I shall begin today to praise the Lord,
I think, for sparing an unworthy heart
An early wound that once might not have healed.
If there lives in me more than should be told,
Not for the world's last oyster would I tell it
To the last ear alive, surely not yours."

"If you were one of the last two alive,
The other might make of you the last," she said,

Laughing. "You are not making love to me,
Gawaine, and if you were it wouldn't matter.
Your words, and even with edges a bit worn
By this time, will do service for years yet.
You will not find that you have dulled them much
On me, and you will have them with you always."

"I don't know now whether I am or not,"
Said he, "and say with you it wouldn't matter.
For Tristram, off his proper suavity,
Has fervor to slice whales; and I, from childhood,
Have always liked this world. No, I should say
That I was covering lightly under truth
A silent lie that may as well be silent;
For I can see more care than happiness
In those two same gray eyes that I was praising."

"Gawaine," she said, turning the same gray eyes
On his and holding them, with hers half laughing,
"Your fame is everywhere alike for lightness,
And I am glad that you have not my heart
To be a burden for you on too long
A journey, where you might find hearts of others

Not half so burdensome. Do you like that?
If you do not, say it was never said,
And listen as if my words were bells of gold,
Or what you will. You will be hanged some day
For saying things, and I shall not be there
To save you, saying how little you meant by them.
You may be lighter than even your enemies
Would see you in their little scales of envy,
Yet in your lightness, if I'm not a fool,
There lives a troubled wonder for a few
You care for. Now if two of them were here,
Would you say what was best, in your reflection,
And on your honor say no more of it,
For one of them alone here to believe
When Tristram goes with you to Camelot?
While he is there, King Arthur, it appears,
Will make of him a Knight of the Round Table—
All which would be illustrious and delightful
Enough for me, if that were to be all.
And though the world is in our confidence,
Your honor as a man will forget that;
And you will answer, wisely perhaps, or not,
One question, which in brief is only this:

What right name should an innocence like mine
Deserve, if I believed he would come back?"
She watched him with expectant eyes, wherefrom
The ghost of humor suddenly had vanished.

Gawaine, who felt a soreness at his heart
That he had seldom felt there for another
Before, and only briefly for himself,
Felt also a cloud coming in his eyes.
"I can see only one thing to believe,"
He said, believing almost he could see it,
"And that is, he will come—as he must come.
Why should he not come back again, for you?
Who in this world would not come back, for you!
God's life, dear lady, why should he not come back?"
He cried, and with a full sincerity
Whereat she closed her eyes and tried to speak,
Despairingly, with pale and weary lips
That would not speak until she made them speak.

"Gawaine," she said, "you are not fooling me;
And I should be a fool if hope remained
Within me that you might be. You know truth

As well as I do. He will not come back.
King Mark will kill him." For so long unspoken,
She had believed those words were tamed in her
Enough to be released and to return
To the same cage there in her aching heart
Where they had lived and fought since yesterday.
But when she felt them flying away from her,
And heard them crying irretrievably
Between her and Gawaine, and everywhere,
Tears followed them until she felt at last
The touch of Gawaine's lips on her cold fingers,
Kindly and light.

        "No, Mark will hardly kill him,"
He told her. Breathing hard and hesitating,
He waited as a felon waits a whip,
And went on with a fluent desperation:
"Mark is in prison now—for forgery
Of the Pope's name, by force of which Tristram
Was to go forth to fight the Saracens,
And by safe inference to find a grave
Not far ahead. Impossible, if you like,
And awkward out of all ineptitude,

And clumsy beyond credence, yet the truth,
As the impossible so often is.
In his unwinking hate he saw Tristram
Too near for easy vengeance, and so blundered
Into the trap that has him.   This was not
For me to tell, and it is not for you,
Upon your royal honor as a woman
Of honor more than royal to reveal.
Mercy compels me to forego my word
And to repeat the one right thing for you
In reason to believe.   He will come back;
And you, if you are wise—and you are that
Beyond the warrant of your sheltered years—
Will find him wiser in his unworthiness,
And worthier of your wisdom and your love,
When this wild fire of what a man has not
Reveals at last, in embers all gone out,
That which he had, and has, and may have always,
To prize aright thereafter and to pray for.
Out of my right I talk to you like this,
And swear by heaven, since I have gone so far,
That your worst inference here is not my knowledge.
He may come back at once.   If otherwise—well,

He will come back with a new vision in him
And a new estimation of God's choice.
I have told you what neither grief nor guile
Would of themselves alone have wrung from me.
The rest will be in you, you being yourself."

"Yes, you have thrown your offices away
And you have left your honor for me to keep,"
She said, and pressed his hands in gratitude.
"Here it will be as safe as in the sea.
I thank you, and believe you.   Leave me here
Alone, to think; to think—and to believe."
She brushed her eyes and tried as if to smile,
But had no smile in answer.   For Gawaine,
Infrequently in earnest, or sincere
To conscious inconvenience, was in love,
Or thought he was, and would enjoy alone,
Without a smile and as he might, the first
Familiar pangs of his renunciation.

He wandered slowly downward to the shore
Where he found Tristram, gazing at the ship
Which in the morning would be taking them
Together away from Brittany and Isolt

Of the white hands to England, where Tristram,
A knight only of Mark's investiture
Today, would there be one of the Round Table—
So long the symbol of a world in order,
Soon to be overthrown by love and fate
And loyalty forsworn. Had Gawaine then
Beheld a cloud that was not yet in sight,
There would have been more sorrow in his eyes
For time ahead of him than for time now,
Or for himself. But where he saw no cloud
That might not be dissolved, and so in time
Forgotten, there was no sorrow in his eyes
For time to come that would be longer coming,
To him, than for the few magnanimous days
Of his remembrance of enforced eclipse.

"Tristram," he said, "why in the name of God
Are you not looking at your garden now,
And why are you not in it with your wife?
I left her, after making love to her
With no progression of effect whatever,
More than to make her laugh at me, and then
To make her cry for you for going away.

I said you would be coming back at once,
And while I said it I heard pens in heaven
Scratching a doubtful evidence against me."

Tristram, in indecision between anger
Deserving no indulgence and surprise
Requiring less, scowled and laughed emptily:
"Gawaine, if you were any one else alive
I might not always be at home to you,
Or to your bland particularities.
Why should a wedded exile hesitate
In his return to his own wife and garden?
I know the picture that your folly draws
Of woe that is awaiting me in Cornwall.
But we are going to Camelot, not to Cornwall.
King Mark, with all his wealth of hate for me,
Is not so rich and rotten and busy with it
As to be waiting everywhere at once
To see me coming. He waits most in Cornwall,
Preferring for mixed reasons of his own
Not frequently to shine far out of it."

"He may not be so rotten as some whose names
Have fallen from my deciduous memory,"

Gawaine said, with a shrug of helplessness,
"But all the same, with Mark and his resource
In England, your best way's away from there
As early and expeditiously as may be.
Mark's arm is not the only arm he uses;
My fear for you is not my only fear.
Fear for yourself in you may be as nothing,
Which is commendable and rather common
In Camelot, as fellows who read and write
Are not so rare there that we crown them for it.
But there's a fear more worthy than no fear,
And it may be the best inheritance
Of luckless ones with surer sight than yours,
And with perception more prophetical
Than yours. I say this hoping it will hurt,
But not offend. You see how lax I am
When I'm away from royal discipline,
And how forgetful of unspoken caution
I am when I'm afraid to be afraid.
I thrust my head into the lion's mouth,
And if my head comes off, it will have done,
For once if only once, the best it might.
I doubt if there's a man with eyes and ears

Who is more sadly and forlornly certain
Of what another's wisdom—born of weakness,
Like all born mortal attributes and errors—
Is like to leave behind it of itself
In you, when you have heard and hated it,
But all the same, Tristram, if I were you,
I'd sail away for Camelot tomorrow,
And there be made a Knight of the Round Table;
And then, being then a Knight of the Round Table,
I should come back.   I should come back at once.
Now let the lion roar."

        He laid his hands
On Tristram's iron shoulders, which he felt
Shaking under his touch, and with a smile
Of unreturned affection walked away
In silence to the ship.   Tristram, alone,
Moved heavily along the lonely shore,
To seat himself alone upon a rock
Where long waves had been rolling in for ages,
And would be rolling when no man or woman
Should know or care to know whether or not
Two specks of life, in time so far forgotten

As in remembrance never to have been,
Were Tristram and Isolt—Isolt in Cornwall,
Isolt of the wild frightened violet eyes,
Isolt and her last look, Isolt of Ireland.
Alone, he saw the slanting waves roll in,
Each to its impotent annihilation
In a long wash of foam, until the sound
Become for him a warning and a torture,
Like a malign reproof reiterating
In vain its cold and only sound of doom.
Then he arose, with his eyes gazing still
Into the north, till with his face turned inland
He left the crested wash of those long waves
Behind him to fall always on that sand,
And to sound always that one word—"Isolt."

As if in undesigned obedience
To Gawaine's admonition, he went idly
And blindly back to the sun-flooded garden
Where sat the white Isolt whose name was not
The name those waves, unceasing and unheard,
Were sounding where they fell. Still as Gawaine
Had left her, Tristram found her. She looked up

With a wan light of welcome flashing sadly
To see him; and he knew that such a light
As that could shine for him only from eyes
Where tears had been before it. They were not
There now, and there was now no need of them
To make him ask, in a self-smiting rage
Of helpless pity, if such a love as hers
Might not unshared be nearer to God's need,
In His endurance of a blinder Fate,
Than a love shared asunder, but still shared,
By two for doom elected and withheld
Apart for time to play with. Once he had seen,
Imploring it, the light of a far wisdom
Tingeing with hope the night of time between,
But there was no light now. There might be peace,
Awaiting them where they were done with time—
Time for so long disowning both of them,
And slowly the soul first, saving the rest
To mock the soul—but there was no peace now.
When there was no time left for peace on earth,
After farewells and vestiges forgotten,
There might be time enough for peace somewhere;
But that was all far off, and in a darkness

Blacker than any night that ever veiled
A stormy chaos of the foaming leagues
That roared unseen between him and Cornwall.

All this was in his mind, as it was there
Always, if not thought always, when she spoke:
"Tristram, you are not angry or distressed
If I am not so happy here today
As you have seen me here before sometimes,
And may see me again. Tomorrow morning
If I am here, I shall be here alone.
I wonder for how long."

                              "For no day longer
Than I'm away," he said, and held her face
Between his hands. "Then, if you like, my child,
Your wonder may come after your surprise
That I should come so soon. There's no long voyage
From here to Camelot, and I've no long fear
King Arthur will engage himself for ever
In making me a Knight of the Round Table.
King Mark . . ."

                              "And why do you mention him to me!"
She cried, forgetful of her long command

Of what she had concealed and stifled from him.
"I should have said King Mark was the last name
Of all, or all but one, that I should hear
From you today.   Were there no better days!"

"King Mark says I'm a knight, but not King Arthur—
Not yet—was all that I was going to say;
And I am not saying that because I love him—
Only that you should hear the difference
From me, and have at least some joy of it.
I shall not feel Mark's sword upon my shoulder
Again until I feel the edge of it;
And that will not befall in Camelot,
Or wheresoever I shall carry with me
One of these arms that are not useless yet."

"And where do you plan next to carry them
To prove yourself a Knight of the Round Table?"
She said, and with a flame filling her eyes
As if a soul behind them were on fire.
"What next one among thieves, with Griffon gone,
Will be the nearest to your heart's desire?"

If her lip curled a little in asking that,
Tristram was looking down and did not see it.

"Where do I plan to carry my two arms
Away with me from Camelot, do you ask?
My purpose is to bring them here with me
To Brittany—both of them, God willing so.
You are not here with me, but in the past
This afternoon, and that's not well for you.
When I'm an exile, as you know I am,
Where would your fancy drive me, if not here?
All that was long ago."

                              "So long ago,
Tristram, that you have lived for nothing else
Than for a long ago that follows you
To sleep, and has a life as long as yours.
Sometimes I wish that heaven had let you have her,
And given me back all that was left of you,
To teach and heal.   I might be sure of that.
Or, to be sure of nothing, if only sure,
Would be a better way for both of us
Than to be here together as we have been
Since Gawaine came from Cornwall in that ship."

"From Cornwall? Are you dreaming when you say it?"
He questioned her as if he too were dreaming

That she had said it; and his heart was cold.
"From Cornwall? Did you not hear Gawaine saying
That he had come for me from Camelot?
Do you see Arthur, who loves Mark almost
As hard as I do, sending ships for me
From Cornwall? If you can see things like that,
You are seeing more of that which never was
Than will be needful where we need so much
Right seeing to see ourselves. If we see others,
Let us, for God's sake, see them where they are—
Not where they were. The past, or part of it,
Is dead—or we that would be living in it
Had best be dead. Why do you say to me
That Gawaine came from Cornwall in that ship?"

There was another gleam now in her eyes
Than yesterday had been imaginable
For Tristram, even had he been strangling her
In some imagined madness. "What?" she said;
"Did I say Cornwall? If I did, perhaps
It was because I thought the sound of it
Would make you happy. So far as I'm aware,
You have not heard that name in a long time.

Did I say Cornwall?   If I did, forgive me.
I should have said that I said Camelot.
Not the same place at all."

                                        Dimly alive
To knowledge of a naked heart before him,
For him to soothe and comfort with cold lies,
He knew that lies could have no cooling virtue,
Even though they might be falling on this heart
As fast and unregarded as rain falls
Upon an angry sea.   Anger so new,
And unforetold, was hardly to be known
At first for what it was, or recognized
With more than silence.   If he recognized it,
Before him in a garden full of sunshine,
He saw it as a shadow in the night
Between him and two dark and frightened eyes
And the last look that he had seen in them,
With music shrieking always in the moonlight
Above him, and below him the long sound
Of Cornish waves that would be sounding always,
Foaming on those cold rocks.   For a long time
He saw not the white face accusing him,

And heard no sound that others might have heard
Where there was once a garden for Isolt—
Isolt of the white hands, who said no more
To him that afternoon. He left her there,
And like a man who was no longer there,
He stared over the wall, and over water
Where sunlight flashed upon a million waves,
Only to see through night, and through moonlight,
The coming after of a darker night
Than he could see, and of a longer night
Than there was time to fear. Assured of nothing,
He was too sure of all to tell more lies
In idle mercy to an angry woman
Whose unavailing alchemy of hope
No longer, or not now, found love in pity.

But with no more display of desolation
Than any one's wife among a thousand wives
Might then have made, foreseeing nothing worse
Than to be left alone for no long time,
She met him without anger in the morning,
And in the morning said farewell to him,
With trumpets blowing and hundreds cheering him:

And from a moving shore she waved at him
One of her small white hands, and smiled at him,
That all should see her smiling when he sailed
Away from her for Camelot that morning.
Gawaine, recovered early from a wound
Within a soon-recuperating heart,
Waved a gay hat on board for two gray eyes
On shore; and as the ship went farther out,
The sound of trumpets blowing golden triumph
Rang faintly and more faintly as it went,
Farther and always farther, till no sound
Was heard, and there was nothing to be seen
But a ship sailing always to the north,
And slowly showing smaller to the sight.

She watched again from the same window now
Where she had watched and waited for so long
For the slow coming of another ship
That came at last. What other ship was coming,
And after what long time and change, if ever,
No seer or wizard of the future knew,
She thought, and Tristram least of all. Far off,
The ship was now a speck upon the water,

And soon, from where she was, would not be that,
And soon was not; and there was nothing left
That day, for her, in the world anywhere,
But white birds always flying, and still flying,
And always the white sunlight on the sea.

VII

Isolt alone with time, Isolt of Ireland,
So candid and exact in her abhorrence
Of Mark that she had driven him in defeat
To favors amiable if unillusioned,
Saw, with a silent love consuming her,
A silent hate inhibiting in Mark
A nature not so base as it was common,
And not so cruel as it was ruinous
To itself and all who thwarted it.   Wherefore,
Tristram it was, Tristram alone, she knew,
That he would see alive in useless fire,
Thereafter to be haunted all his days
By vengeance unavenging.   Where was vengeance
For the deforming wounds of difference
That fate had made and hate would only canker,
And death corrupt in him till he should die?

But this was not for Mark, and she said little
To Mark of more than must in ceremony
Be said, perforce, fearing him to misread
Her deprecating pity for his birthright
For the first meltings of renunciation,
Where there was none to melt. — "If I'm so fair,
Why then was all this comely merchandise
Not sold as colts are, in a market-place,"
She asked herself.   "Then Tristram could have bought me,
Whether he feared my love was hate or not,
And whether or not he killed my uncle Morhaus."
And there were days when she would make Brangwaine
Go over the bridge and into the woods with her
To cheer her while she thought.—"If I were Queen
In this forsaken land," Brangwaine said once,
"I'd give three bags of gold to three strong men,
And let them sew King Mark into a sack,
And let them sink him into the dark sea
On a dark night, and Andred after him.
So doing, I'd welcome Erebus, and so leave
This world a better place."—"If you sew Andred
Into a sack, I'll do the rest myself,
And give you more than your three bags of gold,"

Isolt said; and a penitential laugh
Tempered an outburst that was unrepeated—
Though for a year, and almost a year after,
Brangwaine had waited. But Isolt would laugh
For her no more. The fires of love and fear
Had slowly burned away so much of her
That all there was of her, she would have said,
Was only a long waiting for an end
Of waiting—till anon she found herself,
Still waiting, where a darkening eastern sea
Made waves that in their sound along the shore
Told of a doom that was no longer fear.

Incredulous after Lancelot's departure
From Joyous Gard, Tristram, alone there now,
With a magnificence and a mystery
More to be felt than seen among the shadows
Around him and behind him, saw the ocean
Before him from the window where he stood,
And seeing it heard the sound of Cornish foam
So far away that he must hear it always
On the world's end that was for him in Cornwall.
A forest-hidden sunset filled long clouds

Eastward over the sea with a last fire,
Dim fire far off, wherein Tristram beheld
Tintagel slowly smouldering in the west
To a last darkness, while on Cornish rocks
The moan of Cornish water foamed and ceased
And foamed again. Pale in a fiery light,
With her dark hair and her dark frightened eyes,
And their last look at him, Isolt of Ireland
Above him on the stairs, with only a wall
Waist-high between her and her last escape,
Stood watching there for him who was not there.
He could feel all those endless evening leagues
Of England foiling him and mocking him
From where it was too late for him to go,
And where, if he were there, coming so late,
There would be only darkness over death
To meet his coming while she stood alone
By the dark wall, with dark fire hiding her,
Waiting—for him. She would not be there long;
She must die there in that dark fire, or fall,
Throwing herself away on those cold rocks
Where there was peace, or she must come to him
Over those western leagues, mysteriously

Defeating time and place. She might do so
If she were dead, he thought, and were a ghost,
As even by now she might be, and her body,
Where love would leave so little of earth to burn,
Might even by now be burning. So, as a ghost
It was that she would have to come to him,
On little feet that he should feel were coming.
She would be dead, but there might be no pain
In that for him when the first death of knowing
That she was dead was ended, and he should know
She had found rest. She would come back to him
Sometimes, and touch him in the night so lightly
That he might see her between sleep and waking,
And see that last look in her eyes no more—
For it would not be there.

                         It was not there.
Woman or ghost, her last look in the moonlight
Was not in her eyes now. Softly, behind him,
The coming of her steps had made him turn
To see there was no fear in her eyes now;
And whether she had come to him from death,
Or through those dark and heavy velvet curtains,

She had come to him silent and alone,
And as the living come—living or not.
Whether it was a warm ghost he was holding,
Or a warm woman, or a dream of one,
With tear-filled eyes in a slow twilight shining
Upward and into his, only to leave him
With eyes defeated of all sight of her,
Was more than he dared now let fate reveal.
Whatever it was that he was holding there,
Woman or ghost or dream, was not afraid;
And the warm lips that pressed themselves again
On his, and held them there as if to die there,
Were not dead now. The rest might be illusion—
Camelot, Arthur, Guinevere, Gawaine,
Lancelot, and that voyage with Lancelot
To Joyous Gard, this castle by the sea—
The sea itself, and the clouds over it,
Like embers of a day that like a city
Far off somewhere in time was dying alone,
Slowly, in fire and silence—the fading light
Around them, and the shadowy room that held them—
All these,—if they were shadows, let them be so,
He thought. But let these two that were not shadows

Be as they were, and live—by time no more
Divided until time for them should cease.
They were not made for time as others were,
And time therefore would not be long for them
Wherein for love to learn that in their love,
Where fate was more than time and more than love,
Time never was, save in their fear of it—
Fearing, as one, to find themselves again
Intolerably as two that were not there.

Isolt, to see him, melted slowly from him,
Moving as if in motion, or in much thought,
All this might vanish and the world go with it.
Still in his arms, and sure that she was there,
She smiled at him as only joy made wise
By sorrow smiles at fear, as if a smile
Would teach him all there was for life to know,
Or not to know. Her dark and happy eyes
Had now a darkness in them that was light;
There was no longer any fear in them,
And there was no fear living on a face
That once, too fair for beauty to endure
Without the jealous graving of slow pain.

Was now, for knowledge born of all endurance,
Only beyond endurance beautiful
With a pale fire of love where shone together
Passion and comprehension beyond being
For any long time; and while she clung to him,
Each was a mirror for the other there
Till tears of vision and of understanding
Were like a mist of wisdom in their eyes,
Lest in each other they might see too soon
All that fate held for them when Guinevere,
In a caprice of singularity
Seizing on Mark's unsafe incarceration,
Made unrevealed a journey to Cornwall,
Convoyed by two attendant eminent leeches
Who found anon the other fairest woman
Alive no longer like to stay alive
Than a time-tortured and precarious heart,
Long wooed by death, might or might not protest.
All which being true, Guinevere gave herself
Humbly to God for telling him no lies;
And Lancelot gave his conscience to God also,
As he had given it once when he had felt
The world shake as he gave it. Stronger than God,

When all was done the god of love was fate,
Where all was love. And this was in a darkness
Where time was always dying and never dead,
And where God's face was never to be seen
To tell the few that were to lose the world
For love how much or little they lost for it,
Or paid with others' pain.

                    "Isolt! Isolt!"
He murmured, as if struggling to believe
That one name, and one face there in the twilight,
Might for a moment, or a moment longer,
Defeat oblivion. How could she be with him
When there were all those western leagues of twilight
Between him and Cornwall? She was not there
Until she spoke:

                    "Tristram!" was all she said;
And there was a whole woman in the sound
Of one word surely spoken. She was there,
Be Cornwall where it was or never was,
And England all a shadow on the sea
That was another shadow, and on time

That was one shadow more. If there was death
Descending on all this, and this was love,
Death then was only another shadow's name;
And there was no more fear in Tristram's heart
Of how she fared, and there was no more pain.
God must have made it so, if it was God—
Or death, if it was death. If it was fate,
There was a way to be made terribly
For more than time, yet one that each knew well,
And said well, silently, would not be long.
How long now mattered nothing, and what there was
Was all.

        "Tristram!" She said again his name,
And saying it she could feel against herself
The strength of him all trembling like a tower
Long shaken by long storms, in darkness far
From hers, where she had been alone with it
Too long for longer fear. But that was nothing,
For that was done, and they were done with time.
It was so plain that she could laugh to see it;
And almost laughing she looked up at him,
And said once more, "Tristram!"

                                      She felt herself
Smothered and crushed in a forgetful strength
Like that of an incredulous blind giant,
Seizing amain on all there was of life
For him, and all that he had said was lost.
She waited, and he said, "Isolt! Isolt!"
He that had spoken always with a word
To spare, found hungrily that only one
Said all there was to say, till she drew more
From him and he found speech.

                                      "There are no kings
Tonight," he told her, with at last a smile,
"To make for you another prison of this—
Or none like one in Cornwall.   These two arms
Are prison enough to keep you safe in them
So long as they are mine."

                                      "They are enough,
Tristram," she said.   "All the poor kings and queens
Of time are nothing now.   They are all gone
Where shadows go, after the sun goes down.
The last of them are far away from here,

And you and I are here alone together.
We are the kings and queens of everything;
And if we die, nothing can alter that,
Or say it was not so. Before we die,
Tell me how many lives ago it was
I left you in the moonlight on those stairs,
And went up to that music and those voices,
And for God's reason then did not go mad!
Tell me how old the world was when it died—
For I have been alone with time so long
That time and I are strangers. My heart knows
That I was there too long, but knows not yet
Why I was there, or why so many alive
Are as they are. They are not with me here.
They all went when the world went. You and I
Only are left, waiting alone for God—
Down here where the world was!"

                                    Fire in her eyes,
And twilight on her warm dark-waving hair
And on a warm white face too beautiful
To be seen twice alive and still be found
Alive and white and warm and the same face,

Compelled him with her pallid happiness
To see where life had been so long the fuel
Of love, that for a season he saw nothing,
Save a still woman somewhere in a moonlight,
Where there were stairs and lamps and a cold sound
That waves made long ago. Yet she was warm
There in his arms, and she was not the ghost
He feared she was, chilling him first with doubt.

"We are the last that are alive, Isolt,
Where the world was. Somewhere surrounding us
There are dim shapes of men with many names,
And there are women that are made of mist,
Who may have names and faces. If I see them,
They are too far away for you to see.
They all went when the world went. You are the world,
Isolt—you are the world!"

                              "Whatever I am,
You are the last alive to make me listen
While you say that. You are the world, Tristram.
My worth is only what it is to you.
In Cornwall I was not appraised unduly,
Save as a queen to garnish, when essential,

A court where almost anything with a face
Would have been queen enough.   And you know best
How mu:h I was a queen.   The best I know
Is all there is to know—that some command
In heaven, or some imperial whim of mercy
Brought Guinevere to Cornwall, and brought me
Here to this place that may be real sometime,
And to your arms that must be real indeed.
Let them be real! . . . O God, Tristram! Tristram!
Where are those blindfold years that we have lost
Because a blind king bought of a blind father
A child blinder than they? She might have drawn
A knife across her throat rather than go! . . .
But no—had she done that, she would have died;
And all her seeming needlessness alive
Would have been all it seemed.   Oh, it would be
A fearful thing for me to close my eyes
Too long, and see too much that is behind me!
When they were open you might not be here.
Your arms that hold me now might not be yours,
But those of a strong monster and a stranger.
Make me believe again that you are here! . . .
Yes, you are here!"

All her firm litheness melted
Into the sure surrender of a child
When she said that; and her dark eyes became
For a dim moment gray, and were like eyes
That he had left behind in Brittany.
Another moment, and they were dark again,
And there was no such place as Brittany.
Brittany must have died when the world died—
The world, and time. He had forgotten that,
Till he found now, insensibly almost,
How soft and warm and small so proud a queen
As this Isolt could be. Dimly deceived
By the dark surety of her stateliness
And by the dark indignity of distance,
His love may not have guessed how this Isolt
Of Ireland, with her pride that frightened kings,
Should one day so ineffably become
So like a darker child for him to break
Or save, with a word hushed or a word spoken;
And so his love may well never have seen
How surely it was fate that his love now
Should light with hers at the last fire of time
A flaming way to death. Fire in her eyes,

And sorrow in her smile, foretold unsaid
More than he saw.

                              "You are not sad that heaven
Should hide us here together, God knows how long,
And surely are not fearful," he said, smiling.
"Before there was a man or woman living,
It was all chronicled with nights and days
That we should find each other tonight like this,
There was no other way for love like ours
To be like this than always to have been.
Your love that I see looking into mine
Might have in it a shining of more knowledge
Than love needs to be wise; and love that's wise
Will not say all it means.   Untimely words,
Where love and wisdom are not quarrelling,
Are good words not to say."

                              "If you see wisdom
Shining out of my eyes at you sometime,
Say it is yours, not mine.   Untimely words
Are not for love, and are like frost on flowers
Where love is not for long.   When we are done

With time, Tristram, nothing can be for long.
You would know that if you had been a woman
Alone in Cornwall since those lights went out,
And you went down those stairs. Sometime I'll ask
How far you wandered and what rainy end
There ever was to that unending night,
But now I shall not ask an answer more
Of you than this, or more of God than this;
For this is all—no matter for how long.
Do not forget, my love, that once Isolt
Said that; and wheresoever she may be then,
See her where she is now—alone with you,
And willing enough to be alone in heaven—
Or hell, if so it be—and let you live
Down hére without her for a thousand years,
Were that the way of happiness for you,
Tristram. So long as fate itself may find
No refuge or concealment or escape
From heaven for me save in some harm for you.
I shall not be unhappy after this."

"He that pays all for all is past all harm,"
He said, "I can forgive your thousand years,

And you are sorry for them.   The one harm
Deserving a fantastic apprehension
Is one that surely cannot come tonight.
Only an army of infernal men—
And they would not be men—will find a way
Over these walls, or through them, to find me—
Or you, tonight.   Untimely words again,
But only as a folly to match yours
In feigning harm for me.   Dear God in heaven!
If one such reptile thought inhabited
A nature that was never mine before,
Some woman at hand should watch you properly
While I, like Judas, only running faster,
Might hang myself."

                           He felt her body throbbing
As if it held a laugh buried alive,
And suddenly felt all his eloquence
Hushed with her lips.   Like a wild wine her love
Went singing through him and all over him;
And like a warning her warm loveliness
Told him how far away it would all be
When it was warm no longer.   For some time

He was a man rather by dread possessed
Than by possession, when he found again
That he was listening to the blended gold
And velvet that was always in her voice:

"Your meditations are far wanderers,
And you must have them all home before dark;
Or I shall find myself at work to learn
What's in me so to scatter them. Dear love,
If only you had more fear for yourself
You might, for caution, be my cause for less.
My cage is empty, and I'm out of it;
And you and I are in another cage—
A golden cage—together. Reason it is,
Not fear, that lets me know so much as that;
Also, the while you care not for yourself
Where shadows are, there are things always walking.
Meanwhile your fear for me has been a screen
Of distance between me and my destruction—
Mine, love, and yours. Fears are not always blind.
If love be blind, mine has been so for watching
Too long across an empty world for you;
And if it be myself now that is blind,

I may still hide myself somewhere alone—
Somewhere away from you. Whatever we are,
We are not so blind that we are not to know
The darkness when it comes, if it must come.
We are not children teasing little waves
To follow us along a solid shore.
I see a larger and a darker tide,
Somewhere, than one like that. But where and when,
I do not wish to see."

                    "If love that's blind,"
He said, holding her face and gazing at it,
"Sees only where a tide that's dark and large
May be somewhere sometime, love that has eyes
Will fix itself, and with a nearer wonder,
Upon Isolt—who is enough to see.
Isolt alone. All else that emulates
And envies her—black faggots in red flame,
A sunshine slanting into a dark forest,
A moonlight on white foam along black ledges,
Sunlight and rain, trees twinkling after rain,
Panthers and antelopes, children asleep—
All these are native elsewhere, and for now

Are not important. Love that has eyes to see
Sees now only Isolt. Isolt alone.
Isolt, and a few stars."

                    "Were I the shadow
Of half so much as this that you are seeing
Of me, I should not be Isolt of Ireland,
Or any Isolt alive. All you can see
Of me is only what the Lord accomplished
When he made me for love. When he made you.
His love remembered that; and whether or not
His way was the most merciful, he knows—
Not we. Or was it fate, stronger than all?
A voice within me says that God, seeing all,
Was more compassionate than to let love see
Too far—loving his world too well for that.
We do not have to know—not yet. The flower
That will have withered from the world for ever
With us, will die sometime; and when it fades,
And dies, and goes, we shall have gone already,
And it will all be done. If I go first,
No fear of your forgetting shall attend me,
Leaving with you the mind and heart of love—

The love that knows what most it will remember.
If I lose you, I shall not have to wait—
Not long. There will be only one thing then
Worth waiting for. No, I shall not wait long . . .
I have said that. Now listen, while I say this:
My life to me is not a little thing;
It is a fearful and a lovely thing;
Only my love is more."

                              "God knows," he said,
"How far a man may be from his deserving
And yet be fated for the undeserved.
I might, were I the lord of your misgivings,
Be worthier of them for destroying them;
And even without the mightiness in me
For that, I'll tell you, for your contemplation,
Time is not life. For many, and many more,
Living is mostly for a time not dying—
But not for me. For me, a few more years
Of shows and slaughters, or the tinsel seat
Of a small throne, would not be life. Whatever
It is that fills life high and full, till fate
Itself may do no more, it is not time.
Years are not life."

              "I have not come so far
To learn," she said, and shook her head at him,
"What years are, for I know. Years are not life;
Years are the shells of life, and empty shells
When they hold only days, and days, and days.
God knows if I know that—so let it pass.
Let me forget; and let me ask you only
Not to forget that all your feats at arms,
Your glamour that is almost above envy,
Your strength and eminence and everything,
Leave me a woman still—a one-love woman,
Meaning a sort of ravenous one-child mother,
Whose one-love pictures in her composition
Panthers and antelopes, children asleep,
And all sorts of engaging animals
That most resemble a much-disordered queen,
Her crown abandoned and her hair in peril,
And she herself a little deranged, no doubt,
With too much happiness. Whether he lives
Or dies for her, he tells her is no matter,
Wherefore she must obediently believe him.
All he would ask of her would be as easy
As hearing waves, washing the shore down there

For ever, and believing herself drowned.
In seeing so many of her, he might believe her
To be as many at once as drops of rain;
Perhaps a panther and a child asleep
At the same time."

                              He saw dark laughter sparkling
Out of her eyes, but only until her face
Found his, and on his mouth a moving fire
Told him why there was death, and what lost song
Ulysses heard, and would have given his hands
And friends to follow and to die for.   Slowly,
At last, the power of helplessness there was
In all that beauty of hers that was for him,
Breathing and burning there alone with him,
Until it was almost a part of him,
Suffused his passion with a tenderness
Attesting a sealed certainty not his
To cozen or wrench from fate, and one withheld
In waiting mercy from oblivious eyes—
His eyes and hers, that over darker water,
Where darker things than shadows would be coming,
Saw now no more than more stars in the sky.

He felt her throbbing softly in his arms,
And held her closer still—with half a fear
Returning that she might not be Isolt,
And might yet vanish where she sat with him,
Leaving him there alone, with only devils
Of hell supplanting her.

               "Leave me the stars
A little longer," said Isolt. "In Cornwall,
So much alone there with them as I was,
One sees into their language and their story.
They must be more than fire; and if the stars
Are more than fire, what else is there for them
To be than love? I found all that myself;
For when a woman is left too much alone,
Sooner or later she begins to think;
And no man knows what then she may discover."

"Whether she be in Cornwall, or not there,
A woman driven to thinking of the stars
Too hard is in some danger," he said, sighing,
"Of being too much alone wherever she is."

Her face unseen, she smiled, hearing him sigh—
So much as if all patient chivalry

Were sighing with him. "One alone too long
In Cornwall has to think somewhat," she said,
"Or one may die. One may do worse than die.
If life that comes of love is more than death,
Love must be more than death and life together."

"Whether I know that life is more or not
Than death," he said, "I swear, with you for witness—
You and the stars—that love is more than either."

"If I should have to answer twice to that,
I should not let myself be here with you
Tonight, with all the darkness I see coming
On land and over water." Then she ceased,
And after waiting as one waits in vain
For distant voices that are silent, "Tell me!"
She cried, seizing him hard and gazing at him,
"Tell me if I should make you go away!
I'm not myself alone now, and the stars
All tell me so."

            He plucked her clinging hands
From his arms gently, and said, holding them,

"You cannot make me go away from you,
Isolt, for I believe, with you to tell me,
All your stars say. But never mind what they say
Of shadows coming. They are always coming—
Coming and going like all things but one.
Love is the only thing that in its being
Is what it seems to be. Glory and gold,
And all the rest, are weak and hollow staves
For even the poor to lean on. We know that—
We that have been so poor while grinning hinds
And shining wenches with all crowns to laugh at,
Have envied us, know that. Yet while you see
So many things written for you in starry fire,
Somehow you fear that I may lose my vision
Not seeing them. I shall not be losing it—
Not even in seeing beyond where you have seen.
Yes, I have seen your stars. You are the stars!
You are the stars when they all sing together.
You live, you speak, and you have not yet vanished.
You are Isolt—or I suppose you are!"

He was not sure of her not vanishing
Until he felt her tears, and her warm arms

Holding him with a sudden strength of love
That would have choked him had it not been love.
Each with unyielding lips refused the other
Language unasked; and their forgotten ears
Knew only as a murmur not remembered
A measured sea that always on the sand
Unseen below them, where time's only word
Was told in foam along a lonely shore,
Poured slowly its unceasing sound of doom—
Unceasing and unheard, and still unheard,
As with an imperceptible surrender
They moved and found each other's eyes again,
Burning away the night between their faces.

"Sometimes I fear that I shall fear for you
No more," she said; and to his ears her words
Were shaken music. "Why should I fear for you,
Or you for me, where nothing of earth is left,
Nothing of earth or time, that is worth fearing?
Sometimes I wonder if we are not like leaves
That have been blown by some warm wind of heaven
Far from the tree of life, still to be living
Here between life and death."

                                            "Why do those two
Vainglorious and abysmal little words
Pursue you and torment your soul?" said he.
"They are the serpents and uncertainties
That coil and rustle tonight among your fears,
Only because your fears have given to them
A shape without a substance.   Life and death?
Do not believe your stars if they are saying
That any such words are in their language now.
Whenever they tell you they are made of love,
Believe it; and forget them when they tell you
Of this or that man's living a thousand years.
Why should he wish to live a thousand years?
Whether your stars are made of love or fire,
There is a love that will outshine the stars.
There will be love when there are no more stars.
Never mind what they say of darkness coming
That may come sometime, or what else they say
Of terrors hidden in words like life and death.
What do they mean?   Never mind what they mean!
We have lived and we have died, and are alone
Where the world has no more a place for us,
Or time a fear for us, or death . . . Isolt!"

Her lips again had hushed him, and her name,
As when first he had found her in his arms,
Was all there was to say till he was saying
Muffled and husky words that groped and faltered,
Half silenced in a darkness of warm hair:
"Whatever it is that brings us here tonight,
Never believe—never believe again—
Your fear for me was more than love. Time lied,
If he said that. When we are done with time,
There is no time for fear. It was not fear—
It was love's other name. Say it was that!
Say to me it was only one of time's lies!
Whatever it was—never mind what it was!
There will be time enough for me to die.
Never mind death tonight. . . . Isolt! Isolt!"

VIII

Albeit the sun was high, the breath of morning
Was in the trees where Tristram stood alone
With happiness, watching a bright summer sea
That like a field of heaving steel and silver
Flashed there below him, and as harmlessly
As if an ocean had no darker work

To do than flash, and was to bear thereafter
No other freight than light. Joy sang in him
Till he could sing for joy, and would have done so,
Had not the lowly fear that humbles princes
Constrained him and so hindered him from giving
A little too much to those who served and feared him,
And willingly would listen; wherefore, turning
Away from the white music the waves made,
He lost himself again in a small forest,
Admiring the new miracle of the leaves,
And hearing, if one bird sang, as many as ten.
Now he could see once more the walls and towers
Of Joyous Gard over the tops of oaks
Before him; and while he stared at their appearance,
A cold familiar fear of the unreal
Seized him and held him fixed, like one awaiting
Some blast of magic that would shake them down
To dust, and all within them, and Isolt.
He saw the night-like hair and the white arms
And the wet-shining eyes that half asleep
Had laughed at him again before he left them,
Still shining and still sleepy; and for the while
He saw them, he saw neither towers nor walls;

And for a moment while he could see nothing,
He was not large enough to hold his heart.
But soon he smiled, seeing where nothing yet
Had crashed or vanished, or was like to fail him,
And moved along slowly around the place
To a green field that like a sea of land
Lay flecked and shadowed by the summer wind
That swept it, saying nothing of how soon
Or late the trampling feet of men and horses
Would make a sorry shambles of it all,
And for another queen. He wandered on,
And the green grass was music as he walked—
Until beyond it there were trees again,
And through them was the sea, still silver-white,
And flashing as before. Wherever he looked,
He saw dark eyes and hair and a white face
That was not white, but was the color of love;
Or that was near enough to being a name,
He thought—or might have thought, had he been thinking—
For that which had no name. To think at all
Would be a more perfidious insolence
To fate, he felt, than to forget the sun
That shone this morning down on Joyous Gard,

Where now there was all joy. He felt it shining,
And throughout time and space he felt it singing;
He felt and heard it moving on the grass
Behind him, and among the moving trees
Around him, and along the foaming shore,
And in the ocean where he splashed and swam
Like a triumphant and almighty fish,
Relinquishing the last concern of earth,
Save one that followed him. Below the waves
There were dark laughing eyes and faintly seen
Phantasmal flashings and white witcheries,
Like those of a dim nixie to be trusted
Never to drown him, or not willingly,
Nor to deceive him. For the time it takes
For joy to think of death and to forget it,
He thought of himself drowned. But when his head
Came up and above water, and he was blind
At first with many a shaft of laughing fire,
All shot from somewhere out of violet eyes,
He had thought long enough. Some day or other
He might think more of it, but for some time
He was to live not thinking of his end,
Or thinking of it he was not to live.

On shore again, he wished all mortal choice,
If choice there was, might come only to that.
Whatever it was that filled life high and full,
It was not time. So he had told Isolt
Under the stars; and so he told himself
Under the trees, and was believing it
With all his might and main. Something on him
Had fallen, in all appearance, that fell not
On men that for one reason or another
Were to fill life with time. He stretched his arms,
Laughing to be alive; and over his head
Leaves in the wind that gave them a gay voice
Flickered and ticked with laughter, saying to him.
"Tristram, it is for you to stay or go.
You will not go. If you leave all there is
That fate calls yours—one jewel of a lustre
More than of earth and of all else on earth,
Glowing in more than gold—the gods that live
In trees will tell the others, and there shall be
No place prepared in heaven or hell for one
Who failed in seeing until too late to see,
That for the sake of living it was his life
And all there was of life that he was leaving.

Probably you will not live very long
If you stay here; and the gods who live in trees
Care little how long man lives." He laughed again
To think of that, and heard the leaves and waves
Laughing to think of that.   Like a man lost
In paradise, and before his time to die,
He wandered inland, much at ease with fate,
And in precarious content secure.

Security, the friendly mask of change
At which we smile, not seeing what smiles behind it,
For days and nights, and for more days and nights,
And so for more and more, was unmolested
Through a long vigil over Joyous Gard;
And no dark thunder coming from the west,
Or lightning, shook security, or seared it,
Or touched those walls and towers with even a flick
Significant of irruption or invasion.
He who had laughed at what the laughing trees
Had said, may have laughed well.

                    Summer was going,
When one day Tristram, having heard pleasantly

Isolt's half-hearted and by now less frequent
Reversion to the inveterate whether or not
Of her deserting him in time to save him,
Or of his vanishing, said, stroking her
As if she were some admirable cat,
"Whenever I set myself to count the pounds
Of beauty you have for your not having them,—
Through fear for me, perhaps,—I could affirm
That your disturbance has a virtue in it,
Which I had not foreseen.   Were you too happy,
Your face might round itself like a full fruit,
And all those evanescent little planes
And changes that are like celestial traps
To catch and hold and lose the flying lights
And unseen shadows that make loveliness,
Might go—or rather might not be left the same;
Although if I saw you deformed and twisted,
You would still be the same."

                              "Dear child of thought,
Who forgets nothing if we give him time,"
She said, "if you saw me deformed and twisted,
You might sail back to Brittany so fast

That all the little fishes would be frightened.
Never persuade yourself that you believe
Or need believe, so boundlessly as that.
You will be happier if you leave to me
The love of someone else's imperfections.
I know—but never mind that. It will not come.
We are not for the fireside, or for old age
In any retreat of ancient stateliness.
If that were so, then this would not be so.
Yet when this fragment of your longer life
Has come and gone, it will have come and gone.
There is no doubt of that; and unseen years
May tell your memory more of me than love
May let you know today. After those years
In Cornwall, where my fire of life burned lower
Than you have ever known, I can say this.
Mine is a light that will go out sometime,
Tristram. I am not going to be old.
There is a little watchman in my heart
Who is always telling me what time it is.
I'll say this once to you, and never but once,
To tell you better why harm, for my poor sake,
Must not be yours. I could believe it best—

If I could say it—to say it was all over.
There is your world outside, all fame and banners,
And it was never mine to take from you.
You must not let me take your world away
From you, after all this. Love is not that.
Before you are much older, I suppose
You will go back to Brittany, where Isolt—
That other Isolt—will think, and some day know.
Women are not so bitter if once they know,
And if the other is dead. Now forget that,
And kiss me as if we were to live for ever.
Perhaps we shall, somewhere."

                                          She smiled at him
And shivered, and they were silent for a while.
Then she said, "Do not say it. You'll only say
That if I lost my ears and had no hair,
And I had whelks and moles all over my face,
Your love would be the same as it is now—
So let's believe, and leave it. And if not that,
Your love would find new benefits and rewards
In losing all for me—while yet there's time
Not to lose all. If you think only of me,

You may forget how far a king's arm reaches,
And what reprisals he may buy with gold
And golden promises."

                              "May the kings all
Be damned," he said, "and their reprisals also.
If this that you have hidden from me so well
Hides truth within it—and may God say no!—
I shall have one more right, if more be needed,
Never to let you go while I'm alive.
Tell me you said it only to be sure
There was no truth in it."

                              She said no more,
And only smiled again, shaking her head,
While in her calm and shining eyes he found
Another last look; and it was not like one
That he had seen before and had remembered
Ever since that cold moonlight on those stairs,
And those cold waves below. But though the way
She looked at him this time, and all she told
So silently, and all she did not tell,
Was not forgotten, security remained

Unchanging, and a friendly sentinel;
And neither, as with a hush of understanding,
Save with unwilling eyes now and again,
Said more of shadows; and while autumn came,
Tristram would see no cloud, or a cloud coming,
Between them and the sun. Whether it rained
Or not, the sun was always shining there,
Or wheresoever the hour might find him riding,
Or sailing home with singing fishermen,
Or losing himself in forage of new scenes,
Alone, for the sheer joy of being alone
And seeing Isolt behind him with Brangwaine
And Gouvernail, and with almost a town
Of Lancelot's men and women to attend them.

Love must have wings to fly away from love,
And to fly back again. So Tristram's love,
And Tristram with it, flew, for the sake of flying,
Far as it would; and if he fared alone
Through mist and rain, there were two violet eyes
That made of mist and rain a pleasant fire,
Warming him as he went. If on the sea
That fell and rose interminably around him,

His manful avocation was to feign
Escape from blue-black waves of Irish hair,
There were no other waves worth mentioning.
And if allured by unfamiliar scenes
And distances, he found himself astray,
Or comfortably lost, there was no red
That any western sky might show so fair
Beyond the world as one that was still on it,
A red that mixed itself alive with white,
Never the same way twice. It mantled now
Fairer than phantom flame in a white face
That was itself a phantom, and yet so real
That seeing it fade and smile and fade again,
He trembled, wondering still and still assured
That not far off, and always waiting for him
In Joyous Gard, while he saw pictures of her
That were almost Isolt alive to see,
There was Isolt alive that he could feel
When his hands touched her, and find musical
When his heart listened. There were other women
Who murmured peradventure for men's ears
To hear, yet while his own were not engaged
Or implicated they were ghosts of women,

Dumb in a hell of men that had no ears,
For all they were to him—albeit his love
Of everything, where everything was Isolt,
Would not have had that so.

                      Having outwalked
His hours, he yielded to the setting sun,
And soon enhancing for the eyes of man
With gold of earth, and with his exaltation,
The distant gold of heaven, he borrowed a horse
For a journey, never alone, through falling shadows
And falling leaves. Back to the walls and towers
He went that now held heaven and all but God
To welcome him with wild and happy eyes
And dark hair waving over them, and a flame
Of red that in the firelight was immersed
In burning white, white fire and red together,
And her white arms to hold him while she asked
Where he had been, what insects he had seen,
And who was king of Salem. Leaves and flowers,
Wild roses for Isolt, encumbered him,
But were no bulk or burden as on he rode,
Singing, and seeing always in the firelight

He should find shining at his journey's end—
Isolt, always Isolt. She was not there,
He fancied, smiling; she had never been there,
Save in a dream of his; the towers and walls
Of Joyous Gard were only a dream of his;
But heaven had let him dream for a whole summer,
And he was dreaming still as he rode through
The silent gate, where there were silent men
Who looked at him as if he were a stranger,
Whose tongue was none of theirs. Troubled and vexed,
He felt the stillness of a difference
In their attention, as for some defect
Or lapse of his that he could not remember;
And saying a word about a stranger's horse,
He passed them on his way to the still door
Where joy so often entered and came out.
A wonted sense of welcome failing him,
He summoned it from the twilight on the stairs
And half began to sing with a dry throat
That held no song. He entered the same room
Where first Isolt had found him waiting for her,
And where, since then, he had so often found
Isolt, waiting for him. She was not there—

And that was strange. She was not always there,
But it was strange that she was not there now.
He stared about him, wondering that one room,
Holding so many things that he had seen,
And seen again, should hold at the same time
So much of silence. What had happened there?
Where were those arms, and the dark happy eyes,
Always half wet with joy at sight of him?
He made himself insist that he could smile
While helpless drops of fear came out of him,
And he asked of his heart that beat so hard
Why he should be afraid. It was no mark
In his experience to be found afraid,
But he could find no name warmer than fear
For the cold sickness that was in him now,
Although he named it only to disown it.
"A woman may not be always in one place,"
He thought, and said, "Isolt!" She was not there.
He saw the chimney, and saw no fire was there—
And that was strange. It was not always there,
But there or not there, it should be there now.
"And all fires are not lighted at one time,"
He thought, and said, "Isolt!" There was no sound

In this room, or the next room, or the next;
There was no sound anywhere in the whole house—
Except the pounding of his heart, which felt
To him as if it were the whole of him.
He was afraid, and done with all disowning,
And perilously was not afraid of that.
"Is not one here who dares to answer me?"
He muttered slowly, but he could not move—
Not even when he believed that he heard something
Alive behind the heavy velvet curtain
Where he had heard Isolt, so long ago
That now it seemed that she might never have come,
If now she were not gone. For a gasp of time
That only fooled him to a surer knowing
That this was not Isolt, he told himself
It was—like a man dying who lies to life
For the last empty joy of a last lie.
The sound he heard was not the mouse-like noise
That mice and women make. Be what it might,
He scarcely heard it; and not heeding it,
He stood alone with his hands hanging clenched,
More like a man of bronze than a man breathing,
Until he shook and would have swayed and fallen

Had he not stumbled heavily to a couch
That filled a corner filled already with shadows.
Sitting inert upon the edge of it,
He sent a searching gaze all over the room,
Seeing everything but the one thing he strove
To see; and last he stared upon the floor
Before him, where lay scattered some wild flowers,
Wild roses for Isolt, and saw them there
As if they were a thousand miles away.
Then he looked up again, turning his face
Enough to see in the same room with him,
Rigid and silent, like a friend ordained
To strike again a friend already stricken,
Gawaine from Camelot. Tristram arose,
Propping himself with pride and courtesy,
And stood there waiting for Gawaine to tell him
As much as he might tell.

                   "I have come too late."
He said; and then the look of Tristram vanquished
And routed the battalion of brave words
That he had mustered. "And for that I'm sorry.
Mark is abroad again, and has been free

For just how long the devil himself may know.
The Queen was by the shore, under some trees,
Where she would sit for hours alone sometimes,
Watching the ocean—or so Brangwaine says—
Alone and happy. Your wits will see the rest.
They carried her off with them in a small boat,
And now she's on a ship that sails to Cornwall.
I do not know a land that has a law
Whereby a man may follow a king's ship
For the king's wife, and have a form of welcome
Better than battle. You are not trimmed for that.
Forgive me—we did all we could. I am here,
And here too late. If I were you, I fancy,
I should tear one more leaf out of my book,
And let the next new page be its own story."

Each word of Gawaine's, falling like a blow
Dealt viciously by one unseen, fell slowly,
And with a not premeditated aim,
So accurate and unfailing in its proof
That when the last had fallen—without reply,
And without time to summon will or reason,
Tristram, the loud accredited strong warrior,

Tristram, the learned Nimrod among hunters,
Tristram, the loved of women, the harp-player,
Tristram, the doom of his prophetic mother,
Dropped like a log; and silent on the floor,
With wild flowers lying around him on the floor—
Wild roses for Isolt—lay like a log.

Gawaine, Brangwaine, and Gouvernail all waited
By the couch where they had laid him, but no words
Of any resigned allegiance to a fate
That ruled all men acknowledging its rewards,
And its ingratitudes and visitations,
Were on his tongue to say; and in his eyes
There was no kind of light that any one there
Had seen in them before.   After long time,
He stared at Brangwaine, and his lips moved once,
Trying to speak, but he said nothing then;
And he said nothing that was heard that night
By man or woman.

                    There was a week gone by
When Gawaine, less obscured at each day's end
In his confusions, and far less at home
Than ever, saw fit to feel that his return

Was urging him away. His presence there
Was no contagious good that he could see,
And he felt lonely and unnecessary.
There was no Tristram left that he remembered;
Brangwaine, whenever she saw him, did not see him;
And Gouvernail, to one who had always lived
For life, was only gloom looking for death,
And no right company for Gawaine. Brangwaine,
He learned, was going away with him tomorrow,
As far as Camelot, and he sighed to say so,
Seeing how fair she was. "Brangwaine, Gawaine, . . .
A deal of music in this world is wasted,"
He thought, "because a woman cries and kills it.
They've taken away Isolt, Tristram is mad,
Or dead, or God knows what's the name of it,
And all because a woman had eyes and ears,
And beauty enough to strike him dumb with it.
Why must a man, where there are loaves and fishes,
See only as far as one crumb on his table?
Why must he make one morsel of a lifetime?
Here is no place for me. If this be love,
May I live all alone out on a rock,
And starve out there with only the sea to drink,

And only myself to eat. If this be love,
May I wear blinkers always, or better yet,
Go blindfold through the perils of this world,
Which I have always liked, and so, God help me,
Be led to safety like a hooded horse
Through sparks and unseen fire. If this be love,
May I grow merry and old and amiable
On hate. I'll fix on someone who admires me,
And sting him, and then hate him all my days.
'Gawaine, Brangwaine,' —what else is that than song?
If I were a musician, and had leisure,
I'd surely some day make a tune of it.
'Brangwaine, Gawaine.' " He frowned upon events,
And sighed again that men were not alike.
" 'Gawaine, Brangwaine,' " Brangwaine was fair to see,
And life, while he could sing, was not very long,
And woe not his annoyed him.

       Gawaine went
With all his men, and Brangwaine, the next day;
And Tristram, like a statue that was moving,
Still haunted Joyous Gard, where Gouvernail,
Disconsolate, and half scared out of sorrow,
Followed and feared, and waited for a sound

Of more than Yes or No. So for a month
He waited, hearing nothing of life without,
Barring a word from Camelot of Isolt
In Cornwall, and alive. He told Tristram,
And Tristram said, "Alive!" Saying no more,
He watched the waves with eyes where Gouvernail
Saw not what he would see in them. The light
That had been Tristram was gone out of them,
And Tristram was not there, even when he spoke,
Saying at last, "This is not good for you,
Gouvernail. You are not my friend for this.
Go back to Brittany and forget all this."
Gouvernail's ears were glad and his heart danced
To hear so many words, but long days passed
And went before he heard so many again.
Then came a letter which a stranger brought,
Who, seeing it held by Tristram, rode away,
Saying his work was done. With avid hands
And eyes half blind with hope, he tore it open,
To make whatever he would of words like these:

"Greeting, Sir Tristram, Prince of Lyonesse.
It was a joy to share with you a house

Where I was once. That was a pleasant house,
Say what you will of it; and it was pleasant
Of me to make you safe and comfortable,
Say what you will of that. This will be sent
For your distinguished and abused attention
From my domain, here in this land of Gore,
Which is my land, and is a pleasant land,
As you may say of it yourself sometime.
More to the salt and essence, there's a lady
Alive in Cornwall—or she was alive—
Who is alone and sore bestead, I fear me,
Amort for love of you. If you go soon—
Too soon you cannot go, if you would see her—
And are not burned alive, or flayed alive,
Or otherwise hindered or invalidated,
You may behold once more that Irish hair,
And those same Irish eyes that once engaged
And occupied you to your desperation.
I cannot answer on more authority
Than hope for your reception or return,
But you, being orgulous and full as an egg
Of fate, may find a way through fire and steel
To see that face again. Were I a man,

And were I thus apprised as to the lady,
I should anon be rowelling my good horse,
And on my way to Cornwall.   Peace be with you,
And may no evil await or overtake you.
Farewell, Sir Tristram, Prince of Lyonesse."

Too sorely stricken already to feel stings,
Tristram, with Morgan's letter crushed and wrinkled,
Sat unresponsive, seeing, wherever he gazed,
Foam breaking, and dark stairs, and two dark eyes,
Frightened and wild again as when they left him
That night when he left them.   When he would see
No more of them, he said to Gouvernail,
"Tomorrow I shall go for a far journey,
And may go farther still.   So, Gouvernail,
Go back to Brittany and forget all this,
And tell them there that they were not forgotten.
Nothing that I can send or say to her
Will do much good.   And if I lied to her,
She might remember me—only for that.
Tell her that I meant always to be kind—
And that's a little to tell.   Say there was more
Than I was, or am yet, to be between us—
And that's a little to say to her.   But say it."

"Sometime I will, Tristram, but not tomorrow.
Tomorrow I go with you, unless you kill me,"
Gouvernail said, "and that would be a little
For you to do. I have seen in and out,
And I'm as wise today as when my mother
Was glad because I cried that I was born.
Your mother was not, you say. Well, perhaps not."

IX

Against a parapet that overlooked
The sea, lying now like sound that was asleep,
King Mark sat gazing at Isolt's white face,
Mantled no more with red, and pale no longer
With life. The poor dominion that was his
Of her frail body was not revenge enough
To keep even hate alive, or to feed fury.
There was a needlessness about it now
That fury had not foreseen, and that foresight
Would never have forestalled. The sight of her,
Brought back to him a prisoner by his men
From Joyous Gard, and her first look at him,
Had given to death a smallness, and to life,
Ready for death, an uncomplaining triumph

Like nothing of his.   There might be Tristram dead
By stealth, yet there would always be that face—
Isolt's white face.   He saw it now, and said,
"I am not looking to you for much regard,
Though you might let your eyes, if not your tongue,
Say where I am.   Do they know that I am here?
Why are you looking at the sea so long?"

"The sea was never so still as this before,"
She said.   "It is like something after life,
And it is not like death.   That ship out there
Is like two ships, and one of them a shadow.
When you came, I was asking if the shadow
Might not, if only we knew shadows better,
Be the real ship.   I am not very well;
And lately I've had fancies.   Do not mind them.
I have never seen the sea so still as this."

"Perhaps the sea is like ourselves," Mark said,
"And has as much to say of storms and calms
That shake or make it still, as we have power
To shake or to be still.   I do not know.
I was just saying it for no harm or reason.
I shall do no more harm to either of you

Hereafter, and cannot do more to myself.
I should have lost my nature not to take you
Away from him—but now, having you here,
I'm not so sure of nature as once I was.
If it were fate for man here to be sure,
He might not stay so long. I do not know.
All I know now is that you sent for me,
And that I've told you all, or I believe so,
That you would hear me say. A month ago,
He might have stepped from folly to sure death,
Had his blind feet found Cornwall. But not now.
Your gates and doors are open. All I ask
Is that I shall not see him."

                              Isolt said then,
"There was a time when I should have told God
Himself that he had made you without mercy.
Forgive me that. For there was your side, always;
There were your ways, which are the ways of kings;
And there was blindness everywhere at first—
When there was all that time! You are kind now,
And I thank God that you are merciful."
"When there is nothing left for us to lose,

There's no great mercy in our not losing it,"
He said. "God will not hear you if you thank him
Only for that. A weary spark of sense,
Or a dull feel of reason, is not mercy.
I have not changed. I'm only some days older
Than when they brought you back from there—brought you
And your white face together. You looked at me,
And I saw your white face."

                        She smiled at him,
And touched his hand with hers: "You are good to me.
Whatever you do, I shall not be here long.
Whatever you are, you have been good to me.
I shall not be afraid of you again—
No, nor of Andred. When he knows of this,
He will bow down to your authority
Like a small hungry dog and lick your fingers.
And all his insane hatred for Tristram,
And all his worse than insane love for me . . .
Poor loveless atom!"

                    "Andred?" Mark said. scowling,
And went on with a hoarse unhappy laugh:
"Morgan, when she was here, was playing with him

So much like a damned cat that I believed
His love, if you say love, was all for her.
I wondered that she wasted so much guile
Upon so little grace. The fellow is mad.
I should have seen that he was always mad.
We were all mad—that night. I should have seen.
I should have seen . . ." He rose and stalked along
Before the parapet, and back again;
Then, with a groan that savored of a snarl,
He cried, "God knows what else I should have seen!
Had I been made with eyes to read in the dark
All that was written there, I might have seen,
By straining them, some such effect as this.
How could I see where there was nothing shown
Or told for me to see? There was yourself,
But I believed that home was in your eyes,
Rather than hate, and that a crown to wear
Would outshine all your tears. Had I known early
All that I knew too late . . . I do not know.
I am not sure."

               "Whether you are or are not,"
She said, "you have been kind to me today.
You will not live, though you should live for ever,

To wish this kindness back. You might have given
Me nothing, and I should not have wondered more
Than I have wondered at your giving me this.
I should have suffered, and not thought it strange.
There was a cloud that covered us all, and now
You have been kind. If it was fate, we'll say
Bad fate was like bad weather. Oh, it is hard,
With such a stillness lying on everything
Today, to say that storms have ever been."

"There have been storms enough to sink us all,
And drown us. Yet we are still here afloat—
Here, or somewhere. Not even that ship you see
Will be there always."

       "And ships in their last port,"
She said, "have still a farther voyage to make,
Wherever it is they go. Were it not for love,
Poor life would be a ship not worth a launching.
Is it not true?"

       "I do not know," Mark said;
And for a long time stared upon the sea,
Which told him nothing.

                                    Isolt, watching him there,
And with a furtive sorrow in her heart
For one that was foredoomed to be himself,
Felt presently the coming of quick feet
Up the stone stairs within the walls behind her;
And turning where she lay, saw Brangwaine's fingers
Upon her lips, and saw more in her eyes
Than joy alone, or fear. Only one thing
Was there in life remaining to mean either;
And the wild red came back to Isolt's cheeks,
And to her throat.

                          "He is waiting," Brangwaine said,
"And has the manner, if I may dare to say so,
Of one who should not wait."

                              "Why should he wait?"
Mark answered, with a sullen glance at her;
And then, after one long unhappy look
At where Isolt was lying—or now half lying—
Went through the doorway and led Brangwaine with him,
Leaving Isolt alone to watch the sea
Until there was no sea, and she saw nothing—

Not·even when she felt arms shaking that held her,
And his lips, after so long, on hers again,
And on her cheeks and eyes. When she could see,
She shrank a little away from him for love
And wonder, and then for love and fear she drew
His face down to her heart and held it there
While her heart ached and it seemed right to die.
Searching his eyes to find him, she said only,
"I shall hear all you do not say to me,
Tristram. For you are only one man still,
Which is a thing that one man may forget.
You forget rest."

        "I shall remember it—
Sometime," he said. "When rest remembers me,
There will be time for that. I shall have rest."
Then he sat still, holding her hands as lightly
As if they were two leaves, and stared at her
Like a man back from death. "What has Mark done
That I should find his doors all open for me,
And see no swords, or fire? You have done this.
There is no other woman, and no man,
To do it. I can see now. The king of hell

Would not refuse, if your eyes asked him now,
To open the doors of hell."

　　　　　　　　　　"They are all open,
Tristram, and I shall not go out of them—
Or I shall not go out as I came in.
They are the doors of heaven while you are here,
And shall be so when you are gone from here;
For I shall keep you here.　Mark, I suppose,
Knew that.　Mark has been good to me today—
So good that I might almost think him sorry
That he is Mark, and must be always Mark.
May we be sorry to be ourselves, I wonder?
I am not so, Tristram.　You are not so.
Is there much then to sigh for?"

　　　　　　　　　　　"I am not sighing
For that," he said, and kissed her thin white fingers.
"My love will tell you, if you need be told
At all, why sorrow comes with me . . . Isolt!
Isolt!"

　　　　　　She smiled.　"I am not afraid to die,
Tristram, if you are trying to think of that—

Or not to think of that.   Why think of it?
My cup was running over; and having had all
That one life holds of joy, and in one summer,
Why should I be a miser crying to God
For more?   There was a way for this to be,
And this must be the way.   There was no other;
And I would have no other—not for myself.
Not now.   Not now.   It is for you, Tristram,
That I see this way best."

                    "God knows," he said,
"How well my love, which is the best of me,
Knows what a gulf of trust and understanding
There is in yours, where I would drown and die
So gladly and so soon, could I, by going

That way, leave you behind me here, and happy.
I would be gone from you and be forgotten
Like waves in childhood on forgotten water,
If that were the way left to bring warm life
And warm joy back into these cheeks again,
And these eyes looking at me."

                         The eyes smiled,
And the cheeks flushed with gladness; and Isolt

Said without sorrow, "I would not give two grains
Of sand to stay alive with you forgotten.
But I would give myself, or as much of me
As there is now, for God's word that my love
May not make yours a burden to be borne
Till you be weary of it. If we had seen,
If we had known—when there was all that time!
But no, there's nothing in that. We have known since then
All that we know today. Was it enough?
How shall we measure and weigh these lives of ours?
You said once that whatever it is that fills
Life up, and fills it full, it is not time.
You told my story when you said that to me,
But what of yours? Was it enough, Tristram?
Was it enough to fly so far away
From time that for a season time forgot us?
You said so, once. Was it too much to say?"

Her words had in their pleading an unwilling
And wistful intimation of things ended
That sorrow let escape. But he only smiled,
And pressed her asking hands. "It was enough,"
He said; "and I may tell you more than that,

Perhaps, when I am God, making new stars
To shine for you to see. They are more than fire,
You said; and they will tell you everything
That I may not say now."

              "It was enough!"
She murmured; and her words held happiness
Heard beyond earth, he thought. He turned his eyes
Away from hers that closed in weariness
And peace, to leave her smiling. Never before
Had such a stillness fallen on land or sea
That he remembered. Only one silent ship
Was moving, if it moved. He turned again
To the low couch before him and saw shining,
Under the darkness of her waving hair,
And with a pallid loveliness not pale
With life around them, the same violet eyes
Fixed upon his and with a calm that hurt him,
Telling him what they told, and holding more
Than it was good to tell. But they could smile
And lie for kindness; and she could tell him lies
While he for kindness listened:

              "You will go back
To Brittany after this, and there Isolt—

That other Isolt—" she said, "will, as time goes,
Fill up the strange and empty little place
That I may leave; and as time goes, and goes,
You may be king with her across the water;
Or, if you choose, you will be king, may be,
In your land, Lyonesse. I have never known
A man before with kingdoms at his feet,
Like scattered gold for him to leave or take,
And as he will. You will go back again
To Brittany; and when you are an old man,
You will remember this—this afternoon.
I am so sure of it that I'll not ask you
To tell me more about it." Her white fingers
Closed upon his, and her eyes closed again.

"I shall go back to Brittany, sometime,"
He said, "for whatsoever awaits me there.
There may be nothing. Women have changed before;
And more of them would be more fortunate,
For all I know, if more of them might change."

"I have seen many," she said, "like silent birds
Who could not fly with wings they thought were broken.

They were not broken, and the birds did fly.
I have seen wings that have been healed and mended,
Also. I have not seen many of them, perhaps.
Wings are but once for most of those who fly
Till they see time lying under them like a mist
That covers the earth. We have had wings and flown,
And one of us comes to earth again, and time,
Not to find much time left; and that is best
For her. One will have wings to fly again;
And that is best for him."

                       He looked across
The windless water and forgot what land
It was that lay beyond where he was looking.
He forgot everything, save all there was
For him, and turned again to see it there, lying
So silent, and unendurably so soon
Not to be there; to be so fair there now,
And then to vanish; to be so dark and white
And violet, and to die. And that was best,
She said; and she must know. He heard her saying
And saying again to him that it was best.
She would be saying it all his life to him,

To make him sure, leaving him and his wings
To fly wherever they would. "You do not say
How far I shall be flying, or for how long,"
He told her then, "and that's as well for me.
As for the best, I know no more of that
Than I see in your face and in your love
That looks at me. Love, it was far from here
And far from England and this inchmeal world
That our wings lifted us to let us fly
Where time forgot us. He waited for us here,
But his wings were too old to follow us.
We shall not go so far away from here
Again, till we go farther. It is enough
For me that you should ask if it was so,
And ask it with these eyes."

　　　　　　　　　　　　"I would to God
That we might fly together away from here,
Like two birds over the sea," she murmured then,
And her words sang to him. "The sea was never
So still as it is now, and the wind never
So dead. It is like dying, and not like death.
No, do not say things now. This is not you,

Tristram.   There was a mercy in fate for you
That later will be clear, when you see better
Than you need see today.   Only remember
That all there was of me was always yours.
There was no more of me.   Was it enough?
Tell me, was it enough?   You said it was,
And I have still to ask.   Women have ears
That will hold love as deserts will hold rain,
But you have told Isolt it was enough,
And she knows all there is.   When first we met
In darkness, and were groping there together,
Not seeing ourselves—and there was all that time—
She was all yours.   But time has died since then,
Time and the world, and she is always yours.
Pray God she be no burden.   You that are still
To fly, pray God for that."

                              He raised his eyes
And found hers waiting for them.   "Time is not life—
For me," he said.   "But your life was for you.
It was not mine to take away from you."
He went on wanderingly, and his words ached
Like slaves feeling a lash: "It was not mine.

I should have let you go away from there.
I should have made you go, or should have gone
Myself, leaving you there to tell yourself
It was your fear for me that frightened me,
And made me go."

                    "If you should hear my ghost
Laughing at you sometime, you will know why,
Tristram," she said.   And over her calm eyes
A smile of pity passed like a small cloud
Over two pools of violet in warm white,
Pallid with change and pain.   "It was your life,
For mine was nothing alone.   It was not time,
For you or me, when we were there together.
It was too much like always to be time.
If you said anything, love, you said it only
Because you are afraid to see me die—
Which is so little, now.   There was no more;
And when I knew that I was here again,
I knew there was no more. . . .   It was enough,
And it was all there was."

                         Once more she drew him
Closer, and held him; and once more his head

Was lying upon her with her arms around it
As they would hold a child. She felt the strength
Of a man shaking in his helplessness,
And would not see it. Lying with eyes closed
And all her senses tired with pain and love,
And pity for love that was to die, she saw him
More as a thunder-stricken tower of life
Brought down by fire, than as a stricken man
Brought down by fate, and always to wear scars
That in his eyes and voice were changelessly
Revealed and hidden. There was another voice,
Telling of when there should be left for him
No place among the living any longer;
And there was peace and wisdom, saying to her,
It will be best then, when it is all done.
But her own peace and wisdom frightened her,
And she would see him only as he had been
Before. That was the best for her to see;
And it was best that each should see the other
Unseen, and as they were before the world
Was done with them, and for a little while,
In silence, to forget and to remember.
They did not see the ocean or the sky,

Or the one ship that moved, if it was moving,
Or the still leaves on trees. They did not see
The stairs where they had stood once in the moonlight,
Before the moon went out and Tristram went
From her to darkness, into time and rain,
Leaving her there with Mark and the cold sound
Of waves that foamed all night. They did not see
The silent shore below, or the black rocks,
Or the black shadow of fate that came unfelt,
Or, following it, like evil dressed as man,
A shape that crept and crawled along to Tristram,
And leapt upon him with a shining knife
That ceased to shine. After one cry to God,
And her last cry, she could hear Tristram, saying,
"If it was Andred—give him thanks—for me. . . .
It was not Mark. . . . Isolt!"

                                She heard no more.
There was no more for either of them to hear,
Or tell. It was all done. So there they lay,
And her white arms around his head still held him,
Closer than life. They did not hear the sound
Of Andred laughing, and they did not hear

The cry of Brangwaine, who had seen, too late,
Andred ascending stealthily alone,
Like death, and with death shining in his hand,
And in his eyes. They did not hear the steps
Of Mark, who followed, or of Gouvernail,
Who followed Mark.

              They were all silent there
While Mark, nearer the couch and watching it,
And all that there was on it, and half on it,
Was unaware of Andred at his knees,
Until he seized them and stared up at him
With unclean gleaming eyes. "Tell me, my lord
And master," he crooned, with fawning confidence,
"Tell me—and say if I have not done well!
See him—and say if I'm a lizard now!
See him, my master! Have I not done well?"

Mark, for a time withheld in angry wonder
At what he saw, and with accusing sorrow
For what he felt, said nothing and did nothing,
Till at the sight of Andred's upturned face
He reached and seized him, saying no word at all,

And like a still machine with hands began
Slowly to strangle him. Then, with a curse,
He flung him half alive upon the floor,
Where now, for the first time, a knife was lying,
All wet with Tristram's blood. He stared at it,
Almost as if his hands had left it there;
And having seen all he would of it, he flung it
Over the parapet and into the sea;
And where it fell, the faint sound of a splash
Far down was the one sound the sea had made
That afternoon. Only the ship had moved—
And was a smaller ship, farther away.
He watched it for a long time, silently,
And then stood watching Tristram and Isolt,
Who made no sound. "I do not know," he said,
And gazed away again from everything.

"No sea was ever so still as this before,"
Gouvernail said, at last; and while he spoke
His eyes were on the two that were together
Where they were lying as silent as the sea.
"They will not ask me why it is not strange
Of me to say so little."

				"No," Mark answered,
"Nothing was ever so still as this before. . . .
She said it was like something after life,
And it was not like death. She may have meant
To say to me it was like this; and this
Is peace."

				To make his wonder sure again
That they were there, he looked; and they were there.
And there was Andred, helpless on the floor,
Staring in a mad ecstasy of hope
At Mark, who scanned him with an absent hate
Of nature, and with a doubt—as he had looked
Sometimes at unreal creatures of the sea
Thrown ashore dead by storms. Saying unheard,
With lips that moved as in a tortured sleep,
Words that were only for the dead to hear,
He watched again as he had watched before
The two that were so still where they were lying,
And wondered if they listened—they were so still
Where they were lying. "I do not know," he said,
"What this is you have done. I am not sure . . ."
His words broke slowly of their own heaviness,

And were like words not spoken to be heard:
"I am not sure that you have not done well.
God knows what you have done. I do not know.
There was no more for them—and this is peace."

X

By the same parapet that overlooked
The same sea, lying like sound now that was dead,
Mark sat alone, watching an unknown ship
That without motion moved from hour to hour,
Farther away. There was no other thing
Anywhere that was not as fixed and still
As two that were now safe within the walls
Below him, and like two that were asleep.
"There was no more for them," he said again,
To himself, or to the ship, "and this is peace.
I should have never praise or thanks of them
If power were mine and I should waken them;
And what might once have been if I had known
Before—I do not know. So men will say
In darkness, after daylight that was darkness,
Till the world ends and there are no more kings
And men to say it. If I were the world's maker.

I should say fate was mightier than I was,
Who made these two that are so silent now,
And for an end like this. Nothing in this
Is love that I have found, nor is it in love
That shall find me. I shall know day from night
Until I die, but there are darknesses
That I am never to know, by day or night;
All which is one more weary thing to learn,
Always too late. There are some ills and evils
Awaiting us that God could not invent;
There are mistakes too monstrous for remorse
To fondle or to dally with, and failures
That only fate's worst fumbling in the dark
Could have arranged so well. And here once more
The scroll of my authority presents
Deficiency and dearth. I do not know
Whether these two that have torn life from time,
Like a death-laden flower out of the earth,
Have failed or won. Many have paid with more
Than death for no such flower. I do not know
How much there was of Morgan in this last
Unhappy work of Andred's, or if now
It matters—when such a sick misshapen grief

May with a motion of one feeble arm
Bring this to pass. There is too much in this
That intimates a more than random issue;
And this is peace—whatever it is for me.
Now it is done, it may be well for them,
And well for me when I have followed them.
I do not know."

                Alone he stood there, watching
The sea and its one ship, until the sea
Became a lonely darkness and the ship
Was gone, as a friend goes. The silent water
Was like another sky where silent stars
Might sleep for ever, and everywhere was peace.
It was a peace too heavy to be endured
Longer by one for whom no peace less heavy
Was coming on earth again. So Mark at last
Went sombrely within, where Gouvernail
And silence wearied him. Move as he might,
Silence was all he found—silence within,
Silence without, dark silence everywhere—
And peace.

              And peace, that lay so heavy and dark
That night on Cornwall, lay as dark that night

On Brittany, where Isolt of the white hands
Sat watching, as Mark had watched, a silent sea
That was all stars and darkness. She was looking
With her gray eyes again, in her old way,
Into the north, and for she knew not what
Tonight. She was not looking for a ship,
And there was no ship coming. Yet there she sat,
And long into the night she sat there, looking
Away into the darkness to the north,
Where there was only darkness, and more stars.
No ship was coming that night to Brittany
From Cornwall. There was time enough for ships;
And when one came at last, with Gouvernail,
Alone, she had seen in him the end of waiting,
Before her father's eyes and his bowed head
Confirmed her sight and sense.

                              King Howel paused,
Like one who shifts a grievous weight he carries,
Hoping always in vain to make it lighter,
And after gazing at the large gray eyes
In the wan face before him, would have spoken,
But no speech came. Dimly from where he was,

Through mist that filled his eyes, he pictured her
More as a white and lovely thing to kill
With words than as a woman who was waiting
For truth already told. "Isolt—my child!"
He faltered, and because he was her father,
His anguish for the blow that he was giving
Felt the blow first for her.

                              "You are so kind
To me, my father," she said softly to him,
"That you will hold behind you now the knife
You bring with you, first having let me see it.
You are too kind. I said then to Gawaine
That he would not come back. Tristram is dead.
So—tell me all there is. I shall not die.
I have died too many times already for that.
I shall not ever die. Where was he, father?"
Her face was whiter and her large gray eyes
Glimmered with tears that waited.

                              He told her then
A tale, by Gouvernail and himself twice-tempered,
Of Tristram on his way to Brittany,
Having seen that other Isolt, by Mark's reprieve,

Only once more before she was to die.
It was an insane sort of kinsman, Andred,
Not Mark, who slew him in a jealous hate;
All which was nebulously true enough
To serve, her father trusted, willing to leave
The rest of it unheard, whatever it was,
For time to bury and melt. With Tristram dead,
This child of his, with her gray eyes that saw
So much, seeing so far, might one day see
A reason to live without him—which, to him,
Her father, was not so hard as to conceive
A reason for man's once having and leaving her.
That night the King prayed heaven to make her see,
And in the morning found his child asleep—
After a night of tears and stifled words,
They told him. She had made almost no sound
That whole night; and for many a day to follow
She made almost no sound.

                              One afternoon
Her father found her by the sea, alone,
Where the cold waves that rolled along the sand
Were saying to her unceasingly, "Tristram—
Tristram." She heard them and was unaware

That they had uttered once another name
For Tristram's ears. She did not know of that,
More than a woman or man today may know
What women or men may hear when someone says
Familiar things forgotten, and did not see
Her father until she turned, hearing him speak:

"Two years ago it was that he came here
To make you his unhappy wife, my child,
Telling you then, and in a thousand ways,
Without the need of language, that his love
Was far from here. His willingness and my wish
Were more to save you then, so I believed,
Than to deceive you. You were not deceived;
And you are as far now from all deception,
Or living need of it. You are not going
On always with a ghost for company,
Until you die. If you do so, my way,
Which cannot be a long way now, may still
Be more than yours. If Tristram were alive,
You would be Tristram's queen, and the world's eyes
And mind would be content, seeing it so.
But he is dead, and you have dreamed too long,

Partly because your dream was partly true—
Which was the worst of all, but yet a dream.
Now it is time for those large solemn eyes
Of yours to open slowly, and to see
Before them, not behind. Tristram is dead,
And you are a king's daughter, fairer than fame
Has told—which are two seeds for you to plant
In your wise little head as in a garden,
Letting me see what grows. We pay for dreams
In waking out of them, and we forget
As much as needs forgetting. I'm not a king
With you; I am a father and a man—
A man not over wise or over foolish,
Who has not long to live, and has one child
To be his life when he is gone from here.
You will be Queen some day, if you will live,
My child, and all you are will shine for me.
You are my life, and I must live in you.
Kings that are marked with nothing else than honor
Are not remembered long."

                    "I shall be Queen
Of Here or There, may be—sometime," she said;
"And as for dreaming, you might hesitate

In shaking me too soon out of my sleep
In which I'm walking. Am I doing so ill
To dream a little, if dreams will help me now?
You are not educating me, my father,
When you would seize too soon, for my improvement,
All that I have. You are the dreamer now.
You are not playing today with the same child
Whose dream amused you once when you supposed
That she was learning wisdom at your knees.
Wisdom was never learned at any knees,
Not even a father's, and that father a king.
If I am wiser now than while I waited
For Tristram coming, knowing that he would come,
I may not wait so long for Tristram going,
For he will never go. I am not one
Who must have everything, yet I must have
My dreams if I must live, for they are mine.
Wisdom is not one word and then another,
Till words are like dry leaves under a tree;
Wisdom is like a dawn that comes up slowly
Out of an unknown ocean."

                              "And goes down
Sometimes," the king said, "into the same ocean.

You live still in the night, and are not ready
For the new dawn. When the dawn comes, my child,
You will forget. No, you will not forget,
But you will change. There are no mortal houses
That are so providently barred and fastened
As to keep change and death from coming in.
Tristram is dead, and change is at your door.
Two years have made you more than two years older,
And you must change."

                    "The dawn has come," she said,
"And wisdom will come with it. If it sinks
Away from me, and into night again—
Then I shall be alone, and I shall die.
But I shall never be all alone—not now;
And I shall know there was a fate more swift
Than yours or mine that hurried him farther on
Than we are yet. I would have been the world
And heaven to Tristram, and was nothing to him;
And that was why the night came down so dark
On me when Tristram died. But there was always
Attending him an almost visible doom
That I see now; and while he moved and looked

As one too mighty and too secure to die,
He was not mingled and equipped to live
Very long. It was not earth in him that burned
Itself to death; and she that died for him
Must have been more than earth. If he had lived,
He would have pitied me and smiled at me,
And he would always have been kind to me—
If he had lived; and I should not have known,
Not even when in his arms, how far away
He was from me. Now, when I cannot sleep,
Thinking of him, I shall know where he is."

King Howel shook his head. "Thank God, my child,
That I was wise enough never to thwart you
When you were never a child. If that was wisdom,
Say on my tomb that I was a wise man."
He laid his hands upon her sun-touched hair,
Which in Gawaine's appraisal had no color
That was a name, and saying no more to 'her
While he stood looking into her gray eyes
He smiled, like one with nothing else to do;
And with a backward glance unsatisfied,
He walked away.

Isolt of the white hands,
Isolt with her gray eyes and her white face,
Still gazed across the water to the north
But not now for a ship. Were ships to come,
No fleet of them could hold a golden cargo
That would be worth one agate that was hers—
One toy that he had given her long ago,
And long ago forgotten. Yet there she gazed
Across the water, over the white waves,
Upon a castle that she had never seen,
And would not see, save as a phantom shape
Against a phantom sky. He had been there,
She thought, but not with her. He had died there,
But not for her. He had not thought of her,
Perhaps, and that was strange. He had been all,
And would be always all there was for her,
And he had not come back to her alive,
Not even to go again. It was like that
For women, sometimes, and might be so too often
For women like her. She hoped there were not many
Of them, or many of them to be, not knowing
More about that than about waves and foam,
And white birds everywhere, flying, and flying;

Alone, with her white face and her gray eyes,
She watched them there till even her thoughts were white,
And there was nothing alive but white birds flying,
Flying, and always flying, and still flying,
And the white sunlight flashing on the sea.

MODRED

A FRAGMENT

                              Time and the dark
Had come, but not alone. The southern gate
That had been open wide for Lancelot
Made now an entrance for three other men,
Who strode along the gravel or the grass,
Careless of who should hear them. When they came
To the great oak and the two empty chairs,
One paused, and held the others with a tongue
That sang an evil music while it spoke:
"Sit here, my admirable Colgrevance,
And you, my gentle Agravaine, sit here.
For me, well I have had enough of sitting;
And I have heard enough and seen enough
To blast a kingdom into kingdom come,
Had I so fierce a mind—which happily
I have not, for the king here is my father.
There's been a comment and a criticism
Abounding, I believe, in Camelot
For some time at my undeserved expense,
But God forbid that I should make my father
Less happy than he will be when he knows
What I shall have to tell him presently;

And that will only be what he has known
Since Merlin, or the ghost of Merlin, came
Two years ago to warn him. Though he sees,
One thing he will not see; and this must end.
We must have no blind kings in Camelot,
Or we shall have no land worth harrowing,
And our last harvest will be food for strangers.
My father, as you know, has gone a-hunting."

"We know about the king," said Agravaine,
"And you know more than any about the queen.
We are still waiting, Modred. Colgrevance
And I are waiting."

                        Modred laughed at him
Indulgently: "Did I say more than any?
If so, then inadvertently I erred;
For there is one man here, one Lancelot,
Who knows, I fancy, a deal more than I do,
And I know much. Yes, I know more than much.
Yet who shall snuff the light of what he knows
To blind the king he serves? No, Agravaine,
A wick like that would smoke and smell of treason."

"Your words are mostly smoke, if I may say so,"
Said Colgrevance: "What is it you have seen,
And what are we to do? I wish no ill
To Lancelot. I know no evil of him,
Or of the queen; and I'll hear none of either,
Save what you, on your oath, may tell me now.
I look yet for the trail of your dark fancy
To blur your testament."

                        "No, Colgrevance,
There are no blurs or fancies exercising
Tonight where I am. Lancelot will ascend
Anon, betimes, and with no drums or shawms
To sound the appointed progress of his feet;
And he will not be lost along the way,
For there are landmarks and he knows them all.
No, Colgrevance, there are no blurs or fancies
Unless it be that your determination

Has made them for your purpose what they seem.
But here I beg your pardon, Colgrevance.
We reticent ones are given to say too much,
With our tongues once in action. Pray forgive.
Your place tonight will be a shadowed alcove,
Where you may see this knight without a stain
While he goes in where no man save the king
Has dared before to follow. Agravaine
And I will meet you on the floor below,
Having already beheld this paragon-Joseph
Go by us for your clinching observation.
Then we, with a dozen or so for strength, will act;
And there shall be no more of Lancelot."

"Modred, I wish no ill to Lancelot,
And I know none of him," said Colgrevance.
"My dream is of a sturdier way than this
For me to serve my king. Give someone else
That alcove, and let me be of the twelve.
I swear it irks the marrow of my soul
To shadow Lancelot—though I may fight him,
If so it is to be. Furthermore, Modred,
You gave me not an inkling of the part
That you have read off now so pleasantly
For me to play. No, Modred, by the God
Who knows the right way and the wrong, I'll be
This night no poisonous inhabitant
Of alcoves in your play, not even for you.
No man were more the vassal of his friend
Than I am, but I'm damned if I'll be owned."

In a becoming darkness Modred smiled
Away the first accession of his anger.
"Say not like that," he answered, musically.
"Be temperate, Colgrevance. Remember always
Your knighthood and your birth. Remember, too,
That I may hold him only as my friend
Who loves me for myself, not for my station.
We're born for what we're born for, Colgrevance;
And you and I and Agravaine are born
To serve our king. It's all for the same end,
Whether we serve in alcoves, or behind

A velvet arras on another floor.
What matters it, if we be loyal men—
With only one defection?"

                        "Which is—what?"
Said Agravaine, who breathed hard and said little,
Albeit he had no fame abroad for silence.

"Delay—procrastination—overcaution—
Or what word now assimilates itself
The best with your inquiring mood, my brother.
These operations that engage us now
Were planned and executed long ago,
Had I but acted then on what was written
No less indelibly than at this hour,
Though maybe not so scorchingly on me.
'If there were only Modred in the way,'—
I heard her saying it—'would you come tonight?'
Saint Brandan! How she nuzzled and smothered him!
Forgive me, Colgrevance, when I say more
Than my raw vanity may reconcile
With afterthought. But that was what she said
To Lancelot, and that was what I heard.
And what I saw was of an even bias
With all she told him here. God, what a woman!
She floats about the court so like a lily,
That even I'd be fooled were I the king,
Seeing with his eyes what I would not see.
But now the stars are crying in their courses
For this to end, and we are men to end it.
Meanwhile, for the king's hunting and his health,
We have tonight a sort of wassailing;
Wherefore we may as well address ourselves,
Against our imminent activities,
To something in the way of trencher service—
Which also is a service to the king.
For they who serve must eat. God save the King!"

They took the way of Lancelot along
The darkened hedges to the palace lights,
With Modred humming lowly to himself
A chant of satisfaction. Colgrevance,

Not healed of an essential injury,
Nor given the will to cancel his new pledge
To Modred, made with neither knowing why,
Passed in without a word, leaving his two
Companions hesitating on the steps
Outside, one scowling and the other smiling.

"Modred, you may have gone an inch too far
With Colgrevance tonight. Why set a trap
For trouble? We've enough with no additions.
His fame is that of one among the faithful,
Without a fear, and fearless without guile."

"And that is why we need him, Agravaine,"
Said Modred, with another singing laugh.
"He'll go as was appointed by his fate
For my necessity. A man to achieve
High deeds must have a Colgrevance or two
Around him for unused emergencies,
And for the daily sweat. Your Colgrevance
May curse himself till he be violet,
Yet he will do your work. There is none else,
Apparently, that God will let him do."

"Not always all of it," said Agravaine.
But Modred answered with another laugh
And led the way in to the wassailing,
Where Dagonet was trolling a new song
To Lancelot, who smiled—as if in pain
To see so many friends and enemies,
All cheering him, all drinking, and all gay.

Arthurian Poets

E.A. ROBINSON

INTRODUCTION BY JAMES P. CARLEY

THE ARTHURIAN POEMS of E.A. Robinson were first published in America between 1917 and 1927, to considerable popular acclaim: *Tristram* won a Pulitzer prize. Yet they are almost unknown today, and the present volume restores a powerful and individual writer to his rightful place among Arthurian authors.

Robinson's introspective New England style and quiet tone are often classical rather than romantic, and he has little time for heroics. But he has also inherited much from Swinburne and Tennyson, and the tension between reason and passion that drives the characters of the Arthurian stories is brilliantly caught. These poems are above all studies in personality, and unforgettable for their vivid portraits, which are often unexpected – Merlin, cheerful and fierce; Vivian, enchanting rather than an enchantress; Lancelot in search of 'the Light'.

The sense of vision, and the feeling that the world of Arthur mirrors the fate of all mankind, binds these diverse characters together, and makes Robinson's poems essential reading for everyone interested in the Arthurian legend in the twentieth century.

'E.A. Robinson is too good a poet to be widely popular; his vision is too personal, too relentless to appeal to a crowd. Traditional yet original, realistic but not in the reductive sense, he is too good to be forgotten.'

ROBERTSON DAVIES

Cover illustration: Detail from 'King Arthur', by C.E. Butler, 1903 (private collection).

ISBN 0-85115-545-6

9 780851 155456

£10.95